DICK DAVEY:
A BASKETBALL LIFE RICHLY LED

The coach who discovered Steve Nash, pulled off the biggest upset in NCAA basketball tournament history, and gave his sport four uninterrupted decades of loyalty, integrity and passion.

By Chuck Hildebrand

DEDICATION

This book is dedicated to the true Santa Clara family –
the people who have made it not only a great university,
but an ideal and a sanctuary.

Table of Contents

Foreword

FOREWORD

Even from four hundred miles away, I could smell the stench emanating from the garrison that was Santa Clara University's "leadership" cabal in late January 2007 when it was announced that Dick Davey was "retiring" as the university's men's basketball coach.

I have chronicled in this book the related intrigue, callousness and outright dishonesty of an institution that was a constant in my life from the time I was 9 years old, and that I once loved as much as anybody who isn't Catholic and never attended school there can love it. Even in this situation's aftermath, I'm sure I will always care about Santa Clara, because the vast majority of people connected with it still stand for quality and integrity and not the type of mismanagement and disloyalty that transformed the Dick Davey dismissal into a public-relations quagmire for the school. Maybe it's inevitable, given the state of college athletics today, that even Santa Clara and some of its wealthiest supporters were unable to resist dipping their toes into the big-money, win-at-any-cost bog. Hopefully, this controversy will prove instructive to a university that always has prided itself, usually justifiably, in having the right priorities and adhering to its spiritual and moral mandate in matters involving athletics.

In any case, my outrage over Dick Davey's ouster is not the reason I'm writing this book. The contretemps of the last two months of his 40-year teaching and coaching career should not supersede its first 39-plus years, and

I am writing primarily about the extent and the quality of a man's career, not its end.

I'm writing this book for the same reason I wrote a book about the school's now-defunct football program in 1998. Like the football players who made Santa Clara the Notre Dame of the West in the 1930s and 1940s, and then went on to live even more honorable post-football lives, Dick Davey is a man whose impact on his sport and on the lives of those he mentored needs and deserves to be chronicled for posterity.

I'm not writing this book for profit; in fact, all of the proceeds will be donated to the Global Ischemia Foundation. No book about Dick Davey will ever sell a million copies or be made into a reality-TV show. He never was enmeshed in a scandal. He never professed to have reinvented the sport he spent a lifetime honoring. He never ran roughshod over rules or underlings to win games or shoe contracts or fame. He never worshipped at the shrine of the greed and avarice and self-promotion that permeate college sports in the 21st century.

Instead, Dick Davey did something even more remarkable: He excelled for 40 years in one profession without making a single enemy of consequence.

Even during the ugly denouement of his 30-year tenure at Santa Clara, his energy was spent not on retribution or self-pity, but on deflecting attention away from his situation and making sure his players left his program with the same life tools he had provided his charges since he first got into coaching in 1967. And if this book had been conceived as an attack piece on a place Dick Davey still loves and to which he still feels grateful for 30 fulfilling years, I'm certain he would not have agreed to participate in this project.

I covered San Francisco Bay Area sports throughout my newspaper career, which began in 1979 and lasted until I moved to Nevada in 1997, and I was around many men who were considered great because of their victories and their championships and their ability to manipulate public opinion. But I've always felt that greatness in a man is not always measured in victories, and that being a great coach or a great athlete is not necessarily tantamount to being a great man.

Dick Davey was a great basketball coach, as many people in a better position than I to know will relate on the pages that follow. Even more people will relate the way a man not only reached out to them, but reached inside them to bring forth perseverance and passion and pride and altruism they didn't know they had before they met Dick Davey. I interviewed people who knew Dick during six different decades, and the names – some well-known, many not – are almost interchangeable, because the man was at once a fortress and a sanctuary for everyone whose life he touched.

If you knew Dick Davey, you never quit on the man, and the man never quit on you. I know nobody else who never – as in not once – deviated from that course over such a long period of time and in such a public line of work.

I've never been prouder to have called somebody a friend. And I have two hopes for this book: One, that it does Dick Davey, the man as well as the coach, justice; and two, that future generations will read and heed it and know that this was a man who went beyond living a basketball life well.

He lived it, and still lives it, richly.

Can one give a man a greater compliment? I think not.

Chuck Hildebrand
Winnemucca, Nevada
June 11, 2007

DICK DAVEY:

A BASKETBALL LIFE RICHLY LED

By Chuck Hildebrand

Chapter 1
'I LIKE PEOPLE'

Dick Davey felt almost like Typhoid Mary as he walked along an Atlanta street in April 2007, even though he wasn't sick. Nor was it because he was an unemployed basketball coach for the first time since the Lyndon Johnson Administration.

It was because his peers were approaching him as if he were incurably afflicted, and he didn't want to be mourned, because he wasn't dying or even despondent. Even though he was without a team to coach for the first and only time in a career that had started at Leland High School in San Jose, Calif., in 1967, he always had been as aware as anyone of the tenuous nature of employment in college basketball. Often, in the same setting, he had commiserated with suddenly-unemployed peers he liked and respected.

His eviction as Santa Clara University coach two months earlier was one of 51 such putsches in NCAA Division I during or immediately after the 2006-07 season – one of every seven D-I schools changed coaches during that span – and even though the circumstances were still gnawing at him, he wanted his peers to know he understood and reluctantly accepted the situation, and that he was ready to move on and wasn't interested in having the end of his career eclipse its extent and content.

But in Atlanta, among the thousands of current and former coaches who had converged for the Final Four as they do each year, Davey was inundated by well-wishers, and he was trying to figure out a way to convey his appreciation while deflecting any pity or sympathy. The solution fell to Bob Burton, the Cal State Fullerton coach who is one of Davey's longest-standing friends in the coaching profession – partly because he has the same puckish sense of humor as Davey.

"We're at the Final Four having breakfast, and two or three people came up during breakfast, reached their hand out and said, (in funereal tones) 'How ya doin?'" Davey recalled, grinning. "As Bob and I are walking down the street after breakfast, two or three other guys, coaches I knew, came up to shake my hand. They had that same kind of befuddled look … 'how ya doin?' I kept telling everyone I'm doing great, everything's fine, how are you doing? … Finally, Bob got mad. He said, 'OK, goddammit, next time somebody comes up to you and says 'how you doing?' like that, I want you to go into a tirade. 'I'm so goddam pissed off at those son-of-a-bitching bastards, I'm kicking my walls in at the hotel and I'm pissed and I'm never gonna forgive them for this.'

So I said, 'OK, I'll do it,' Sure enough, 30 seconds later another guy, I don't even remember who he was, puts his hand out like I've got cancer, and I give him the spiel. 'Goddam son-of-a-bitching bastards, I'll never forgive those bastards.' The guy kind of backs off, and he looks a little bit nervous. Finally I gave in and told him I was just pulling his leg, that we were having some fun with this stuff."

"This stuff" was a series of events in February 2007 that tore at the anchor tenets of a Santa Clara basketball program that has existed since 1904, usually fielding good teams and occasionally clambering to the competitive summit while adhering far more strictly than most Division I schools to the premise that academics and friendship and loyalty and honesty and trust always came before athletic conquest.

At age 64, Davey was in the final year of his contract at Santa Clara. He had led the Broncos to three NCAA tournaments – and perhaps the most monumental upset in that event's history, a 64-61 first-round win over Arizona in the first round of the 1993 tournament – in his first four years as head coach after 15 seasons as an assistant under Carroll Williams. During those four years, Davey and his assistants took Steve Nash, an unimposing acne-faced Canadian best known at the time as a soccer player, and gave him the tools that he was to use to transform himself into the NBA's Most Valuable Player in 2004-05 and 2005-06.

Davey had been the West Coast Conference Coach of the Year three times and was closing in on the 250-win mark, eventually finishing at 251-190, second on the WCC career win list behind only Carroll Williams, his Santa Clara predecessor and mentor. Of the other 63 head coaches in the 1993 NCAA tournament, only four – Duke's Mike Krzyzewski, Arizona's Lute Olson, Connecticut's Jim Calhoun and Coppin State's Ron "Fang" Mitchell – were still directing the programs at the same schools during the 2006-07 season.

"Going around the country, I've talked to guys like Roy Williams, Jim Boeheim, Tubby Smith ... when they talk about Santa Clara and Dick, they refer to him as one of the best coaches in the country," former Santa Clara radio play-by-play announcer Dave Lewis said. "He's not playing with McDonald's All-Americans. They break Santa Clara down on film and they say, 'Jesus, look at what he's doing with these guys.' He's appreciated more around the country than he is within the walls of his own university."

Roy Williams' 2004-05 North Carolina team, which went on to win the national championship, was ambushed 77-66 in its season opener by Davey's Santa Clara squad. The friendship between the two men dates all the way back to 1982, when both were assistant coaches and North Carolina came west to play Santa Clara in a non-conference game. Williams, of course, later became head coach at Kansas, and the Broncos and Jayhawks played four times during Davey's tenure as head coach, including a meeting in the second round of the 1996 NCAA tournament in what turned out to be Steve Nash's final game as a Bronco.

That the two became friends is not surprising when one considers the way their lives and careers paralleled each other, even though Davey is eight years older and has functioned in a lower-profile sphere than Williams.

Both grew up in small towns – Davey in Ceres, Calif., Williams in Biltmore, N.C. – and both were good but not great players who began preparation for their coaching careers long before they graduated from college. Both began as high school coaches. Both served long apprenticeships as assistants to highly-respected college head coaches (Williams under Dean Smith, Davey under Carroll Williams) before taking over programs themselves. Both inspire fierce loyalty among their former players, and remain part of those athletes' lives long after those lives cease to include basketball. Both have two children, one boy and one girl – and both of their daughters are named Kim.

Davey says he has met no contemporary coach for whom he has more admiration and respect than Roy Williams, whose program, to many, represents the zenith of college sports in terms of producing quality basketball on the court and quality individuals away from it. Williams, in a 2007 interview for this book, said the feeling long has been reciprocal.

The two, in fact, played golf at Cypress Point on the Monterey Peninsula the day before Santa Clara pulled off the 2004 upset over North Carolina, and they served together for two years on the National Association of Basketball Coaches board of directors toward the end of Davey's career.

"I've always watched other coaches during games, just to observe the way they do things," Williams said, "and it got to the point over the years where I just really enjoyed watching Dick and watching his teams play. We also went on trips (when both were representatives of the same shoe company) and we had a lot of fun together. The year we played golf at Cypress, there were only three of us, and I called Dick (to create a foursome) because I don't like to play 'business golf.' I was out there to have fun, and with Dick there, I loved it."

Williams was asked how he thought Davey might fare in the Atlantic Coast Conference, North Carolina's league, if he had ACC-level resources with which to work.

"He'd do great," Williams said. "Of course, a (larger school like) North Carolina is going to attract a higher caliber of athlete than a (smaller school like) Santa Clara can, and his teams didn't have the talent or size our teams did, but they were always very, very well-coached. It wasn't a deal where we got to know each other because we were thrown together for 12 days at any one time. It was an accumulation of respect that just got higher and higher as I saw how serious he was about coaching and teaching.

"Dick has always understood that what's good for our game is most important. What was good for (specific schools) was never the biggest factor with him (when the two worked together on NABC matters), and I knew I had an ally when it came to that. To be compared to Dick Davey … that's flattering, and I'm very sincere in saying that. I want him to come out here before next season and watch practice; maybe I can pick up some ideas from him.

"The two best compliments you can pay a man are if you can say he's a coach's coach, and if you can say you'd be thrilled to have your son play for him. I can say both those things very easily about Dick."

Burton said Davey was one of the first people he called in 2003 after he got the Cal State Fullerton job, his first Division I head coaching position in a career that began at Leigh High in San Jose in 1970 – the year he first met Davey, then coaching at Leland.

After assistant-coaching stints at Leigh and Westmont high schools, Burton was head coach at Willow Glen, another San Jose school, from 1972 through 1980 – at which point he accepted the head-coaching job at West Valley, a community college in nearby Saratoga. His teams there won 488 games over 21 seasons and reached the California juco championship game five times. Burton then was an assistant at Fresno State, his alma mater, before going to Fullerton, where in 2004-05 he led the program (which had had 10 straight losing seasons before his arrival) to its first 20-plus win season since 1983.

"He was one of the first guys I'd ever call about anything," Burton said of Davey. "I always wanted to know what he had to say about anything, because he was one guy who was never enamored of where he is. It wouldn't matter if he was coaching Leland High or Santa Clara or the L.A. Lakers … he'd still be the same guy. He has a tremendous love for the people who work and play for him, and he's the most loyal and hardest working guy you'll ever find.

"More than anything else, he was a great inspiration to me. I was a high school coach and then a JC coach for a long time, and he was always a D-I guy after he left Leland. He really took me under his wing, even though we're close to the same age. We'd spend hours together. I'd go with him to watch him recruit kids and just to be with him … he was a tremendous guy to be around, so much fun.

"We were always great friends through basketball, but we both also got into fishing, fly fishing, at the same time. The difference between me and Dick is that Dick's really good … he really understood it, and I was just kind of learning how.

"One thing about Dick that's so funny, and what makes him so great as a coach and as a person, is that he's very stubborn on things. Like this one time … we're out in the middle of nowhere, and there was a little store on this lake we were fishing. We went in there and bought some flies and stuff, and he bought some candy, and right when we were leaving, I bought some (of the same kind of) candy. We decided to go to another lake because we weren't catching anything, so as we're driving off, I pull out my candy and he says, 'That's my candy.' I go, 'What do you mean?' He said, 'It's *my candy.*' Now we're arguing … 50-year-old men arguing about candy. I ate mine as slow as I could right in front of him, and he's yelling at me; he's really ticked. 'I watched you in there (the store) and you never bought anything.' So we get there and go into the water with our waders on, and what falls out of his waders but the candy. He accused me of planting that on him. He refused to believe I didn't steal his candy. I don't think there's anyone I love to tease more … I get him fired up, and he goes right back at me and just kills me.

"He and Carroll (Williams) are dinosaurs in this business today … this long at one place, the way D-I is now, and doing it the way they did it. You've never seen more of a family atmosphere than (with) him. He was really an inspiration to me on everything … he was the guy who always slowed me down and brought me back to the reality of why we went into coaching. It's not about D-I or the crowds or any of that stuff, and nobody has been in it more for the right reasons.

"Coaching has lost one of the truly tremendous teachers of the game. I hope he stays in it some way because the game needs him more than he needs the game. There aren't a lot of Dick Daveys out there anymore. I'm going to miss him. He's still got a lot of passion and a lot of love for the game and the kids. I really wish I was (living and working) closer to him, because I'd have him come over and help coach our team."

UCLA coach Ben Howland, another of Davey's close friends and frequent fishing companions, first met Davey in 1985, when Howland was an assistant at UC Santa Barbara and Davey was a Santa Clara assistant.

According to Howland, it was Davey who suggested that Howland take a discerning look at Brian Shaw, who was in the process of transferring out of St. Mary's after two seasons there. Howland took Davey's advice and UCSB signed Shaw, who went on to become arguably the best all-around player in the Gauchos' history, recording all five of the triple-doubles in the UCSB record book as of 2007. As a senior in 1987-88, Shaw led Santa Barbara to the first NCAA Division I tournament berth in school history before going on to a 14-year NBA career during which he won championship rings with the Los Angeles Lakers in 2000, 2001 and 2002, and was in 127 playoff games – a full NBA season and a half.

"He probably saved my job," Howland said of Davey. "If it wasn't for him, I might be selling insurance right now."

After 12 seasons as a UCSB assistant – from the dues-paying perspective, Howland's career paralleled that of Davey to a large extent – Howland got his first head-coaching job in 1994 when Northern Arizona hired him. He then went to Pittsburgh, where he made the Panthers national-title contenders, and after moving to UCLA, he took the Bruins to the national title game in 2006 and the Final Four in 2007.

Davey is predictably self-effacing when he is asked about the story; his version is that Howland already knew about Shaw and merely asked Davey's opinion of the player – at which point, Davey said, he told Howland, "he'd have rocks in his head if he didn't try to get Shaw, because the guy was damn good.

"Ever since then, he's said I'm the guy who got him out of Santa Barbara," Davey said, smiling. "I don't know about that, but we've been friends ever since."

UC Riverside athletic director Stan Morrison was head coach at Pacific, Southern Cal and San Jose State during Davey's coaching career, and took all three programs to NCAA tournaments. He also played for the 1959 University of California, Berkeley squad that won the NCAA championship under coach Pete Newell. Davey wound up with 17 more career wins than Newell – considered by many the best college basketball coach who ever lived – even though he was a head coach for only one more season than Newell, who went 234-123 over his 14-year career. (Newell's winning percentage of .655, though, was significantly better than Davey's .582 mark, and Newell won two national championships, the NIT with the University of San Francisco in 1949 and the NCAA crown with Cal in '59.)

"He is one of the most uncomplicated men I've ever known," Morrison said. "He was brutally honest and that was difficult for a few people and a few players, I suspect. Those who appreciated his honesty, players being treated like men, developed a bond of loyalty that was incomparable. When I have had an opportunity to occasionally run into one of his players, they were always gentlemen and spoke of their coach with the highest level of respect and appreciation because 'we always knew where we stood with Coach Davey.'

"I believe his team rule about punctuality describes him quite well. He once told me, 'Everyone is going to be late *once*. You never know . . . a flat tire, run out of gas, forgot, etc. No problem. Get to class and/or practice and continue on. The next time you are late, you are off the team. No arguments, no questions, no nothing. That's it.' I found this to be very revealing. All black and white. No gray. It was simple and to the point. It said to me, don't get strike one because you will be gone with strike two. Protect the margin for error. Don't be late!

"Dick Davey is one of the 'good guys.' He would never cheat. He valued the institutional, conference and NCAA rules. He made sure that his staff and players always respected the fact that they were representing not only themselves, but the institution and the game of basketball. He is truly one of the keepers of the game. There was never a whisper, glance, or rumor about him or his staff with respect to recruiting and the conduct of the program. I will guarantee that there are lots of clean programs in the NCAA. None was or is any squeaky-cleaner than the Santa Clara Broncos under Dick Davey.

"The entire Bay Area and the game of basketball are better because Dick Davey cast his shadow on that court on the Santa Clara campus. He is a values-based decision maker who commands the attention of the entire coaching fraternity because he is straight and would never compromise an ideal for the sake of winning. Don't misunderstand, he wanted to win! More than any of us could possibly know. I loved seeing him with a huge smile after the games. His glasses would be a little fogged up. He still had sweat falling from the hair on the back of his neck. But, he was happy. And, he relished winning the old-fashioned way: fundamentally sound, playing unselfishly, playing physically, and playing with an understanding of the game plan. And, his teams always, *always* played hard. That fact, along with some great game planning, propelled the Broncos to some incredible upsets during his tenure at SCU. History will record them for all of us to reflect on in the years to come. If he lost, he didn't give excuses. He was gracious to the winning coach. He congratulated the opposing team players. He knew. It was their time. Tomorrow, it would be his time and the time for his players too."

Dennis Awtrey, who arguably achieved more at Santa Clara than any player in the program's history, particularly appreciates Davey's loyalty to Santa Clara and those who represented it – even those, like himself, who were there before Davey's arrival.

Awtrey was the junior center on the 1968-69 Santa Clara team that spent much of that season as the No. 2-ranked team in the country behind Lew Alcindor and UCLA. He averaged 21.3 points and 13.3 rebounds that year, and 21.2 and 14.1 for the 1969–70 squad, which went 23-6. Awtrey went on to play 12 NBA seasons for six teams, including the Phoenix Suns, whom he helped reach the NBA Finals in 1976. Though never a go-to offensive threat in the pros, Awtrey was valued for his rebounding and defense, especially against Alcindor/Kareen Abdul-Jabbar.

Because of his NBA travels and the fact he never lived in the Bay Area after he graduated from Santa Clara, Awtrey's ties with the program were relatively distant after his graduation until Davey became head coach in 1993. In fact, he says Santa Clara re-entered his life because of Davey.

"I wasn't very close to the program (during and for the first decade after his NBA career) just because I wasn't around," he said. "I didn't even know Dick at all for a while after he first came on board (as an assistant in 1977), but we became friends after he became head coach because he was really interested in bringing the old Santa Clara players back into the program … he thought it was important for the program to have a relationship with its past.

"He started having reunions and oldtimers games, and I even worked one of his camps for a week and met some of his players at the time. I would have liked any of his players to have dated my daughter, and he really made me proud all over again that I was from Santa Clara. I'll always be grateful to him for that.

"I've seen schools where I wouldn't let any of their players get anywhere near any daughter of mine … a coach is supposed to be a model, somebody who teaches his players how to be productive citizens. Dick does that. When I was a high school and college player, we didn't lose very often, but when we did, it was like ripping a part of my heart out. In the NBA I learned that you're going to play 82 games and you're going to lose some, and although I've never been in one of his locker rooms, you can see the values he instills (regardless of the outcomes of games or seasons), even though he wants to win as bad as anybody."

Dave Frandsen, who directed the same Leland High program that Davey had started in 1967, has a more personal insight into the compassion that dovetails with his passion.

One of Dave Frandsen's sons, D.J., was diagnosed with cancer at age 6. Despite his illness, he ran cross country and played basketball and tennis at Bellarmine Prep in San Jose, and was headed to Loyola Marymount when he relapsed and had to stay in the San Jose area to undergo chemotherapy for kidney cancer.

After Davey found out about the situation, he called D.J.'s father to inquire about the possibility of D.J. joining the Santa Clara program. Frandsen transferred to Santa Clara, and became the Broncos' team manager.

"Dick was instrumental in helping (his son transfer to Santa Clara)," said Dave Frandsen, whose younger son Kevin made his major league baseball debut with the San Francisco Giants in 2006. "He got D.J. to come over and help out and run the scoreboard and D.J. got on the court with the guys. Dick would spend hours with us in the hospital. He was so good in being (supportive) for D.J. He didn't have to do that. He made him an assistant there on the bench his last year."

D.J. Frandsen died on September 16, 2004 at age 25 of complications from Wilm's tumor, a form of recurring kidney cancer. The top-sixth-man award at the Cable Car Classic, the tournament hosted by Santa Clara each December, is named after him.

Before going to Santa Clara as an assistant to Williams, Davey had been an assistant for five years at Cal. Before that, he had taken the Leland program that he started to a California Interscholastic Federation sectional Final

Four – the equivalent of a state tournament most places in the country – in only the school's fourth season of existence. In all, he probably was on the winning sideline in at least 600 games on the college and high school levels.

He coached six Santa Clara student-athletes – Nash, Kurt Rambis, Marlon Garnett, Harold Keeling, Mark McNamara and the late Nick Vanos – who went on to play in the NBA, and all except McNamara, who transferred to Cal after two seasons, received their degrees from Santa Clara. At least twice as many other young men who played for him went on to become millionaires through their business acumen and not the accuracy of their jump shot. (Another, Ronnie Reis, gained another sort of fame, as the World Wrestling Federation's "Vanilla Gorilla.") Forty-six of the 50 players who spent their full careers at Santa Clara while he was head coach went on to obtain their degrees, and all six of the 2006-07 seniors graduated with their class. No Santa Clara player ever had an entanglement with the law during Davey's 30 years there, and the school's program never was investigated by the NCAA for improprieties. Only two players transferred elsewhere while he was in charge of the program, even though few coaches anywhere are more demanding and insistent that the integrity of the sport and the university be honored.

"When he came to my house (on a recruiting visit), he sat down at my table and showed me the Santa Clara course catalogue and went through the courses I would be taking as a freshman," said Mitch Burley, who played for Santa Clara from 1985-89 and was the program's first 3-point shooting specialist. "I knew even then that I was going to be an engineer (which he has been since graduation) and he was the only (college) coach to show me anything to do with academics. I had other coaches come in and tell me how much fun it was gonna be and this and that. That's what separates Santa Clara in my mind, because I was a serious student, and the character he showed … he never swayed from that. He's a hero. He changed my life."

"I feel like I always had a special bond with Dick, paralleling with what I remember about my father (who died when he was 12)," said Steve Kenilvort, a backcourt starter – and in many ways Davey's on-court alter ego – for the Broncos from 1982-86. "When I first met Dick, I was 17; when I left, I was 21, and now that I'm in my 40s, we have a totally different relationship. He was always hard on me, and I learned early on that if Dick's on you, it's a good thing, because he won't waste time on people he doesn't think have a chance (to improve themselves as athletes and individuals). So, goofy as it sounds, it was flattering when he was all over my ass, because I knew he believed in me and expected more of me and really *knew* me."

However, the fact Davey changed lives, often won against foes with vastly superior physical and financial resources, and enriched his profession mattered not at all to Davey's superiors, and to the owners of two of the heftiest wallets in the Santa Clara alumni hierarchy.

After the three NCAA appearances in Davey's first four seasons as head coach, Santa Clara was only 70-78 in the five years that followed a 20-12 showing in 2000–01. But Davey's 2006-07 team got off to a 14-6 start, with five of the losses coming to Air Force, Kentucky, Nevada, California and Gonzaga, all in or near the national rankings at the time Santa Clara played them. The fact that the six losses came by an average margin of 18.5 points was disconcerting to Davey, but Santa Clara did post victories over strong Utah State and Stanford squads during that stretch.

The Broncos appeared headed for their first postseason appearance since 1996 when the university's reputation for requiting its employees' loyalty liquefied like landfill in an earthquake.

The seismic event was a 79-77 home loss to winless Loyola Marymount on January 27, a Saturday. Three days later, on the morning after a 77-75 victory over Pepperdine, Davey was called into athletic director Dan Coonan's office and, as Davey put it, "they told me I was retiring" at the end of the season. Worse yet, he was told that he had to announce his departure immediately instead of waiting until the season's conclusion.

"He comes in and tells me I have to announce it now," Davey said of Coonan, who later walked out of the Santa Clara senior awards banquet after one of the players criticized the administration for its handling of the Davey matter. "I tried to barter a little, hold off on announcing it until the end of the season, but he said, 'They said you have to announce it now.' He never did tell me who 'they' were. So I said, OK, I'll do it after the next weekend's games. I called my assistants in and told them that the university has asked me to announce my retirement now, and I've told them I'll announce it next Tuesday. Steve (assistant coach Steve Seandel) said, 'You can't wait. It (the news) will spread, and it'll be a problem.' So I called Coonan and told him I'd changed my mind (and would make the announcement immediately)."

The subsequent announcement was startling the moment it was uttered because of the awkward, if not downright bizarre, timing. (Just three weeks before, the school had honored Davey by staging a "Dick Davey Argyle Sweater Night," asking fans to wear Davey's favorite courtside attire to the Broncos' home game against Gonzaga.) The situation spiraled into a public-relations fiasco for the school after Davey, in response to questions by reporters who already knew the answer to their own queries, acknowledged that the "retirement" decision had not been his. It was an untidy and utterly unnecessary situation that, had Davey so wished, might have become downright scandalous for a school that historically had made much of its desire to strike a balance between the school's educational and spiritual missions and the financial realities of big-time college sports.

Santa Clara's Jesuit hierarchy had resisted the encroachment of checkbook athletics for decades, dating all the way back to 1952 when the school dismantled its football program – which had won two Sugar Bowls and one Orange Bowl while making itself the Notre Dame of the West in the 1930s and 1940s – when confronted with the need to dramatically increase its funding and perhaps sacrifice its academic standards to remain competitive in two-platoon major college football. (When the Broncos beat Bear Bryant's Kentucky team 21-13 in the 1950 Orange Bowl, supposedly costing Jimmy "The Greek" Snyder a $500,000 bet and driving him away from plunging and into bookmaking, they had only 54 players in the program to Kentucky's 100-plus, and the Wildcats wore new-fangled plastic helmets in that game while Santa Clara was still using leather headgear. And Santa Clara won despite the fact the team had endured a four-day train trip to Miami, long after most big-time college teams began flying to road games as a matter of course.)

Santa Clara's athletic-budget monitors had been as vigilant – some would say, downright cheap – during Davey's tenure as they had been during the football program's halcyon years. Most within the Santa Clara basketball inner circle felt that the financial factor, not Davey's coaching or recruiting, was the main reason Santa Clara fell behind Gonzaga in the late 1990s and early 2000s, when the Bulldogs became annual entrants in the NCAA tournament and built a national following. The insiders feel that had Davey, who was the lowest-paid coach in the WCC at the time of his dismissal – and at the time of his original hiring as well – been given means comparable to Gonzaga's at the time that school first ascended the national heights, he might well have continued and even expanded upon the success the Steve Nash-led teams had enjoyed.

After the Loyola Marymount loss, those who felt otherwise quickly went to work and covertly – they thought – engineered Davey's removal.

It developed that university president Paul Locatelli and two of Santa Clara's wealthiest boosters had conversed at length the night of the Loyola Marymount game, which was played in the afternoon. The three principals were Locatelli; Devcon Construction president Gary Filizetti, a former Santa Clara football player; and billionaire John Sobrato, owner of a Cupertino-based development firm. Locatelli probably had no choice but to listen to Filizetti and Sobrato, even if he had been disinclined to do so; their wealth aside, Sobrato was a member of the school's Boards of Trustees and Regents, and Filizetti was a regent.

Nobody except Locatelli and the boosters, who remained mum on the subject, knew exactly what was said at that impromptu meeting. But it became apparent within three days that a deal had been cut: If Davey were to be taken out of the picture, with or without his assent, the school wouldn't have to worry about having the financial resources to hire a new coach from a upper-tier program and increase the basketball budget so that it was consistent with those at programs like Gonzaga. Nor, for that matter, would it have to worry about completing the library that was under construction – and under-funded – at the time.

(Santa Clara subsequently hired Kerry Keating, an assistant coach at UCLA who had no prior head-coaching experience, and signed him to a contract that included a $300,000 annual salary – more than twice the $130,000 Davey was making – and a promise of new perks, most notably an increased recruiting budget and the addition of a third full-time assistant-coaching position. Davey had three assistant coaches, but the salary of one, Lloyd Pierce, was financed through fund-raising and outside sponsorship and was not part of Davey's budget.)

Media members and bloggers, and most of the program's longest-standing supporters, didn't like the way a 30-year coach who had graduated almost all of his players, never been in trouble with the NCAA, and had been competitive every year against strong national schedules was shunted aside at a school that through most of its history had never fired coaches except for outright insubordination. Most of all, they didn't like the clandestine manner with which the school's administration, particularly Locatelli, handled the matter from the time Davey was "retired" until the day that Keating was hired. That wasn't until two months after Davey's ouster, even though the administration claimed that the timing of Davey's "retirement" announcement was attributable to the need to sign a new coach as soon as possible.

Coaches throughout the country also expressed their displeasure – including Gonzaga's Mark Few, the winningest eight-season coach in NCAA history, whose success with the Bulldogs raised expectation bars at each of the other seven WCC schools and indirectly led to coaching changes at all seven. During the 2006-07 season, the only two WCC coaches who had held their jobs when Few took over the Gonzaga program were Davey and San Diego's Brad Holland, who also was fired at the end of the season.

Few told the *Spokane Spokesman-Review:*

"Firing a guy to protect yourself in case his team goes on a run is insane … That's so incredibly backward, it's ludicrous. Pull the plug on a guy in case he goes on a run? It reminds me of what you see in baseball – 'We've got a six-game homestand coming up, so let's get rid of the manager now in case he goes 6-0. Let's saw him off before it gets too crazy.'

"Guys have been losing jobs in this league long before we started our run, and for the same old reasons. But if that is the case, then the presidents and ADs need to be held accountable for not raising the level of support the way (we) have here. What they're allowing their teams to do in scheduling, in facilities, support, everything. It just seems like the tenor and landscape is changing. The impatience is at an all-time high and the expectations don't reflect reality. And the Internet as a place to vent and voice untruths and see those gain a lot of traction has increased to a dangerous point."

"My first reaction (when he first heard Davey was retiring) was, 'Oh, great, he's getting out on his terms,'" Roy Williams said. "But later, I spoke to a couple of people who knew what was going on there, and they said it wasn't very smooth, that it could have been ugly if Dick had wanted it to be. For somebody who has done what he's done, it was sad to see, and I wish it could have been handled a little differently."

"Dick Davey is one of the best guys in college basketball," former Stanford coach Mike Montgomery, who for a time was mentioned in some media accounts as a possible successor to Davey, said at the time Davey's imminent departure was announced. "The game needs people like him. I don't know any of the circumstances, but the timing of it is odd. They have a chance to win this thing (WCC title) ... I think Dick will handle it with his kids, but it's just a little unsettling."

Brian Katz, who coached with Davey and Williams at Santa Clara in the late 1980s and in 2007 was in his ninth year as head coach at San Joaquin Delta College in Stockton, called Davey's dismissal "the greatest travesty in college basketball."

"Dick Davey is a phenomenal coach, but he's a better friend," Katz told the *Stockton Record*. "If there was a disaster or a problem here and I called Dick, he'd be here as soon as it took him to drive his car here.

"You've got a guy who won, who overachieved. He graduated his players and he won. And he never had a brush with the NCAA in terms of a violation. And he was respected in the coaching community. What else is there?"

The *Contra Costa Times*' Eric Gilmore received an unexpected e-mail from Matt Wilgenbush, who played for Williams and Davey from 1983-87.

"After I graduated from SCU in 1987, I contracted leukemia and was in for the fight of my life," Wilgenbush wrote to Gilmore. "One of the first people to come to the hospital was Dick Davey. He would come up a few times a week to check on me. I was thinking (when he wrote Gilmore) about my past and have to give much of the credit for my surviving a bone marrow transplant to the attitude I developed from my years playing for Dick Davey. I don't know why I'm writing this. I'm just very frustrated at the way he is being treated by the administration at SCU and wanted a place to vent."

In a subsequent interview with Gilmore, Wilgenbush – who beat his leukemia and went on to become a high school coach before unrelated health issues forced him to give up that job – continued to vent.

"These are people who don't understand – and this is what my main focus is, what I want to get out (is) what basketball means to a person. It supersedes money," Wilgenbush said, choking back tears. "It's a team. It's the whole attitude that you've got. … I go play golf with Coach in the summer. He comes out and sees my parents. It's beyond the court. It's beyond wins and losses. It's what they make of you, the attitude you get."

Those were only samplings of the outpouring of support for Davey and indignation toward the Santa Clara administrators who dismissed him.

"I think (through e-mails, letters and phone calls) maybe 300 different coaches (contacted him with their thoughts and condolences)," Davey said. "Some high school coaches, some college coaches … guys like (former Purdue coach)

Gene Keady, (former Los Gatos High coach) Jim Marino, one extreme to the other. Everybody you knew … even assistant coaches from schools in our league. If you put it (a random coaching name) down, you'd probably be right."

Even though Davey deflected the focus away from himself and his situation during the final month of his coaching career, that didn't mean he and those closest to him didn't feel anger and betrayal.

"We were really, really depressed," recalled Jeanne Davey, Dick's wife. "I remember coming back from the last game in the (WCC) tournament (at Portland, against Gonzaga). We got all the kids' luggage together and got them into their cars and on their way home, and the two of us just sat their on the steps (of Leavey Center, Santa Clara's arena) and just sat there and stared straight ahead. We must have sat there a good half-hour. Our life was over as we knew it. All that time promoting the university, telling so many people what a wonderful place it was, and look at what it goes and does to you.

"(Later) they tried to get my husband to go down with Kerry Keating to L.A. with (Filizetti) and Coonan on his (Filizetti's) private jet. They wanted him to go to L.A. to try to talk the alumni down there into giving money again. Imagine that … my husband flying on the jet of the guy who got him fired. *That's* audacity."

(Davey refused at the time the request was made, but later, after he accepted a fund-raising position at the university, he did agree to make the trip.)

"I was going to send my daughters to Santa Clara," Mike Davey, the oldest of Dick's two children, told a reporter, "but not now."

Because of his age and the fact he was in the last year of his contract, Davey's dismissal would have caused only a minimal stir if it had not become a matter for public consumption at midseason, and if his bosses had not concocted the voluntary-retirement fable. So, after the controversy had subsided, why was this firing any different than the other 50 in NCAA Division I basketball that season? Why was – is – this man different than any of the other 50 coaches who found themselves without coaching work at the end of the 2006-07 season?

Listen to two Scotts, one of whom played for Dick Davey before the other was born, and you have your answer.

Scott Lamson came to Santa Clara in 1981 after a distinguished prep career at Fremont High in nearby Sunnyvale. At 6-foot-5, he was a positional "tweener" – too small to be a prototypical power forward, not a good enough shooter to be recruited as a "three," and not quick enough to defend guards on the perimeter. But he oozed energy and toughness, and at Santa Clara, he made his own position – that of team stevedore. His father was a coach (and later a high-level school administrator) and his mother was a junior high school principal, so the quest for knowledge and learning were embedded in him almost from the crib. And his coach at Fremont was Phil Kelly, a basketball Archimedian for whom athletes who didn't have a team orientation simply didn't play, no matter how talented they were.

Santa Clara and Air Force (then one of the dregs of Division I) were the only schools to recruit Lamson out of high school, yet he became a starter on Santa Clara teams that posted three straight 20-win seasons and earned two NIT berths from 1982-85.

"The thing I remember most (about Davey) was that he wouldn't let anybody settle for second best," said Lamson, who moved successfully into finance and then real estate after college. "It didn't matter how good you were or if you were a top recruit or a walk-on; he treated everyone the same. He gave 100 percent effort and he demanded 100 percent effort. He challenged guys to fights … he kicked Nick (Vanos) out of the gym his freshman year. But I think if you look at all the guys who showed up at his last game and all the alumni games he had … everyone respects him because of the person he is. He made everybody a better person and not just a better basketball player.

"He's honest as the day is long, (and he's) as competitive in golf or cards as he is in basketball. I remember him telling us, 'If they don't score, they can't win.' He was about fundamentally doing things soundly, whether it's raising kids or doing your job. He taught us a whole life lesson about building from the basics and building from the foundation."

Lamson went through a family crisis in the mid-1990s when his younger brother Jeff, a high school football coach in nearby Cupertino, lost his job and served prison time after being convicted of a felony. Scott Lamson said his experiences at Santa Clara and the coping mechanisms he learned under Williams and Davey helped he and his family weather their ordeal.

"Things happen, and they happen for a reason," he said. "He gave me an understanding … you don't dwell; you move on to the next thing and make a positive out of anything that happens."

Scott Dougherty began his Santa Clara career in 2002, 17 years after Scott Lamson played his last game in a Bronco uniform. Like Lamson, he was virtually unrecruited out of high school (in Portland, Ore.), and he first made the Santa Clara team as a non-scholarship walk-on. Even after he was put on scholarship, the early segment of his career was punctuated by injuries. But he blossomed as a fifth-year senior in Davey's final season, averaging 14.9 points per game and attaining first-team all-conference honors while shooting 47 percent from beyond the 3-point arc.

"To be honest, the first thing that set in was absolute shock," Dougherty said of the team meeting at which Davey announced he wouldn't be returning. "Not only was he retiring but he was going to be forced to deal with this issue midseason.

"Certainly there was anger, not at anyone in particular but (because) it was something that had to be dealt with in the middle of the season. But I think it speaks volumes that it was never about Coach; it was always about the team. He doesn't want the limelight. He wants everything for us. He told us, 'I'm sorry you have to deal with it, but we'll get through it, it's over (for the present) and we won't deal with it again until the end of the season.' I know it sounds cliché, but we did try to make our best effort to come together for him and win the league and get to the postseason. We feel awful about that (not attaining those goals) and in some ways we felt like we let him down.

"I consider myself honored and blessed to have been here for five years. (Davey has) done so much for every single guy. (As far as) what type of person I want to strive to be, he'll be alongside my mom and my dad as one of my big role models. When I make a big life decision, I'll think, 'How would Coach Davey reflect on this decision I'm about to make?'"

Those players, and most of the others who played for Santa Clara during his 30 years there, understood and benefitted from the dichotomy that was Dick Davey – the soft-spoken, ready-listening, accommodating, gentle, even courtly away-from-the-floor presence who became part of their families and would drop everything at any time to come to their assistance in times of crisis, and the fiery, on-court drill sergeant who seemingly was intent on making their ears bleed and their lungs shriek during practice.

"One of the things about him that's really good is you don't have to worry about where you stand," said former SCU sports information director Mike McNulty.

"He always lets you know. I still remember I had my office right near the entrance (to Toso Pavilion, which was rebuilt in 2000 and renamed Leavey Center) and they were having practice on the floor one day. Because of the (air-supported Fiberglas) roof at Toso, you could hear what was being said on the floor because the echo was so great. All of a sudden we hear this enormous *eruption* … 'JESUS CHRIST, JEFFTY, WHAT IN THE HELL ARE YOU DOING?' He (Jeffty Connelly, a guard at Santa Clara from 1988-91) had made the critical error of not running hard enough in practice, and I swear you could hear Dick in Milpitas (about 15 miles away)."

But Connelly, and other Santa Clara players from 1978 through 2007, knew and know Davey as the man who embodied former coach Rick Majerus' line about players not caring how much you knew until they knew how much you cared. They knew and know him as a man who could demand much from them because they knew he would return more. He remained a presence in their lives long after those lives ceased to include intercollegiate basketball – a man whose teaching style was to show his pupils that every problem contained its own solution, and then give them the tools to find that solution.

They knew, and know, him as somebody who was all too aware of their basketball warts, but also saw beneath their skin and into their hearts. They experienced the abrasive on-court side, but they saw and felt and were touched by the compassion, the Joe Torre-like calm in times of upheaval, and the willingness and eagerness to make the stranger and the newcomer feel at home. They saw the laughter, the love of family, the sense of humor and fun, and most of all the wisdom that shouted even when it was muted.

His approach to basketball, family and life always reflected his parents and his rural Central California upbringing in a more genteel and unwired time. He never owned or made any significant use of a computer, and his telephone and his car remained his communications conduits right to the end. He never sent a text message and almost never read his e-mail. He didn't barricade himself in his office with doors and secretaries and voice mail as his buffers; indeed, he estimates that he averaged 15 to 20 *outgoing* telephone calls on non-game working days, in addition to fielding every incoming call to his office. Unlike most Division I head coaches, he didn't have a personal secretary.

"When I heard about Mike Montgomery resigning at Stanford (at the end of the 2003-04 season, for an ill-fated two-year sojourn with the NBA's Golden State Warriors), I remember what he said about (his distaste for) recruiting," Davey said. "That wasn't the case for me as much, because of the kind of kid we recruited. Monty was up against a Duke or a UCLA for his kids, and we're recruiting more against the people on the same level as us. I never got involved (with the meat-market element of new-age recruiting for which Montgomery developed such an extreme distaste), and maybe that's one thing (his detractors) didn't like about me. Ours was more hands-on and more about talking to people (directly rather than through self-serving intermediaries). I didn't do anything with the AAU programs, although my assistants did some. There are a couple of AAU people I know and like, but generally I didn't want to deal with those kinds of people.

"I think the one thing I've been able to do … I like people, and from my perspective I think I've developed tremendous friendships with a number of people in different areas. I don't like e-mail, partly because I'm not smart enough to figure it out, but mostly because when I want to talk to somebody I want to *talk* to them, have verbiage with them back and forth.

"I came back from vacation after my first year as head coach and I called the admissions office and asked the lady there, 'Charlotte, we have this kid that's trying to get into school and I don't know what to tell him. Is he admissible? I know you've had his paperwork, so where are we with him?' She said, 'Dick, do me a favor … I just got back from vacation and I've got 272 e-mails to answer. Can you wait a week until I figure out where I stand? I have to go through all this stuff and see where we stand.'

"I said 'Charlotte, you just helped me out a lot. Now I know I don't want e-mail. If I have to go through that kind of thing, I don't want to do it.'"

And he never did.

His first overture to recruits, many of whom had become accustomed to being praised and patronized, often involved a detailed discussion of their *worst* basketball characteristics – even when he desperately wanted to sign them, as in the case of his first interaction with Steve Nash on the steps in front of Nash's high school gym in Victoria, British Columbia.

Late in games, he loosened his grip on his players rather than tightening it, and he obliged his players to play through difficult spells by refusing to bail them out with a timeout. His wardrobe contained more sweaters than suits. Whatever was said to his players in anger one day would be a blank splice in his memory the next day. And unlike the coaches who start a new job by sending an updated resume somewhere else, all three of his job changes in 40 years were made without Davey burning any bridges or breaking any contracts or commitments.

"We need to have guys (at Santa Clara) that have that grit about them," he said. "I don't think I've ever run into a recruit where I've said, 'You're the answer to our prayers.' If you have that kind of program, you'll have a bad program. The kids won't respond properly, and you'll have a negative atmosphere. I think we researched kids reasonably well before we recruited them, and we had a pretty good idea where a kid was coming from before we went into the home and started making real contact. We had it organized it ahead of time. Occasionally we got surprised, but in general we were prepared ahead of time.

"We have a kid there now, (2006-07 junior) Brody Angley, who sort of epitomizes what the kind of player we wanted was about. He was the all-time leading scorer in North Coast Section football (at Enterprise High in Redding, 165 miles north of Sacramento), and some Pac-10 schools were looking at him. I walk into his house and we're sitting at the table with Brody and his parents, and I said, 'Brody, here's what I think. I think you should play football. You're just a natural.' Brody looked at me and said, 'I don't want to play football. I love basketball.' So I said, 'OK, that's the end of that conversation, because that's all I wanted to know. Now let's talk about Santa Clara.' And he's (the personification of) what my father taught me about keeping your mouth shut and playing hard. He never misses a practice, and he never complains."

Angley's father Jamie died in May 2007 after a year-long battle with cancer. Dick and Jeanne Davey both made trips to Redding during the final stages of his illness, and drove there again to attend the funeral. For Dick Davey, there is no such thing as a former player … only somebody who was an important part of his life then, and remains so now.

Williams, who was the Broncos' head coach from 1970 to 1992 and became athletic director after his retirement from coaching, was Davey's most profound recruiting and coaching influence. Davey described him this way, and in doing so described himself to a large extent:

"From my perspective, here's a guy with not a big ego who really wants to help people get better at what they do. Another way of getting an idea of what he's like is you go out in a car and there's three or four of you, and

35

Carroll always looks for the back seat. He wanted to let you be in the front seat. 'You get up there, you need more legroom than I do.' It was not about Carroll; it was about other people."

A month or so after returning from the Final Four, Dick Davey had "his" weekend – a surprise 65th-birthday party at his son Mike's house on a Sunday afternoon, followed the next day by his final awards banquet as Santa Clara coach, followed that night by a liars-dice session at The Hut, a bar adjacent to the Santa Clara campus. Well over 200 people showed up for the party and at least that many came to the banquet, and both crowds were chronological and occupational cross-sections. Mark Bruening, who played only one year for Davey (as a senior at Santa Clara during Davey's first year as an assistant there) was at the party, and Dan Glines, a former San Jose State head coach who got out of the business while Davey was still at Leland, was at the banquet. There were children and grandparents and corporate executives and blue-collar workers, and at least one player from most of Davey's 30 Santa Clara teams.

On a veranda overlooking his backyard and his party guests for the day, Mike Davey looked down, and smiled – something he had rarely done since his life came unraveled on a January day in 2004. He and his mother both are lifelong Los Angeles Dodger fans, and it was obvious he had had fun creating this backyard, where there is a baseball foul pole on the far-left corner, a sign reading "Davey Ravine," and two seats that once were anchored in the stands at Dodger Stadium. The pool and the mini-meadow of grass beckon to visitors, but this was one of the few occasions in 3½ years that chatter and laughter have been the prevailing sounds in this yard and this house.

Far more often, it has been enveloped by the sound of silence, and the house has been a manor of despair.

"I really think if not for the tremendous family support … if not for what I've been taught all these years, I would have checked out," Mike Davey said.

Chapter 2
BEAN

Editor's note: All of the proceeds from this book will be donated to the Global Ischemia Foundation, founded by Mike Davey to encourage and eventually fund research in the area of central nervous system ischemic accidents such as the one that felled Kathleen Davey. For more information on the foundation, log on to www.globalischemia.org.

The body once ran distance races, bore and nurtured two beautiful daughters, and was medically decreed to be in "Olympic shape" only days before its cruel and ultimate betrayal. The brain once enabled Kathleen Davey to practice law and delight all who knew her with her wit and insight. Now it has been stilled, most likely irreparably.

Three years and three months after she was stricken with a cardiac arrest at age 37, Kathleen – "Bean" to her family and friends – lay in a converted bedroom within the Campbell, Calif., home in which she and husband Mike Davey shared a life that once was everything that two people in unabashed love can possibly share. The smile that radiated every day before January 24, 2004 is twisted into an impassive grit. Her wrists are bent at 90-degree angles, with the hands extended as if seeking solace. Tubes and sensors monitor the flicker of life that remains.

"I don't know if my wife is ever going to come out of what's happened," Mike Davey said. "We're hoping for a miracle, essentially."

About all that's left of the Kathleen Davey that her husband and daughters and family and friends loved, aside from her will to live and their memories of her before she was stricken, are her eyes, which are wide open and still seem to search and summon and penetrate the darkness beneath. Sometimes, her loved ones and caregivers say, they seem to focus and follow movement, as if signaling an impending miracle.

"She's now looking like there might be something there," Jeanne Davey said. "For three years, it was a complete blank. Now you get the feeling something's going on, but it's hard to imagine that you'll ever get back anything (that had characterized Kathleen before she was stricken)."

It's those eyes that have been Mike Davey's beacon through his own darkness. Those eyes, his family, and his upbringing.

"If it wasn't for basketball and for my father, I would have committed suicide, to be honest with you," Mike Davey said in a voice that tells you he's still looking for some sort of meaning to the events on and since that murky January day. "I thought about it, and if it wasn't for Kathleen (still) living I think I would have committed suicide too. I see it as an absolute quitting thing, but I was so devastated … my relationship with her was my life in many ways.

"I see my life completely differently from that point on. I preached it so many years (as a teacher and parent and basketball coach, like his father), about absolute commitment ... I don't care if we're down 20 points with one minute to play; you're gonna get after your man and play hard until the final buzzer sounds. I preached it and lived it for so long that one night when I was (thinking about) driving into a pole ... I think I would have kept driving if not for that. It would have been an absolute sellout of my daughters, whom I love ... and my goal and my life now is to get them to adulthood and have them be respectable young ladies, for lack of a better term."

Mike Davey, the oldest of Dick and Jeannie Davey's two children, has a lot of the best characteristics of both his parents – his mother's ever-uplifting sunny disposition and ability to illuminate others intellectually and spiritually, and his father's loyalty, his knack for organization and motivation, and his ability to say the right thing to the right person at the right time. Those who were close to the Santa Clara program in the 1980s remember Mike as a quiet but open and perceptive teenager whose mind was so organized that he could speak in paragraphs while most kids his age were limited to clauses and sentences. He constructed his value system around that of his parents, but with his parents' encouragement, he had chosen his own career path, which didn't swerve back to parallel those of his parents until after his graduation from Santa Clara.

Just as Dick Davey started his adult life as a teacher and basketball coach at Leland, Mike teaches social studies and coaches basketball at Saratoga High School, nestled in the foothills bracketing the southwest corner of the Santa Clara Valley. Saratoga is one of the wealthiest communities in the San Francisco Bay Area – the median price for a home there in 2007 was $1,660,000 – and most residents have the wherewithal to send their children anywhere they wish, but choose Saratoga High because of its academic reputation, which rivals that of any other high school, public or private, in the Bay Area.

Mike Davey had attended Bellarmine College Preparatory, which once was part of Santa Clara University and continues to be one of its primary sources of incoming students. With his parents paying his way, and with nobody in academia doing him any favors because of his last name, he graduated from Santa Clara with degrees in history and political science. He had considered entering the political arena after working for John Vasconcellos, a Democrat who served on the California Assembly and Senate during a political career that spanned 38 years. In fact, it was Mike Davey who first broached and then helped push through the idea of transforming the abandoned Fort Ord military installation in Monterey County into a state university. Today, Cal State Monterey Bay stands and functions as evidence of his foresight.

"I went to those meetings," he said, "and I said why doesn't somebody make it a (state university)?," he said. "They all laughed … it was like nobody had even seen it, which was part of my discouragement with the (political) process. I'd been there and saw that it had buildings that would be perfect for dorms, a gymnasium, lots of room and open space … what more could you want?

"I enjoyed the people I met (in politics), my fellow interns and my boss … my mom (who taught for 40 years and still is much in demand as a home tutor) had told me that I'd be a great teacher, but she said there just wasn't any money in it. But what I had avoided all along was that I wanted to teach."

He got that opportunity when Barry Mendenhall, then the Saratoga basketball coach and a friend and confidant of both Carroll Williams and Dick Davey, offered Mike a position as his assistant. Mike took the job with the understanding that he would be offered a teaching job at Saratoga as soon as an opening occurred. That happened soon after he began working with Mendenhall, and when Mendenhall resigned a couple of years later, Mike replaced him.

His teams usually finish in the 17-to-19 win range and qualify for the Central Coast Section tournament, even though many of his players lack size and the year-round basketball experience that is common among players at most of the other schools in the area.

"Basketball (at Saratoga) kind of went into a shell in the late 1980s (after producing three NCAA Division I players in the late 1970s and early 1980s, including Randy Arrillaga, who was on the 1980 UCLA team that reached the national championship game)," Mike said. "Barry brought that back and made it a great experience for me. Our kids come from different backgrounds than you usually see, but they're intelligent basketball-wise … in some ways they sense they have to work harder to play, but at the same time they're wealthy too and have been given a lot.

"I guarantee you we run more plays than anyone in the state of California … we can because the kids are so bright."

(They also have been sources of solace for Mike in his time of need. Right after Kathleen fell ill, the players began to shout "Bean" as they broke their huddles after timeouts, and many of them have committed their time and energy to the various fund-raising campaigns on behalf of both Kathleen and the Global Ischemia Foundation.)

As a teacher and coach, Mike found the perfect vehicle by which to impart his sense of commitment and quest for one's best – just as his parents had done. He says his relationship with his father made him understand that life contains few entitlements, and that responsibility and challenge are to be confronted and not ducked, no matter how unfathomable or painful.

"There were certain expectations (while he was growing up)," he said. "When you met them, you were rewarded, and when you didn't, you weren't. Quitting was a big factor in my dad's estimation, not only on the basketball court but in our household. 'Are you trying as hard as you can? If you are, you'll be rewarded.' Maybe (he absorbed his father's postulates) grudgingly over the years, but I've taken it and tried to instill it (in others).

"My mother is a fantastic teacher, and not only myself but my daughters have benefited tremendously from her.

With my dad, if anything, he was less supportive than I wanted when I was a kid. He didn't want to be the dad who had the son who was that (pampered). He watched my Little League games from the parking lot ... he didn't want to be out there with the parents (because he wanted to have Mike perceived and acknowledged on his own merits and not as his son).

"He never coached me except for once when I asked him to ... it was my last basketball camp, in Helena, Montana, and it was an experience I'll always remember. I told him, 'All these years you never drafted me (on a camp team). Would you draft me for my last camp?'

"I'll remember that forever. We went all the way to the finals, and I learned a lot just from that one camp experience about how to coach. We were *horrible.* Maybe there were two of us who could play, but we made it to the championship game because he made us into a good team in just that one week."

Mike played basketball at Bellarmine, but his father always gave him an out because he didn't want Mike playing basketball for his, Dick's, sake, and because academics were the No. 1 priority in the Davey household. Just before his senior year, he took that out.

"I was a sometime starter on the Bellarmine freshman and later JV team, but after that, no," he said. "I wasn't a very good basketball player then; I think I actually got better after I got out of high school. My dad told me my senior year, 'You need a 4.0 (grade-point average) to get into Santa Clara. Let's sit down and talk … you can ride the bench for the rest of the year and play out your string, or (dedicate more time to schoolwork and) get the grades you're going to need to get into Santa Clara. And I'm not paying for anywhere else.'

"It wasn't that I didn't want to go to Santa Clara, but it was then that I really became a student. Life sunk in at that point. I quit the team my senior season, and I don't think I regret it to this day because I learned a lot about life from that. I got the 4.0, went to Santa Clara and then went from there. It really wasn't about the grades to me; it was about learning. I overloaded, but I absolutely loved college. I didn't enjoy the classroom at all until my senior year in high school."

Even more important, he met Kathleen McGrath – whose father Jerry had been a dean at Santa Clara – in a "Politics of China" class. Mike walked her across campus every day, trying to get up the nerve to ask her out, when she pre-empted him and suggested their first date. They married soon after both graduated, and their love for each other has never diminished.

"We were Hollywood … a princess-bride-fairy tale story," he said. "We got along so well, and that's why it was so devastating. I was always 'Sorry guys, I can't go play poker tonight, I want to go home and spend the night with my wife on the couch.' That was my reality … at the end of the day I just looked forward to going home and being with her and the girls. And when the girls went to bed at 8 o'clock, it was *our* time … reading, playing cards, watching TV, it didn't matter. I could *always* tell when she walked in the room. I can't tell that anymore, and it's so hard. She's still with me all the time, but it's not the way it was before.

"She had an infectious laugh that her co-worker described as somewhere between pixie bells and harp music. My sister wrote to her in the hospital: 'You are my best friend Bean, and I love you so much not because you are my brother's wife because you are you. You are the best listener, who shares her heart and compassion with all you love sacrificing *anything* for them. You have laughed with me, cried with me and stood by during the most difficult of times! I need you to know that you are the most incredible woman I have ever known.'"

Geoff Lamotte, who played basketball for Mike Davey at Saratoga, expressed his feelings about Kathleen in a letter, written before she was stricken and addressed to "the mother of our basketball program."

"We all love you dearly, Kathleen – your positive attitude, calming smile and your endless support and patience for our basketball team and Mike's coaching along with your indomitable will inspires us all. The Davey family name is qualified by love, selflessness, and a special influence on the Saratoga community. You have taught us to never give up on ourselves or on each other and we will demand the same from you. We are who we are as people because of your influence. May the most you wish for always be the least you get. Always with you in unequivocal love and support."

Weeks before she was stricken, Mike and Kathleen had considered an opportunity to leave the Bay Area's urban congestion and move to New Mexico. While they were pondering that option, Bean wrote to Mike:

"I was thinking about you today and how much I love you. Things seems to be crazy lately and we are going in all sorts of directions, but I wanted you to know that you truly are my soul mate, and I know how lucky I am to have you. Whatever the end of this year and next year brings, I know that we can meet anything that comes our way together wherever. I look forward to our continuing life adventure together wherever we end up. I know that I can live anywhere as long as I am with you."

When he talks about Kathleen, Mike's voice is tinged with wistfulness … and he acknowledges that when he isn't feeling wistful, he's feeling angry. Angrier than he ever thought he could feel before January 24, 2004.

Kathleen had been having chest pains and feeling weak for a couple of weeks before she was stricken, and had visited a Kaiser Foundation medical center for a checkup. She was told that her fears were unfounded, that she was as fit and healthy as any 37-year-old woman could hope to be, and that she should continue her exercise regimen. She collapsed at home after suffering a cardiac episode while doing pull-ups in the garage, and averted death then and there only because her older daughter Samie, then 6, had the presence of mind to call 911.

Police arrived within five minutes to administer CPR, and an EMT unit restarted her heart with a defibrillator and rushed her to a hospital. But speedy as the response time was, it wasn't fast enough to provide an adequate supply of oxygen to her brain. The result was cerebral damage that in most similar cases had proved immediately or imminently fatal. She was given last rites at the hospital that night, and though she made it through the night, doctors told the Daveys for the next few days that she was clinging to life by a day-to-day thread.

She refused to relinquish her grip on that thread, and before long was tightening it. She eventually stabilized to the point where she could be transported to a specialized-care facility, and in 2006 she came home after the Davey residence was remodeled extensively to accommodate her needs and those of her caretakers. Her bedroom has all the accouterments of a hospital room, and she must be monitored virtually around the clock, but Mike and his daughters have made Kathleen's room their sanctuary as well as hers.

That didn't make it any easier for the Davey family to cope with the situation, even more than three years after the fact.

"You don't think anything like that will ever happen to your family," Mike's sister Kim said. "I think because there was so much focus on me and my ballet success (she was a top performer for ballet companies in San Francisco and Seattle), there were times when my brother was really lonely, and (in Kathleen) he had found somebody who meant the world to him. Kathleen was his world, and

I can't tell you how painful that (Kathleen's illness) was for me as his sister. We're so close, and I knew what she meant to him. She was his rock … he's such a great guy, and to see him have to suffer in the way he has suffered just doesn't make any sense.

"He lived to be with her. He's come out of it a little bit but he'll never be the same … I've lived through the pain with him, and the pain and the tears don't stop. My brother's life is just not easy, and it's hard for me to watch that. But I'm happy to see him where he is today (in 2007) over even a year ago. He's getting stronger and stronger. As a family, it's amazing what they've been through."

"I can't say enough about my family and her family and how they've rallied around us," Mike Davey said. "I'm really lonely, but it's loneliness for what it used to be with Kathleen and I, not from not being around people who care for me. People have said that (at least they had their years together before January 24, 2004) … it doesn't help, but would you rather have not loved at all?"

Besides being angry at the cruelty of the blow to Kathleen, Mike remained infuriated by what he believes has been a lack of sensitivity by Kaiser during the four years of his family's ordeal. He said he was told by more than one Kaiser doctor after Kathleen was stricken that there was no hope whatsoever for any kind of meaningful recovery, and he said Kaiser has been slow at best and obstinate at worst when it came to trying any sort of treatment beyond basic stabilization.

Mike also is incensed with politicians, particularly President George Bush and others who reflect and represent the religious-right segment of the Republican Party and have blocked the stem-cell research that constitutes Kathleen's only real hope for emerging from her darkness. He is hoping that the progressives in the House of Representatives eventually can do as the Senate did in early 2007 and obtain enough votes to override Bush's veto of a bill that would expand stem-cell research. That failing, Mike was considering taking Kathleen to China, where major breakthroughs in the field have taken place because the Chinese government is far more proactive than its U.S. counterpart in terms of funding and encouraging stem-cell research.

"Government (in the U.S.) doesn't do anything for it; in fact it curtails it to a certain extent," Mike Davey said. "With the type of brain injury my wife has, there's almost nothing going on. Our goal for the Global Ischemia Foundation is to endow a chair at a medical center. That's about a million dollars ... we've raised $70,000 through fundraisers so far. I know nobody (in the U.S.) is doing research now, which makes it real discouraging, not only for her but for everybody else (suffering from anoxic brain injury). Dozens of people have contacted me and told me the exact same thing happened (to someone close) to them. 'Nobody's helping me. How do I get help?'"

The Kaiser advertising slogan is "Thrive," and Mike feels clenched in anger whenever he hears the word.

"Apparently since Kathleen's ear is no longer bleeding, her injury is not worth checking," the April 24, 2007 entry on his blog reads. "Since the doctor doesn't currently have the equipment to look in her ear and she is training a new doctor to go to homes, Kathleen will not be seen this week. She will make a visit this month, however. If her ear starts bleeding again we are to take her to Emergency. Thrive!"

"Everything changed when Kathleen's accident occurred," Jeanne Davey said. "It was heartbreak, just heartbreak. That first year, I cried every day … it's like losing your daughter. Now it's like you have this perpetual sadness in you because your child is so unhappy and your grandchildren are so unhappy. It's changed me forever; I'm always, always worried about Mike and the girls. It's been really, really hard … so much goes in, so many emotions.

"It's been very tough on the entire family. What to do, what not to do? What's right to say to somebody, and what might offend them? You're afraid … it's like walking on eggs all the time. I used to be a lot more outgoing, vivacious, and now I'm more reserved. My thing is, what can I do to try to make this up to them in some little way? What can I do to help fill the void? We used to talk about retiring in Hawaii or somewhere. Now we're here to stay."

"A doctor would tell you no, and probably I would tell you no at this point," Mike said when asked about Kathleen's chances of ever improving beyond her "minimally responsive" status. "But if there's any, any, *any* chance … there have been people, like a case in Australia that was just like hers. Somebody woke up after five years and said, what time is it?

"At the same time, what are the other options? There are no other options in my mind. It's not like there's a breathing machine you unplug. She's there, she's alive, and at times you think she's reading what you say. You don't *know* ... so as much as I can, I like to provide her something of the girls' childhood in case she does. That (Kathleen's bedroom) is our family room ... the girls go in there to read or watch TV of their own volition, and maybe they sense it too, that they need to do that."

Mike said his daughters – Samie, who was 9 in 2007 while her sister Rachie was 7 – were doing as well as could be expected under the circumstances. Both girls attend therapy sessions once every two weeks to help them deal with their grief and sense of loss, and Samie has immersed herself in softball, for which she has aptitude as well as affinity.

"(The girls are doing) much better than last year," Mike said. "There's really been a reawakening from them in the last year, going back to sports, and for Samie it's softball. She's an all-star but not a superstar ... her friends mean more than anything to her. It's more about the friends and it's also the effort and commitment together. Those are the same things I had when I was little ... it's a magical experience for her that she really needed."

Mike said the support from his family and that of his wife, and the continued involvement of the Campbell and Saratoga communities, helped make the ordeal manageable – if not yet totally bearable – for him. Dick and Jeanne are at Kathleen's side whenever their schedules permit it, and babysit their granddaughters regularly. Dick acknowledged during the 2004 season that his passion for basketball had been partially diverted by Kathleen's situation.

"A (Campbell) chiropractor who read an article on it (soon after Kathleen was stricken) has seen Kathleen three times a week for the past 3½ years, no charge," Mike said. "Campbell's a great town ... I teach at Saratoga (about eight miles away) and I want the girls near me, so they go to school there, but all the softball is Campbell and it's unbelievable. Samie's having a sleepover party next week ... there will be 10 girls there and five of them are from her softball team. That means so much to her. I haven't met a bad member of this community yet.

"The community has supported me much longer than I expected, and the families have been unbelievable. Kathleen's mom comes over three times a week to take her to therapy and see the girls. Her brother flies in from Arizona. Their other brother came to (Kathleen's) therapy two times a week for me, and they're always here to help with the girls. Her sister drives out every other weekend from Fort Bragg, which is four hours each way, and my sister Kim moved in for a year. The girls benefit from that so much ... they see everyone who was closest to Kathleen and get a sense of motherhood from her."

Mike was asked how he has tried to directly apply his upbringing to the ongoing crisis.

"There's the Lance Armstrong never-give-up perspective … maybe it's knowing what matters in your life," Mike said. "I've seen (his father) cry three times in my life, and none of them have been about 'woe is me.' It's been about things that really matter – (Jeanne) having breast cancer, my wife's accident, and his father's funeral. I know (his firing) really affected him, getting axed, but I never saw him cry about it. Saw him close, after the last game against Gonzaga, but it was about 'I'm not going to see these guys anymore.'

"He absolutely loves these guys. That was the hardest thing for him. He told me 'I don't give a crap about me; I want to be there for these guys.' He must have told me 50 times how he's letting Brody Angley and these other guys down. I told him 'You're not doing that. You're not letting anybody down. You gave all those guys everything you had for all those years.'"

Just as Mike learned that sort of commitment from his childhood, so did his father.

Chapter 3
'KEEP YOUR MOUTH SHUT AND PLAY HARD'

"The world isn't going backward, if you can just stay young enough to remember what it was really like when you were really young."

— A.J. Liebling, 1955

When he thinks about the Central California town of Ceres in which he was born in 1942, Dick Davey remembers a canopy of earth-grown green ... as might be expected from a town that took its name from the Roman goddess of agriculture.

Today, its population of 35,000 is more than four times what it was when Davey graduated from Ceres High in 1960. Ceres, 95 miles east of San Francisco and 80 miles south of Sacramento, in 1960 was surrounded and in some places infiltrated by farmland and grazing acreage, and the completion of the peach harvest late each summer often determined the starting date of school in the fall. By 2007, Ceres was surrounded and in many places infiltrated by the metropolitan sprawl of northern neighbor Modesto, which up until the 1980s was a lot like Ceres is now, but in 2007 had about 200,000 residents. Most of what farmland remains in Ceres has been given over to almonds, which are far less labor-intensive to grow than peaches.

Ceres High School, built in 1908, still is on Central Avenue, as is the Odd Fellows building downtown, and the Sequoia Super Market on North Central Avenue still is owned by the same family that operated it when Dick Davey went there to buy the bubble-gum packages that contained the baseball cards of Mickey Mantle and Rocky Colavito and Ted Williams and Yogi Berra. The main street still is bracketed by trees and brick buildings. The park, now known as George Costa Field, where Dick Davey took his first steps and sprints and leaps in athletics is still there, and the high school baseball diamond where Davey played still feels the churning of cleats, although they are softball cleats now. Both of the gyms in which Davey played high school basketball still stood in 2007, although the older one, which was Ceres High's basketball home until 1957, has been remodeled to accommodate new classrooms and no longer is used for basketball.

Otherwise, Ceres hardly would be recognizable to those who lived there a half-century ago and haven't seen it since. While the town was self-contained in 1960, today it is home to many who commute two hours each way to their jobs in the Bay Area because housing is well-nigh unaffordable in urban Northern California.

But Dick Davey remembers the Ceres of the 1950s vividly, and says growing up within its borders did much to shape him as an individual, family man, teacher and coach.

"It was small, maybe 8,000 people," he said. "You knew everyone, especially since we lived right in the heart of town. You had to be into agriculture there then. I swamped peaches, and picked grapes and boysenberries in the summer. My parents were friends with a grower in town who later became state director of agriculture under Ronald Reagan (when he was governor of California). We were also close friends with the (wine-growing) Gallo families; they'd come up to (the Daveys' cabin in) Pinecrest and we'd play dominoes on the deck up there. We had a two-bedroom house, and I lived in the same room with my sister (through most of his childhood)."

Dick Davey most often was called Rich as a youngster and into his early 20s – his wife Jeanne still calls him that – because his father, also known as Dick, was an exalted figure in town by virtue of being the Ceres High basketball, baseball and football coach, and one of the town's best-ever athletes before that. "Scuffer" Davey quit coaching in 1950, when Dick was 8, and went into the insurance business, but Dick still tells vignettes about the times, and the values that were instilled in him as a boy.

"All of my basic foundation of living came from my dad and family," he said. "It was a household where discipline was a key ingredient. He was the high school coach before I was there, but he talked about principles to live by. That was how he coached, and I remember all the high school coaches in the area would come over after games and talk to my dad, even after he left coaching, because they all respected him as an authority on teaching and coaching.

"He was very successful in all three sports. He was a great athlete before he went into coaching, but he never went out and played anything with me unless I asked him. He never said, 'Hey, let's go out and play.' I had to tell him I wanted to, because he wanted me to make decisions on my own."

Another reason was that the elder Davey didn't want his son to be dwarfed by his athletic reputation, which was considerable. After a year at Modesto Junior College, he played football at the University of San Francisco from 1940-42. The Dons' football program, which was disbanded in 1951 and never revived beyond the club level, played its home games at 60,000-seat Kezar Stadium and had lively rivalries with St. Mary's and Santa Clara, both of which were national powerhouses between the two World Wars and into the late 1940s.

"At 40 years old, he could punt a football 60 yards – consistently," Dick Davey said of his father, who was deferred from World War II military service because of a back injury suffered in college. "He played pro baseball for a year or so after he left college. Another summer, he went to a summer school at Huntington Lake, just out of Yosemite. At the time the world record for the pole vault was 15-6 … I think Bob Richards held it. In that summer camp, my dad went 15 feet in crude conditions. He could do anything.

"I can remember sitting with him in a boat up in Bridgeport … we're fishing, and we're about halfway through the day and he has nine fish and I have none. I'm about 11, 12 years old … I said, 'OK, I want to use your rod and everything you have on your rod, and you use mine.' That was fine with him, so we proceeded to fish another couple of hours and he caught nine more and I caught one.

"I realized it wasn't the rod, it was the guy handling the rod ... he was so unique in every way from my perspective. He was a really bright guy, and he had a great ability to needle you and have fun with you without you even knowing it."

Dick's mother, Marian, grew up under modest circumstances in the Fresno and Modesto areas, and met Dick's father while both were attending Modesto JC. Like many long-time residents of the Central/San Joaquin Valley at the time, she was of Armenian descent. Although she worked part-time at a Ceres dress shop, she was devoted to her family above all else, and Dick says she always imparted the lessons she had learned from growing up during the Great Depression and being obliged to extract the maximum from the minimum.

"My mom ... she was kind of the family organizer," Davey said. "She was the only one in my family (including his younger sister, who in 2007 still lived in Modesto) who didn't become a teacher. She was highly organized, loved sports and she loved being around athletics. We did everything together as a family ... we ended up building a place in the Sierras because both my dad and I were big into fishing. She was just a great mom ... (for pregame meals) she always made sure we had poached eggs on toast, which was the thing at that time."

One of Davey's earliest memories is from the final year of his dad's tenure as basketball coach, when Dick was 8.

"A lot of the athletes my dad had who are still alive, I've stayed in contact with," he said. "They were my heroes because they were good athletes when my dad was coaching there. We had one of those old-style gyms, where the bleachers were upstairs, and I was standing up there one time laughing at the guys because my dad had them running. I was standing by a window ... one guy stopped, picked me up and threw me out the window into a hedge. In the old days you did things differently ... (you could get away with) a lot more shenanigans."

Davey, of course, was too young at the time his dad was coaching to give much thought to the basketball tactics and philosophy his father employed, and the *modus operandi* that evolved later at Leland, Cal and Santa Clara was an amalgam of what he learned and adopted along the way. But one of the first things his father taught him about athletics, and life, was one of the things he never forgot.

"He had one mantra: Keep your mouth shut and play hard," Davey said of his father, who died in 1989 (his mother passed away in 2002). "That was his epitome of what a player was about. This was how you acted, responded, carried yourself. Never let the opponent know what you're thinking.

"I don't know why, but I remember vividly making a decision in fourth grade on what I wanted to do. Most kids don't decide until they're 20 … hell, a lot of kids *never* decide. But I said I wanted to play pro baseball and then coach basketball (as his dad had done). Those were the two things I wanted to do. I played sports every second I wasn't having to study or do chores. I remember Jim Presto, this kid across the street who was a baseball player … we were friends, but in seventh grade, for some reason, we'd get in fights every day. We'd meet at the phone pole every day and he'd beat the living crap out of me, and every day for about a month I'd come home with a bloody nose. Finally I said to myself, 'You can't beat this guy so you better stop doing this.'

"I got a little goofy then, but other than that, I was always playing ball somewhere. I remember playing all the time, *all* the time … I'd come home from school, and I'd go out in the backyard where we had a little basket area, or I'd go out in front and play catch with my dad. The kids in the house behind us had a little pole-vault pit, and we'd go out there and pole vault. You name it, we tried it … the only thing I never remember doing as a kid was snow skiing. Other than that, we played baseball, basketball, track, football, tennis, golf, swimming … at that time in our development, everybody tried everything (athletic).

"In the summer we'd work in the fruit; it was a way of making a couple of bucks and making it a little easier on the family. It was a struggle to make ends meet and own a home … when my dad bought a home in '47 or '48, I think it cost $8,000, which was a lot of money then. Traditionally every summer, you'd play ball and work in the fruit all summer long, and then we'd have a one-week vacation. Every year we'd go to Kennedy Meadows or Strawberry or Pinecrest or somewhere else up in the Sierras.

"Finally, in 1956 when I was 14, my mom decided we were not going to the Sierras this year; we were going to Las Vegas instead. We had a brand-new '56 Buick; you know, the model with the three portholes and the fins and everything. So we took off for Vegas; we had enough (money) to stay at the Sahara (one of the destination resorts during Las Vegas' early history) and what I remember was that it had a pool about the size of six basketball courts. We were there about a day and a half. Finally, we got into the car after the second day, got on (U.S. Highway) 395, and spent the rest of the vacation in the Sierras, because that's what we did."

It soon developed that Dick Davey had the same athletic prowess as well as the sense of propriety that characterized his father.

"I played baseball, basketball and football," he said. "I think we had about 160 in our senior class and maybe 600 in the school (about one-third the 2007 size of Ceres High, which no longer is the only high school in its district). It was a good athletic school, and we had some good teams … I still keep in touch with some of (his teammates) … in fact, every year in Spokane, I see Jerry Kanada, a guy who was two years ahead of me at Ceres and always goes to the (Gonzaga-Santa Clara) games."

Long after he left Ceres, Davey never forgot where he was from … and during his last season at Santa Clara, the basketball gods seemingly went out of their way to remind him.

"I know Coach Davey, I have seen him speak at clinics and have brought one of my better post players to his post-play camp," Jason Martin, the Bulldogs' coach in 2007, said. "We actually bumped into each other (during the 2006-07 season). Santa Clara had just beaten UOP, and we were on the way home from winning a preseason tourney in Brentwood. We saw each other at an In and Out (fast-food restaurant) in Tracy. Right when he saw me and our Ceres sweat suits, he told all of his players, 'Look – Ceres High, my alma mater.' I think Coach Davey has been an outstanding coach and an icon for Bay Area college sports. He is a great person."

Some of the schools – Manteca, Sonora, Oakdale – that in 2007 opposed Ceres in the Valley Oak League were also in Ceres' league during Davey's high school years, and the rivalries were intense because they were as much town against town as they were school against school. One of Ceres' most intense rivalries was against Tracy, which since has moved to a different league. Davey particularly remembers Tracy High's Nick Eddy, who later starred in football at Notre Dame and played five seasons for the NFL's Detroit Lions.

"I played baseball for four years on the varsity, basketball and football for three and track for two," he said. "You could play baseball and run track at the same time then … I high jumped and broad jumped. What you'd do … there'd be a track meet going on right next to the baseball diamond, so you'd run out of the baseball field, do the high jump, go back to the baseball game, do the broad jump, and go back to the baseball game. I wasn't that good in track … I think the best I ever high-jumped was 6 feet. One time I ran the 440, and I'd never run it before. So I'm running along, doing OK, not great, and all of a sudden I just died. I finished, but I finished last. I never had tried out for the 440 or practiced it, and after that I had a much greater appreciation for what 440 guys did."

"We had a few guys sneak around behind my back and do that," Art McRae, the Ceres baseball coach at the time, said with a laugh. "We'd have a game and a track meet going on simultaneously, and I'd pick up the paper the next morning and read about one of my players winning the pole vault."

McRae, a Montana native who had just received his teaching credential from Fresno State, came to Ceres High as head baseball coach and biology teacher at the start of Davey's senior year, 1959-60. McRae, at 24, wasn't much older than his players, and as a newcomer to coaching and to the school, he knew establishing a working relationship and a rapport with the Bulldogs' senior leaders would be essential if he were to attain his short- and long-term objectives for his program.

Davey, as the catcher and No. 2 pitcher, was the acknowledged team leader, and McRae said Davey's commitment to him and to the team was immediate and total. McRae began his career with a successful team, led by Davey, and that pattern continued throughout a Ceres career that spanned 37 years and included 550 victories, a CIF Sac-Joaquin Section championship in 1990, and nine league titles. At the time he retired in 1997, he had more victories than any baseball coach in Stanislaus County history.

"He had so many positive attributes," McRae said of Davey. "He was definitely the team leader, and he was very determined. I wouldn't say he was an overachiever, but he definitely got everything out of the ability he had. He had great concentration and intensity. I felt really fortunate to have that kid as a senior on my first team, and I became very good friends with him and with his family. You could do more things socially with your players' families than you could later, and Dick Sr. was a guy I never felt uncomfortable around. He was Dick's mentor, but he was pretty reserved (in terms of making suggestions to McRae about how the program should be run and how his son should be coached).

"Dick had great potential (beyond high school) and I always thought baseball was his best sport. As a catcher, he was very durable, and I don't remember him ever wanting to come out of a game. We had a No. 1 pitcher who was a pretty tough guy to handle, but Dick really knew how to work with pitchers. He had great knowledge, and his going straight to UOP and doing well there certainly opened up a lot of things for our (Ceres) athletes after that."

McRae stayed in touch with Davey throughout his coaching career, and in 2005 when McRae helped form the Ceres High Schools Alumni Association, Davey immediately purchased a lifetime membership. In 2007, as the school approached its centennial, Davey was named one of Ceres High's five most outstanding graduates, although he was unable to attend the ceremony because of his Santa Clara schedule.

"We stay in touch and we see each other occasionally," McRae said. "He spoke at my retirement banquet here 10 years ago. I also walked with him during a fund-raising event at West Valley College (for Kathleen Davey) last year (2006). It gave us a good chance to reminisce."

Considering his fourth-grade vow to play pro baseball and coach college basketball, it was surprising that Davey's first profound sports imprint was made on the football field. As a quarterback and linebacker, he became one of Ceres' first national-level recruits.

"Most of the scholarship offers I got were for football," he said. "USC and Oklahoma were involved. In baseball (which didn't implement its amateur draft until 1965) I had a chance to sign with the Pittsburgh Pirates out of high school … one of the scouts was a former Pirates player who lived in Ceres. The Pirates had taken a look at me, but I didn't want to sign because I had decided I wanted to go to college.

"I probably feel coming out of high school, my best sport was football, but I'd always wanted to play professional baseball, and basketball was probably the sport that I liked the most of the three. So I had a little interest for different reasons. There's no feeling like running onto a football field before a game, with the thrill and the anticipation, but at the same time, there's nothing like the quick-decision making of basketball. That was something I really wanted to play in college, and (he also wanted to play) baseball, which I probably wouldn't have been able to do at other schools."

Although Davey didn't choose football as a collegiate pursuit, he did choose a football-oriented school that was in the midst of one of its worst stretches ever in both basketball and baseball.

At the time, the University of the Pacific – which had just changed its name from College of the Pacific – in nearby Stockton was seeking to become in football what Fresno State became much later: "The Valley's program." (Fresno State football players in the early 2000s began wearing green Vs on their helmets, symbolizing the program's commitment to recruiting and signing players from the Central/San Joaquin Valley.) Though COP was one of the smallest schools playing major-college football at the time, and remained so until it dropped its football program in 1996, its administration and boosters were ambitious. They hoped to establish a constituency similar to those of Santa Clara, St. Mary's and USF before all three schools dropped football in the early 1950s.

Amos Alonzo Stagg, one of the sport's pioneers, was forced into retirement in 1932 by the University of

Chicago after coaching there for 40 years and winning 242 games and seven Big Ten Conference championships. (Chicago, which dropped out of the Big Ten in 1940, is the only charter member that no longer is in the league.) But he didn't stay retired long, and in 1933 COP hired Stagg, then 70, as its head coach. Amazingly, he stayed until 1946, and after that was an assistant coach under his son at Susquehanna College in Pennsylvania until 1952. He ended his career at age 98 as an advisory coach at Stockton Junior College (now San Joaquin Delta College) and died in 1965 at the age of 102. Stagg High in Stockton is named after him.

The energy and attention that Stagg had generated were sustained well beyond his tenure. In 1950, on land donated by Stagg himself, COP built Memorial Stadium, which had 30,000 seats and was expandable to 44,000. The Tigers fielded quality teams throughout the 1950s, sending two of their stars – running back Dick Bass and quarterback Eddie LeBaron – on to the NFL, where both had successful careers.

But Davey said any thoughts he had about playing college football at COP or anywhere else were dashed late in his senior year at Ceres, when he was invited to play in the North-South Shrine all-star game at the Los Angeles Coliseum. Bob Garibaldi from Stockton also was chosen to play in the game.

"I knew there were a lot of good players who were going to play in the game, and I was pretty excited," Davey said. "I was a quarterback and linebacker, and I punted. We go to camp before the game ... we're punting a little on the side. I'm reasonable, not great, and the first time I saw Garibaldi punt, I knew I wasn't going to be the punter anymore. He throws a pass, and I saw I wouldn't be the quarterback either, so now I'm down to linebacker. I broke my hand before the game ... I played almost every play defensively anyway, but I didn't play on offense at all. I never thought about playing football after that, except for when I was a senior at UOP, but by then I'd been out too long."

Garibaldi was offered considerable money by major league baseball teams to sign out of high school, but instead went to Santa Clara, and in 1962 pitched the Broncos into their only College World Series, in which they reached the championship game before losing in 15 innings to Michigan. He subsequently signed with the San Francisco Giants for one of the largest bonuses awarded an amateur player up to that time, but his major league career lasted only 15 games and 26 2/3 innings over four seasons. He was far better known to later generations as a longtime West Coast basketball official, and he worked many of Davey's games during the latter's coaching career at Santa Clara.

While Davey never supplanted Garibaldi as the Valley's baseball/football paragon, he did attain, by signing with COP, the first objective that he had set forth for himself as a fourth-grader. He says one reason he went to COP was its location, but the main consideration was the fact it was the only school that would permit him to play both basketball and baseball.

Perhaps because Pacific was sinking the bulk of its available assets into its football program, the basketball and baseball teams suffered during Davey's career there. He says he never regretted selecting UOP, but he played for only one winning team out of eight during his four years there.

In basketball, the Tigers were the playthings of the West Coast Athletic Conference, which was dominated by San Francisco; Bill Russell, K.C. Jones and the Dons had seized NCAA titles in 1955 and 1956 while winning a then-NCAA record 60 straight games. Under coach Van Sweet, with whom Davey remained close long after his graduation, Pacific went winless in WCAC play in both 1961 and 1963, and was 5-21, 10-16 and 4-22 during Davey's first three seasons. The Tigers had Ken Stanley, who averaged 24 points (still a school record) in 1960-61 and subsequently was drafted by the NBA's New York Knicks, and Leo Middleton, who scored 1,044 points from 1962-64, but not much else during Davey's first three years. They improved to 14-12 in 1964 under new coach Dick Edwards, who crafted a 169-72 record and took UOP to four NCAA tournaments during his nine-year tenure.

The baseball situation was little better, as Pacific went 33-63 from 1961-64. Davey, by now exclusively a catcher, batted .359 to lead the team his senior season, but the Tigers finished only 8-17.

Four decades later, Davey remembered his UOP experience primarily for the education he received and for the fact he met his future wife during that time. Jeanne had started college at UOP, transferred to Penn State, and then returned after a year. They married in 1965.

In 1964, after the conclusion of his senior baseball season, Davey signed with the San Francisco Giants organization and was assigned to their Decatur, Ill., affiliate in the Class A Midwest League.

"I was signed by (Giants scout) Eddie Montague, who had signed Willie Mays (and whose son of the same name became a longtime major league umpire)," Davey said. "I think I got a little extra time because it was him who signed me."

Davey played 89 games for the Decatur Commodores in 1964, and the only statistical memory he has of that season was the dubious distinction of leading the Midwest League in passed balls – even though, in reality, he didn't. "We only had two catchers," he said, "and the other catcher got hurt, so I wound up playing those 89 games all in a row."

(Davey actually was an improvement over the man he replaced, DeGold Francis, who had 47 passed balls. The Commodores, who finished the season 61-63 and placed sixth in a 10-team league, wound up with 83 passed balls for the season.)

One of only two college graduates on a team that included about 20 players, Davey said he came to a quick realization that riding buses between small towns, playing every day in the oppressive Midwest heat, subsisting on per-diem meal money that barely was sufficient to buy greasy-spoon café food, and spending five or six months among baseball "lifers" each year wasn't his idea of a career. Beyond that, he came to an early underst anding that he didn't have the talent to make a long-term living in baseball.

"In that league, we would play a night game at Decatur, get on a bus and drive all night to Appleton, Wisconsin and play the next night," Davey said. "It was an eight-hour drive, and I still remember Richie Klaus, our manager, taking a 12-pack of beer on the bus, sitting in the front seat and throwing an empty can out the window every 30 minutes. It kept us awake. There wasn't a lot to do on the road … at that time (as a diversion to while away time) guys got a kick out of spitting on (each others') sanitaries (white socks) until they turned them black.

"One excuse I had for the problems I had was the lighting in our park (Fan's Park, which was demolished in 1974 after Decatur lost its Midwest League franchise) was so bad you could hardly see. We had a guy from Oakland, Jim Black, who probably threw about 98 (mph) … he couldn't see my signs and I couldn't see his pitches. But I knew pretty early on that I wasn't going to be good enough (to have a chance to make the majors)."

One of the few highlights for Davey during that summer of 1964 was a photo op. Future Illinois Sen. Charles Percy was running unsuccessfully for governor, and during his campaign, he made a stop in Decatur while the Commodores were home. Davey posed for a publicity picture with Percy before one night game.

"Rick Reichardt (who had just signed with the California Angels for a bonus so huge that it led directly to the adoption of the major league draft in 1965) was going to play his first professional game (with Quad Cities) that night," Davey said. "The picture had Reichardt batting, me catching and Percy dressed up as an umpire, holding a lantern.

"There was one other college graduate on the team, and everybody else had different agendas. I enjoyed the guys, but it's a different lifestyle … a really tough deal. I got a taste of it and found out I wasn't good enough, and that was what it (his minor league experience) was about, finding out what it was about."

Davey suffered a broken wrist while playing in a pickup basketball game during the 1964-65 offseason. At that time, most minor league players who weren't "bonus babies" usually were released outright if they suffered injuries that appeared likely to keep them out of action for any length of time. Davey was spared that fate, but only briefly.

"Even now, I can't bend back that wrist," he said. "I went to spring training with the Giants (in 1965), but my hand was fried. I was only two weeks out of a cast, and I was dribbling the ball back to the pitchers. After a month I could swing the bat a little, and the Giants sent me to

Twin Falls (Idaho, in the rookie-classification Pioneer League). I never would have even gotten to go there if it hadn't been for Montague, because he had some confidence in me and helped me stay on a little while longer. But I only lasted about two weeks at Twin Falls. I just couldn't throw."

The only thing Davey remembers about his short stint at Twin Falls was his honeymoon, such as it was.

"A couple of days before workouts began in Twin Falls, I went up there and got a flyrod and convinced Jeanne to go fishing with me," he said. "She was going to knit while I fished. Well, the mosquitoes just tore us up, and I finally had to get out of the stream. We weren't exactly living the lifestyle of two college graduates.

"Some honeymoon," Jeanne said, grinning. "I sat in the car just about the whole time."

After the Giants released him, Davey – who already had graduated from UOP, and had married Jeanne – returned to Stockton to complete work on his masters degree. Next, he began his search for his first coaching/ teaching job.

"I sent out 105 applications (to teach and coach), and I got seven interviews," he said. "One was at Compton High (an inner-city school near Los Angeles), for an assistant's job, and another was at Leland (as head coach). The Leland job was coaching basketball, baseball and C-and-D basketball, and teaching U.S. history, world history, state requirements (health and drivers education), American government, and P.E."

In the San Jose area, school districts were and still are a hodgepodge, with both high-school-only districts and K-12 entities serving a valley that in the 1940s had experienced the first of a series of growth surges that ballooned San Jose's population from about 75,000 in 1940 to 204,000 in 1960 and to over 950,000 by 2005. The San Jose Unified School District's boundaries extended in only one direction – south – from the city's oldest central neighborhoods; consequently, the district was and still is smaller than most of its metropolitan counterparts.

San Jose High had been around since long before the turn of the 20th century, but was the only public high school in the city until 1942, when Lincoln opened to serve the expanding and relatively affluent western part of the city. Companies like General Electric and Sylvania that had come to San Jose to fulfill war-related contracts from 1942-45 decided to stay and expand after the war, and San Jose's population began to swell. Willow Glen High opened in 1950 to accommodate an exclusive series of neighborhoods that extended from downtown San Jose's western edge. In the early 1960s, Pioneer was built at what then was the southern edge of the city, but there still was no school to serve the Almaden Valley, which yawned across what was then largely unincorporated Santa Clara County land in the southern foothills, and had been the scene of extensive mercury-mining operations many years before.

Leland, which much later became known as the alma mater of future NFL player and War on Terror casualty Pat Tillman, was conceived almost a decade before it opened in the fall of 1967, and the 55-acre parcel on which it and an adjoining junior high school were built was acquired in 1960. Because the Almaden Valley was filling up rapidly with young, upwardly-mobile families who wanted a relatively rural lifestyle within an urban area, it was immediately apparent that Leland would soon become the district's flagship high school. Consequently, the staff was carefully chosen.

"Our first principal had been the director of personnel for the San Jose district," Davey said. "He hand-picked a lot of people he'd known from other schools to come to Leland, and he knew exactly what and who he wanted. And he did a great job. We had great support at Leland … there were 33 staff members that first year (1967-68), and at least 25 of them came to every one of our home games even though we were probably the worst team in America. Everyone supported everyone else, and it was the greatest community … it seemed like 99 percent of the kids there were college bound. Thank God he hired me."

The principal was Aaron Seandel, a former San Jose State basketball player, who stayed at Leland until 1973 and later became SJUSD assistant superintendent. His son Steve was an assistant coach under Davey throughout his 15 years as head coach at Santa Clara … and to complete the cycle, Steve was hired as head coach at Leland in the spring of 2007 after Davey was relieved of his Santa Clara duties and Seandel wasn't retained by incoming coach Kerry Keating.

Davey was 25 at the time he took the job, and like many young, inexperienced coaches before and since who are not far removed from their playing days, he approached the task of building a program the same way great athletes approach on-field obstacles – straight ahead and without subtlety or tact.

"When you're young and an immature and unaware guy trying to start a program, you do some things," Davey said. "One was that I wanted the keys to both gyms – women's sports weren't in vogue yet – and I wanted to be able to use them at any time, and I wanted every kid in the program to have the keys. We didn't get 100 percent on that one, but we finagled our way around it. I also remember, before the season started, bringing in all the parents and setting the groundwork. 'Here's who's in charge … I appreciate your calling and I know all of you want your sons to be starters, but I'd have rocks in my head if I didn't play the best guys because the object is to win games, not satisfy parents.'"

Leland had opened with 610 students, far fewer than most of its opponents, in three classes, and some athletes who had been involuntarily moved from Pioneer had no inclination to try to contribute to the sports teams at their new school. Because of that, and because Davey by his own admission was still learning the nuances of coaching, the Chargers struggled during their first three seasons.

"I remember my first game as a head coach was against Branham (another brand-new high school in San Jose), and they had Gary Radnich (later a sports anchorman at San Francisco television station KRON for many years)," Davey said. "He went for about 40 against us ... (in subsequent years) I used to tease him about scoring and then going to the water fountain to get a drink while his teammates went back to play defense. He was a hot dog, but a hell of a player."

Leland won two games in December 1967 while capturing the consolation championship of the Westmont tournament in Campbell, but won only one game during the balance of the year. The next season, the Chargers didn't win a single game, and Davey, wrapped too tightly by his frustration and impatience, was beginning to establish a reputation for inflexibility and volatility rather than for his basketball acumen and ability to relate to players.

"I started showing films of games to the parents to help them understand the game a little better and see why maybe their kids weren't playing," Davey said. "Of course, you never have a (high school) parent who completely understands. They still think their kid should be playing more. It was a learning time for me too. At the end of practice that first year, at 6 o'clock after three-hour practices, we split the kids into two groups and they couldn't leave until (each group) made five straight free throws on one end and five straight on the other. The first day, one group gets out about 6:30. The other group ... when it was about 9:15, I'm still working with the other group. And we would have gone until 6 in the morning if we had to. We weren't going to fail at that task. We were a horrible team, but we had to find a way to develop discipline."

The problem was that Leland simply didn't have enough quality players during Davey's first two years to compete with programs like Santa Teresa Athletic League rival Willow Glen, which went 27-0 and won the Central Coast Section title in 1969 under Andy Locatelli. Locatelli later became a Santa Clara assistant coach, before Davey was hired there, and remained a friend of Davey's during a subsequent period as director of athletic facilities at SCU.

It was during this period that Davey adopted another of the precepts that were to guide him throughout his coaching career: That a coach must support his players regardless of their talents, and that all a coach has a right to expect from his players is their best effort.

"If you don't have good players, you won't be successful," he said. "None of us has this magic wand. My wife was a critical clement for me during my second year at Leland. We were pretty strong on the disciplinary side and I think the kids appreciated it, but they were kind of scared of it too. I'd be walking down the halls of the school and one of my kids might be 100 yards away … he'd see me and dart into a room or in another direction because he was in fear of me. The discipline may have been a little too severe.

"One day Jeanne told me, 'Your disciplined approach may be giving you a problem because you don't let them be themselves.' So on a Saturday morning a couple of weeks after that, we had the team over to the house. We talked some basketball, barbecued, chased the cat around, had some interchange, and I think they started to see me more as a human being, and we developed a better relationship.

"We still have guys from those teams come to our (Santa Clara) games. They love to tell stories about how goofy I was."

Just as Davey's former Leland players remembered their coach almost four decades after playing their last high school basketball game, they remember their "team mom" just as readily and fondly. The bond between Dick and Jeanne Davey was a partnership from the start, and even though she had her own distinct life niche that didn't involve basketball at all, she enjoyed being a basketball wife ... and she truly loved being a "basketball mom."

Chapter 4
JEANNE AND KIM

They saw a movie starring Rock Hudson on their first date, and almost from that point on, Dick Davey had an anchoring rock in his life – someone with whom to share and shoulder the peaks and precipices of his profession while she was establishing a profound identity of her own.

Dick and Jeanne Noble first met in 1962, when Dick was a sophomore at University of the Pacific and Jeanne was a freshman there. "He had a friend ask me if I would go out with him," Jeanne recalled almost a half-century later. "I knew who he was (because of his status as an athlete) and I said yes, so the friend set us up. We went to a movie … *Giant*, with Rock Hudson (and James Dean, in his last role before his death in 1955).

"At that point, I wasn't dating any one person. I was so young, and I was a Catholic girl from a Catholic upbringing. Then, when I was a sophomore, he asked me to a dance and a party, and after that we started dating regularly."

Even though Dick was an achiever of considerable stature in the athletic realm, his new girlfriend quickly broadened the limited horizons of a country boy from a small town who'd spent most of his youth playing sports and picking peaches. By the time she reached college, Jeanne had already lived all over the world and had been exposed to the most pristine of the world's beauty and the most shameful of its ugliness.

Jeanne's father was Major Gen. Charles Noble, one of the most versatile and accomplished military men of the 20th century. Upon his graduation from West Point in 1940, his engineering expertise prompted the Army high command to choose him to participate in the then-nascent Manhattan Project, which culminated in the development of the two atomic bombs that were dropped on Japan in 1945. Jeanne was too young to remember that event, but she does remember knowing virtually nothing about what her father did within the military. She also knew that her dad's profession made her an "Army brat" who would spend almost her entire childhood moving all over the world.

"I didn't know about it (the Manhattan Project)," Jeanne said. "Mom didn't know it. We never knew where he was or what he was doing, and we never asked. It wasn't declassified until I was an adult with kids. He was in charge of the plutonium, believe it or not, and he was based in Oak Ridge, Tennessee. He'd go to New York and have meetings, then fly with (Dr. Robert) Oppenheimer out to New Mexico. His title was (being) in charge of Ohio Valley flood control, and he was doing that while he was still involved with the other things that we didn't know about, that were covert.

"When he was heavily involved with Oppenheimer, he 'based' us in Syracuse for two years. We also lived in Harrisburg (Pa.) for a year … that's where I got my braces. It's funny why you remember certain cities."

After his work on the atomic-bomb project was completed, Noble (then a colonel) was put in charge of creating temporary housing for the millions of European Jews who had been incarcerated in the Nazi concentration camps. As part of that assignment, he was with one of the first Army units to liberate a death camp, in what was then Czechoslovakia, days before the end of the war in May 1945.

"He built the prison at Nuremberg where the (Nazi war) criminals were housed while they were being tried there," Jeanne said. "He definitely saw everything, but he never told us any of this until a few years ago. He was with a platoon that freed one of the concentration camps. He was shocked, absolutely shocked … they'd heard rumors (about the atrocities committed during the Holocaust) but they didn't know for sure until then. He was shocked at how emaciated they were … it's hard to believe today that there are people who say it never happened. My father was there, and he saw it.

"Because of my childhood and because of what my dad went through, I am fiercely defensive of Jewish people and African-Americans. I know what they went through. Maybe I'm too much that way, but I'm very, very protective of both groups. Every one of my students (in her subsequent teaching career), I've had read *The Diary of Anne Frank*, and there's another book written by Alicia Appleman-Jerman (who was the only member of her family to survive a death-camp imprisonment in Poland). I know her personally; we swim at the Y together. It's a story of courage and survival ... she's a wonderful lady and I've become very, very close to her. I want all of my students to understand what happened (because of Hitler and the Third Reich)."

After the war, Noble was promoted to brigadier general and was assigned to Gen. Dwight Eisenhower's NATO staff in France for three years. Jeanne, by then eight years old, said her time there was another major factor in the shaping of her life and character.

"I think that's why I love history so much ... I lived it as a child," she said. "When we lived in France, all our field trips were to places like the Eiffel Tower and Arc de Triomphe and the Royal Château de Fontainebleau (where the Treaty of Paris was signed in 1814, ending 50 years of almost-continuous Franco-British warfare). I saw the bed and the nightgown that Napoleon died in. There was a (restored) medieval village called Mont Saint-Michel that I saw when I was 9, and I remember it as though it were yesterday. As a child, if you see remarkable things, they always impact your life."

Jeanne didn't remember seeing any of the vestiges of the Nazi death camps, but she has never forgotten another sort of ethnic cleansing upon her family's return to America. Her father was stationed at Fort Benning, Ga., and the family lived in Atlanta.

"It was such an awakening for me because as a child, to me, there was no such thing as black or white," Jeanne said. "I lived in the Army world. We were all one. When I lived in Paris, we lived in Versailles while the SHAPE village was being built. It stood for Supreme Headquarters Allied Powers Europe, which became NATO. We lived with children from all over the world who spoke different languages. I learned (to speak) French fluently, but I also learned to communicate with kids from Italy and all over. That's why my experience in Georgia during (the start of) the civil rights movement was so profound to me. This was during the time of (Alabama governor and two-time presidential candidate) George Wallace and (Georgia governor) Lester Maddox (both of whom were ardent segregationists).

"I went to an all-white segregated school because that was the only school they had near the post. I can remember other kids saying 'I don't want to go to school with Negroes or colored people' or worse things that they called blacks. I remember them throwing things out the windows of the school bus at black kids, and I remember looking out the window and seeing the shacks they lived in. In town, the water fountains were 'colored' or 'white' and so were the restaurants, but the most shocking thing was that blacks could only go to town on Tuesdays. That was 'black day.' One time my sister and I went down to the radio station, and there was nobody on the streets and I didn't understand why. I didn't know until then that I was in town on 'black day.' I also remember seeing our cleaning lady work all week for $5. That whole experience made me very, very angry with whites for the way they treated black people.

87

"I also remember (seeing on TV) how obnoxious the people were to those black children who were trying to integrate the schools (in Little Rock, Ark., after the *Brown vs. Board of Education* decision by the U.S. Supreme Court). I remember the crowds screaming at the innocent little black girl, and being so appalled. All of that marked my life more than anything. I remember thinking how horrible they were and being appalled at (the behavior of) Maddox and Wallace."

The Noble family's next stop was Indiana, where Jeanne found what he hoped would be a permanent home. "My father was stationed in Louisville, and we stayed across the river in Indiana," she said. "That was probably the happiest time of my childhood, other than Paris. It was a nice high school, and I was accepted. I went to Girls State, I was on the student council, and high school basketball there was just *unbelievable*... they'd (vocally) take the roof off the place. Things were finally falling into place for me, and then Sputnik went up and my father was shipped out again to build missile bases in California. I was in culture shock that first year I was in L.A."

After graduating from Bishop Montgomery High in Torrance, Jeanne traveled to Northern California to attend UOP, on the recommendation of her two aunts, both of whom graduated from there. "It was the right place for me, because it was so small," she said. "But when Rich and I were dating during my sophomore year, my father was transferred to the Pentagon and wound up being chief of engineers in Vietnam. He wanted me back there, so I transferred to Penn State for a semester. I was miserable; I stayed in my room the entire semester and got a 4.0 grade-point average. With that, I applied for a scholarship to UOP and got it, so my parents had to let me go back."

Dick and Jeanne Davey knew even then that they were destined to spend the remainder of their lives together, but the Vietnam War accelerated their matrimonial timetable.

"This is the joke of it," she said. "Here my father is a two-star general and the chief of engineers in Vietnam, and my husband graduates from college and goes to play professional baseball. I'm still in school, and my husband gets a 1-A draft notice. He either had to get married or go to war. So we got married (in 1965), and my father was fit to be tied ... here I was marrying a draft dodger (laugh). When he was in graduate school, the draft rules changed, and you had to have a dependent (to be deferred from the draft). That's when Mike came along.

"My father later said we should never have been in Vietnam in retrospect. It's the same thing as with Iraq now ... what a terrible mistake. You wonder why people don't learn from the past."

Her spirits, unlike her clothes, undampened by the "fishing honeymoon" at the tail-end of Dick's brief minor league baseball career, Dick and Jeanne Davey settled in San Jose and began their careers as teachers and parents. Kimberly, their daughter, was born late in 1970, and Jeanne said neither she nor Dick gave much thought during his Leland years to merging into a faster career lane. She loved being a teacher and a mother, and she reveled in her first experience as a "team mom" who made her husband's players feel as if they were part of her family.

"We were going to relax and live a nice quiet life," she said.

Then Dick accepted the assistant's position at Cal in 1972, and the family moved to Walnut Creek, in the East Bay.

"It's hard being married to a college coach; you don't see him much," she said. "There's never enough time in the day to improve your team, so family unfortunately has to take a back seat if they're going to succeed. And at Cal, I was never a 'team mom' because I was an assistant's wife and assistant coaches' wives didn't do that (there)."

Happily for Jeanne, they did at Santa Clara, where Sue Williams, Carroll's wife, was immersed in her husband's program throughout his tenure as head coach. Sue Williams and Jeanne became close friends, and Jeanne, like Sue, adopted many of the Santa Clara players as her own – particularly the young men who at first found the urban, mostly upper-middle-class environment at Santa Clara difficult to which to adjust initially.

"I love geology," Jeanne said. "I took a course at UOP that I just loved, and I have all of these rocks I've collected … sedimentary, metamorphic, igneous, gemstones. I love to find little bits of copper, and Indian arrowheads. Sue loves rocks too, and she loves cats, just as I do. We're absolutely two peas in a pod."

Yet while she derived considerable pleasure and satisfaction from the bonds she formed with Dick's charges during his Santa Clara career, Jeanne flung herself even more eagerly into her own dual career as teacher and parent.

As she spoke in 2007, she was sitting at the dining table adjoining the Daveys' kitchen. Areas on three sides of the table that in most homes would be pantries are bookshelves, and books are jammed into every spare millimeter. Hundreds of small paperback books are on those shelves, and Jeanne says she has more than a thousand titles in the house. On the wall, there's a clock adorned with depictions of birds, and as the top of each hour arrives, the clock's "chime" is a chirp, each specific to a certain variety of bird.

It's in that kitchen that Jeanne tutors children, some of whom have been with her since she taught them in kindergarten. Like the rays of sunlight that cascade through the kitchen windows, and the smile and warmth that radiate from her even in the midst of the Davey family's recent crises, her mission and her passion are – always have been – to illuminate young minds. She left teaching when Dick got the Santa Clara head-coaching job, but just as Dick says he doubts he will ever remove himself entirely from the basketball realm, Jeanne says she can't see herself ever foregoing teaching. The rewards, to her, are too precious.

Even while she was still teaching, Jeanne based her entire approach on creating and developing a love of reading within her pupils. Now, freed from the curricular limitations of schools, she has even more freedom to help kids embark on learning adventures through books.

"I think the biggest thing is just being excited about it yourself," she said. "It's just getting them to books you know will stimulate and excite them ... leading them to books you know they'll love. Then as soon as they finish, you present them with a stack, and they can't wait to get at them because they loved the first one so much. I hand-picked all of those books (pointing to a stack of about 10 small books, tied together by string) for one child only; there's another one, and here's another.

"I tended to lean (as a classroom teacher) toward science and history. When you've lived as long as I have, you see things you saw once happening all over again, like a circle.

"My greatest love was kindergarten, I taught different levels, but kindergartners were my favorites ... they are so amazed at what you have to teach them. At that age, you get them almost *carte blanche*, and they're really open to learning, and once you've got them, they're turned on. They never lose you. Look at this graduation announcement. This girl is about to graduate from USC, and I had her in kindergarten. You get these wedding invitations, graduation announcements ... you go to bar or bat mitzvahs, and these are my babies for life. Even the kids on the basketball team don't know how young they really are ... they're just kids.

"I remember when Steve Nash was sick in Birmingham during a tournament we played there one Christmas, I remember bringing him chicken soup. Just a baby ... my baby."

With Dick often on the road or holed up in his office trying to maximize Santa Clara's basketball resources, Jeanne assumed most of the responsibility for raising their two children.

"My day would be, get up at 5:30, leave for work at 6:30, teach all day, get in the car, drive Kimberly to San Francisco, come home at 7, sometimes even 9, feed the kids, spend time with Mike and help him with his homework, get them to bed, go to bed, get up at 5:30 and make their lunches," she said. "That was my day, every day."

Kim Davey was born pigeon-toed, and her parents started her in classical ballet at the age of 6 on the advice of an orthopedic surgeon. She began while Dick was at Cal and the family still lived in Walnut Creek, and when Dick moved to Santa Clara in 1977, Kim's teachers, seeing her talent, suggested that Jeanne try to get her into the San Francisco Ballet School, one of the top instructional facilities in the country.

"They raised her in the ballet world ... I really knew nothing about it (ballet)," Jeanne said. "I'd sit in the car with my cat while she was in there, just the two of us. I'd do my teacher homework, and then the cat and I would cuddle up together and take a nap. It was a half-Siamese, half-Persian cat ... I loved her, she was so gentle.

"What we tried to do was expose both the kids to everything we could. Kimberly was doing theater and art and piano lesson and gymnastics and Girl Scouts, but she kept eliminating things … ballet was all she wanted to do. With Mike, the hard thing was that he didn't have a dad (constantly) at home to help him with his sports. He was small, a towhead, and he really didn't start to fill out until he was a senior in high school. It was hard for him.

"At one point (while Mike was a freshman at Bellarmine) he said, 'Mom, I want to quit baseball.' But he was scared (of his father's reaction). All I said was 'Sweetie, are you happy playing?' He said no. So I said, 'Quit then.' Mike was identified as mentally gifted from the time he was in kindergarten, and I always tried to make him realize how mentally talented he was and what a gift it was and how he could use that to help his fellow mankind. That was my mission (both as a parent and as a teacher): Find each child's gift and help them find their niche."

In 1992, after Dick was promoted to the head-coaching position at Santa Clara, Jeanne found a new niche of her own – as fulltime "team mom."

"When Rich got the head job, I was teaching kindergarten and was director of kindergarten at Harker Academy (a private school about five miles from the Davey home)," she said. "It was administrative as well as teaching. I loved the kids, but I wanted to be part of the (Santa Clara) team. That was Steve Nash's freshman year …

we go to Utah and we beat Arizona, and it was like, 'OK, I'm quitting this job so I can be part of it. This is a once-in-a-lifetime opportunity that I can't pass up.' So I became a dedicated team mom. With every player, I made a memory book for him, and I took pictures constantly. I just really, really loved the kids ... even if they lost, I knew they'd done the best they could and tried their hardest. I made up 'care packages' for them on each road trip, just stuff like granola bars and apples.

"Steve (Nash), Marlon Garnett, Kyle Bailey ... here's a picture of Kyle (with his arm around Jeanne) ... he brought me ice cream the day after I had surgery for breast cancer. That was my first game back ... he was like a son to me. They all were."

Jeanne was diagnosed with breast cancer during the 2002-03 season.

"It was the year before Kathleen (Mike's wife) went down," she said. "It was just a shock ... nobody in our family had ever had it. They caught it early, thank God, and I didn't have to do (chemotherapy) because it wasn't into my lymph nodes. It really impacted my husband's job. When they called and told me, I was here getting ready to go to the game; my husband had already gone and I decided not to go to the game because I was in such a state of shock, but I didn't want him to know until after the game. It was pretty evident that he was shaken up, but he didn't know until after the game.

"The kids brought cards, candy, ice cream, and this beautiful, beautiful plant. Jim Howell was like the team leader … he was just the greatest kid."

Through the remainder of Dick's tenure as coach, Jeanne remained the "team mom," although the focus necessarily shifted to Kathleen Davey after she was stricken in January 2004.

Meanwhile, the sacrifices that Dick and Jeanne had made for their daughter had earlier come to fruition when Kim Davey came closer than even her father to super-stardom. Her chosen field was ballet, and she made the equivalent of what major league baseball players call "The Show."

"I feel my parents were a little surprised when they found out how serious I was about dancing at 6," Kim Davey said, "but they did nothing but support me. I think my dad gave up a lot of his dream for me … I think he had gotten other offers to go to big-time schools, but he passed them up because he knew I was sort of settled in San Francisco and he wanted me to live out my passion. My dad and I always had that link through that commitment. I couldn't have done it without their support. As you get older and have your own kids (her son Niko was born in 2006), you realize how much they sacrificed for you."

In 1987, at age 17, Kim earned full ballerina status, and she performed for five years with the San Francisco Ballet and nine more with the Pacific Northwest Ballet Company in Seattle before retiring and enrolling at Santa Clara, from which she subsequently graduated with a degree in communications.

She said she came to identify with her father even more as her career progressed because of the degree to which she had to invest time, energy and emotion to reach the pinnacle of her profession.

"I can remember (as a kid) waking up at 11 at night and my dad wasn't home yet and my mom was sitting in bed eating ice cream," she said. "It's hard, but you make sacrifices when it's something you love and you're passionate about. I know I was coming home at 11 for many years after performances, and I can understand how hard it was.

"I retired when I was 31 … I probably could have danced another five or 10 years, but I wanted to leave the field in one piece. I didn't want to have any major injuries that I couldn't work out for the rest of my life. One of my friends has no cartilage in her knee, and she was only a couple years older than I was. My dad also said he hoped I would be able to come to Santa Clara because he didn't know how much longer he would be there, and I was ready. I'd done everything I wanted to do … you can keep doing the same roles, but honestly, I used to think about Michael Jordan (and the two anticlimactic seasons he played for the Washington Wizards after retiring from the Chicago Bulls).

"It's not like I was anything like Michael Jordan, but I didn't want to be like athletes who hang onto their careers too long, and then people say 'You're not like you used to be.' I wanted to leave when I felt I was at the top of my game."

As with her father and basketball, though, Kim couldn't divorce herself entirely from ballet – and in time, she determined that she didn't want to.

"I was teaching ballet when I came down here while going to school," she said, "and I just can't seem to draw myself from teaching ballet ... I love it so much. I thought 'Oh, I'm going to have a completely different life. I'll be in the corporate world doing PR or something like that.' But I couldn't bear to leave it. I love teaching young kids the love of dance. We've been fortunate in our family in that each of us has found our passion and never lost it.

"I think my parents set a really good example for Mike and I. They loved their family and were wonderful to us, but they also had something (else) they were so passionate about. It taught us that when you really want something, you really have to go after it. If you only half-go after something, you're only going to be half-good.

"I really just hope to spend a lot of time with my parents (in the aftermath of her father's retirement), just as much time as possible. Now that my dad is not as busy and not as stressed I want him to be able to enjoy his life and I want my parents to be able to do things like traveling. Kathleen's accident taught me ... it's not really paranoia, but you have a fear of losing people close to you after you go through something like that. I think you learn how to value every single second you have with them. That's what I want to do with my father and mother. When you're a parent yourself (in addition to her son, Kim and her husband Alvaro were expecting a second child in the fall of 2007), you so know what your own parents went through and all the feelings they had for you and how much they wanted good things for you.

"I want my family to be at peace, and I want my parents and brother to be happy."

Chapter 5
MATURITY

Although Davey describes himself as periodically "goofy" with ambition and impatience during the years he coached at Leland, he wasn't at all goofy when it came to learning his craft. Toward that end, he considers himself fortunate to have had the opportunity to study and communicate with some of the veteran coaches who were operating at the time in the Santa Clara Valley, where the quality of the athletes, coaches and programs reflected the fact that the area was one of the fastest-growing suburban regions in the country.

In addition to Locatelli at Willow Glen, Davey had to contend with coaches like Dave Morgan at Del Mar in San Jose, Dan Fitzgerald at Archbishop Mitty in San Jose, Bob Hagan at Gilroy, Phil Kelly at Fremont High in Sunnyvale, Ray Snyder at Monta Vista High in Cupertino, and Mike Gervasoni at Silver Creek in San Jose. Jim Brovelli and Dan Belluomini, both of whom later were head coaches at USF, were assistants under Locatelli at Willow Glen. Future NFL quarterback Steve Bartkowski played basketball as well as football at Buchser High (now Santa Clara High) in Santa Clara, and Ray Townsend, who went on to UCLA and then the NBA, played first for Mitty and then for Camden. Another top Santa Clara Valley basketball player from that era was Branham's Pat Hughes, who went on to a distinguished baseball broadcasting career that continued through 2007 and has included play-by-play positions with the Chicago White Sox, Chicago Cubs and Milwaukee Brewers.

Davey and Fitzgerald coached together under Williams at Santa Clara in 1977-78, and their friendship continued unabated almost four decades after it started. Their relationship also became a rivalry after Fitzgerald took the Gonzaga head-coaching job in 1978, the year before the Zags switched from the Big Sky Conference to the WCAC. Over a 17-season stretch (1978-81 and 1985-97) he went 254-169, and although he wasn't able to take Gonzaga to its first postseason appearance until the Zags won the WCC tournament title in 1995, it was his blueprints – both as coach and athletic director – that Dan Monson and then Mark Few used to construct the program that gave the WCAC/WCC national prominence on a level unseen since the Bill Russell era at USF in the mid-1950s.

"When I first got the (assistant's) job at Santa Clara in 1977, the first night Fitz went and bought a case of beer and we sat in the car in front of the gym from 11 that night until 7 the next morning," Davey said, grinning. "In the morning we threw the (empty) case in the garbage, walked into the office and started work. That was my first 'day' … we had a 'training session' in the car that night.

"We've always been close, and Jim Fitzgerald, his brother, is also a good friend. When I was coaching Leland and he was at Mitty, he invited me to work his camps … he's a great talker but he also has a lot of substance in what he says. He understands basketball as well as anyone I've ever been around. I always admired him for his knowledge. We were enemies when we coached against each other, but friendly enemies. When the game was over, it was over."

Fitzgerald was fired as Gonzaga coach and athletic director in 1997 after accounting irregularities in the athletic department came to light, but he remains prominent in Spokane basketball circles as a speaker, camp operator and individual tutor. "In fact, one guy who helps him is (former Santa Clara player) Phil Von Buchwaldt, who is in banking up there," Davey said. "I think Fitz always kind of resented what happened there. I don't know the details, but I felt bad for Dan and I do know he wasn't ready to leave the game.

"I also know Jud Heathcote (the former Michigan State coach who moved to Spokane after he retired) ... he'll call every three months or so and say, 'Well, kid, it looks like you're having some problems down there' or, 'It looks like things are going pretty well down there.' He and his wife Bev are good friends (with the Daveys), and he once told me, 'When you come up to play Gonzaga ... we're big Gonzaga fans, as you know, but if the Broncos beat the Bulldogs, I won't be too upset.' I said that to Bev, and she said, 'Neither would I.' He called to congratulate me after we won up there (in 2007), and whenever we're up there I have breakfast with Jud and Fitz.

"I don't get many words in, but it's great to listen to those two talk."

103

Although he gravitated toward coaches like Fitzgerald who were close to him in age, Davey also found himself taking mental notes when he watched and worked against long-time coaches like Morgan and Hagan.

Morgan started the basketball program at Del Mar when the school opened in 1959, and won seven league titles and never had a losing season before departing in 1979. He later resurfaced in the San Joaquin Valley, and coached at Denair and Delhi high schools before retiring in 2004 with more than 800 victories and 18 league championships. Mark Bruening, a burly pivotman who played for Davey during his first year as a Santa Clara assistant, is a Del Mar graduate, and so is Mark McNamara, who later played at Santa Clara and Cal and earned an NBA championship ring with the Philadelphia 76ers in 1983. Morgan also sent Bill Drozdiak and Bruce Posey to the University of Oregon in the late 1960s, and Drozdiak was taken by the Miami Floridians in the 1971 ABA draft.

Hagan was the coach at Gilroy from 1950 until he died of a heart attack during the 1977-78 season. Because of him, Gilroy – then a distinct farming community and not the southern suburb of San Jose it has since become – was known for basketball long before it became famed for the garlic that is its main agricultural export. His career record was 457-209 and he won 14 league championships and four regional titles, and the plaque honoring him in the Gilroy gym reads simply that he "made Gilroy High School one of the best, year after year."

Both Hagan and Morgan were steadfast in their insistence that basketball should be played within narrow parameters of their choosing, and while Davey never adopted their tactics as a body, he did draw from the approaches of both throughout his coaching career.

"Bob Hagen was a good friend ... I'd met him through Andy Locatelli at Willow Glen," Davey said of Hagan, who was perhaps most notorious for cranking up the heat in the tiny Gilroy gym to unbearable levels to sap opponents' energy. "He was the old master ... a sly old fox, and very competitive. You noticed that most on the golf course, because he'd take you for everything you had.

"Morgan was unique. We stayed in contact over the years. His teams were the most unique I've ever seen ... only five guys played, and you never saw a guy come off the bench. (Morgan didn't even let the non-starters in the huddle during timeouts, and because Morgan was so resistant to change of any kind, Del Mar was the last school in the Santa Clara Valley to maintain wooden backboards in its gym.) They were a fast-break team that played 2-3 zone all the time ... he had his own style, but he had some really good teams and he was very successful doing it his way. He was a crusty old guy. Probably a lot of guys who played for him weren't happy with some things he did, but I really liked Dave and he was good to me. He and Hagan came out of the same vintage ... tough-minded guys, no nonsense."

Snyder had the remarkable distinction of coaching championship teams 30 years apart – in 1957, when his Fremont team went 29-0, and in 1987 when Monta Vista won the CCS title led by 7-foot center Ronnie Reis, who went on to a good career at Santa Clara under Williams and Davey. Kelly, who had played for Snyder at Fremont in '57, led the Indians to the first CCS title in 1968, captured another in 1983 and reached the sectional semifinals four other times. Scott Lamson, a three-year starter for Santa Clara in the early 1980s when the Broncos won 20 or more games three times and earned two NIT berths, and John Prunty, San Diego's starting point guard in 1984 when the Toreros reached the NCAA tournament, were among the many college players Kelly produced during his 30-plus years in coaching.

Gervasoni, who'd played for Santa Clara from 1964-67, founded the Silver Creek program when the East San Jose school opened in 1969, and over the next decade produced five Mount Hamilton Athletic League championships and the 1978 CCS title team, along with future Santa Clara guard Vester Robinson. He later became the women's coach at De Anza College in Cupertino, and was married to Nevada coach Kim Gervasoni – one of his former players – and was serving as her assistant coach when he died in an auto accident in Reno in 2004 at age 59.

Even in such a challenging coaching incubator, Davey proved he belonged. With the improved player-coach relationship beginning to manifest itself, Leland reached double figures in wins in 1969-70, Davey's third season. Then, in 1970-71, the program blossomed.

Led by forward Guy Leo, the Chargers wrested the STAL championship away from the Willow Glen-Gilroy axis, and advanced to the CCS Final Four by crushing Oak Grove 79-51 and easily beating Leigh 62-49. But even though Davey had the same type of burly, forceful, no-squiggly-lines team that characterized the Santa Clara program later, he then ran into a team from Alisal High in Salinas that measured 6-foot-10, 6-8 and 6-8 across the front line. (Danny Cunningham, one of the 6-8 starters, went on to play for UNLV and San Jose State.) Alisal also had Mark Haddan, who during his four-year prep career treated defenders like Peter Townshend treated guitars. His 65 points in a game earlier that season remained the CCS record almost 40 years later, and he later played for Fresno State.

Leland never was in contention against eventual CCS champion Alisal, losing 86-65 before coming back to beat Fremont in the third-place game.

With most of that team set to return for the 1971-72 season, Davey and the Chargers figured the Alisal loss was more of an investment in their future than a reflection of their present, and they thought they had an excellent chance to win the sectional title. It didn't happen that way, despite the returnees and the unexpected presence of a newcomer who was to thrust Davey into the vortex of a controversy for the first and only time before the furor that surrounded his "retirement" from Santa Clara in 2007.

The new player was Jody Desin, who had been the star of the Leigh team that Leland had beaten in the regional championship game the year before. Desin, a 6-3 guard who would be termed a "combination guard" today because he could function either at the point or shooting positions, reminded many of a young Paul Westphal, then a star at USC. Consequently, Desin was perhaps the most widely recruited player in Santa Clara County at the end of his junior season at Leigh.

But early in the 1971-72 school year, Desin was suspended from Leigh and kicked off the basketball team after he and a friend entered an unlocked locker room and stole a couple of T-shirts.

"This is before basketball practice started," Davey said. "His dad contacts Leland and talks to the administration and tells them he wants to transfer his son to Leland. He gave his Leland address to our vice principal at the time, Jack Mahaffey ... Mahaffey goes over there and knocks on the door at that address. His dad answered the door, so we knew he had established residency and that he was eligible to play for Leland (under the CCS rules at the time). My dilemma is ... I barely know this guy, so do I allow a guy to play who was suspended from another school for something fairly serious?

"We always had only 10 guys on the team when I coached at Leland, and Jody would make 11. I talked to one of our guys, Bobby Isaacson, who was a sophomore at the time. I told him, 'We're in the process of doing this, and if he comes, you'll probably get less playing time because he's pretty good. What's your thinking on this?' As it turned out, he'd played with Jody in summer leagues and liked him, and said he'd like to have him on the team.

"I also called my dad. He said, 'That's a tough deal, but does he deserve a second chance? If he doesn't, don't take him, but if you think he does, go ahead and take him.' I knew we'd be a lot better if we took him, so I sat down with him and gave him the lay of the land. I also called the coach at Leigh and asked him what he thought. He was pissed at the kid and didn't think he should have another chance, but I've never had a kid who didn't deserve a second chance."

After due deliberation, Davey allowed Desin to come out for the Leland team, which he joined just before the midway point of the season. At a time when it was very rare for student-athletes, especially ones as prominent as Desin, to transfer from one public high school to another in the midst of a season, much was made in the San Jose media of Desin's presence on the Leland roster.

Davey acknowledges that the situation was a distraction, especially in the days immediately after Desin joined the team.

"It wasn't a difficult decision, really, but I knew I would make some enemies," Davey said. "I knew guys would be pissed off and in general upset because you're getting a good player by way of him screwing up somewhere else. But he turned out to be a great kid, and that's one thing you hope is the result of giving guys a second chance ... you want them to take advantage of it, and he surely has."

Thirty-five years later, Desin said Davey's impact on his life had remained continuous, even though Desin wound up playing only half a season for Davey at Leland.

At 53, Desin lived and worked in Billings, Montana, where he founded and owned Montana International Supply, a wholesale supplier of spare parts for mobile mining equipment. His family included his wife and six children, ages 14 to 27 – including Mark, who accepted a football scholarship from Montana State in 2006 after establishing himself as one of the top high school athletes in Montana history. Mark Desin completed his football career with more than 9,500 passing yards, by far the top total in Montana annals, while throwing 65 touchdown passes and running for 27 more. In basketball, he scored more than 1,000 points and led the state in scoring (21.8), assists (7.8) and steals (4.3) as a senior.

Montana International Supply was one of three businesses Desin operated in 2007, and while his post-Leland basketball career was fraught by numerous detours and ultimately was ended by injury, his post-basketball life has been one of serenity and success. He gives Davey much of the credit for that, and the two remained close, 35 years after Desin graduated from Leland.

"It was really kind of a minor thing that happened at Leigh, not something I think warranted my removal from the team," he said. "They said we had keys to the locker room, and that other stuff was missing, which wasn't true. The football coaches, and I had a couple of them as teachers, weren't happy with me even before that because I wouldn't play football; I never got into the football mentality. (Leigh is perhaps best known athletically as the alma mater of baseball All-Star Ken Caminiti, but it was a football power at that time.) But we were wrong, and it was my screwup. I was being recruited by every school in the Pac-8, along with Long Beach State (coached by Jerry Tarkanian, just before he moved to UNLV), and it was gonna *kill* me. I was pretty stupid about a lot of things back then ... I didn't go to class all the time and I goofed off a lot.

"My dad talked to the people at Leland, and we rented an apartment in their district. I don't remember the exact circumstances, because I had never talked to Coach Davey before that, but after I enrolled at Leland, Coach Davey pulled me aside and said, 'I want to tell you what the situation is. I'm allowing you to play for us, not because it will make us a better team, but because I talked to my dad and he convinced me to give you a second chance because everybody deserves that.' It meant a lot to me at the time, because I didn't know what I was going to do (if he had been denied the opportunity to play his senior season), but it means even more now than it did then.

"The first thing he did after I started practicing with the (Leland) team was run my ass off in front of everyone ... baseline to free throw line, baseline to midcourt, baseline to free throw line, over and over. He made me prove myself, and he wanted me to show what kind of character I had. It was a great thing for him to do, because I understood then that I had to earn anything I got there and that I wasn't going to get any special treatment.

"My coach at Leigh was a history teacher (who doubled as a basketball coach). Coach Davey was a *basketball coach* who knew the game very, very well, even then. He became my mentor in a very short period of time, and our relationship just kept getting better."

Desin remembers his first game in a Leland uniform.

"It was against Pioneer," he said, "and the first time I touched the ball, I made a (no-look) pass to Guy Leo for a layup, and the place went absolutely *crazy*. It was like they had never seen a pass like that before; I was looking the other way, but I knew where Guy was. He really wanted me to be there (on the Leland team) and soon we became very good friends. I took three shots in that game and made all three and got a three-point play, and I think I had about as many assists as I had points. I didn't get a lot of time at first … with Coach Davey, it was all part of an earning process."

"He might have been the best player I've ever coached, physically," Davey said. "He was the best I've seen at getting fouled on penetration and still scoring. He was so strong you could bang him and he would still score the ball."

"Coach (Carroll) Williams met with me and with Coach Davey," Desin said. "We had lunch, and (Williams) said, 'I want to offer you a scholarship to Santa Clara. I know you had a problem at Leigh, but Coach Davey has told me that he thinks you deserve this chance, and it's on his recommendation that I'm offering you this scholarship.' When I was a kid, Santa Clara had Awtrey and the Ogdens and that was the program you followed, and my dad took me to a lot of games. Santa Clara was where I had hoped to go."

Shortly thereafter, though, Davey was hired as an assistant at Cal. In those days, binding letters of intent did not exist and verbal commitments were considered just that, so Desin remained free to change his college choice. In his new capacity, Davey convinced new Cal coach Dick Edwards to take a look at Desin during a Saturday pick-up game in Berkeley; Edwards liked what he saw, and offered Desin a scholarship.

"I said OK," Desin said. "I signed the papers, and soon after that my dad and my older sister and I went to Europe (on vacation). While I was there, I got a call from one of my other sisters telling me I'd been refused admission to Cal because of a D I'd gotten in English as a sophomore at Leigh. They (the Bears) were on (NCAA) probation and they'd just brought in a new admissions person and I got rejected.

"Years later, Coach Davey told me, 'I had the only copy of that (grade) transcript. I knew about the D, and I considered changing it. I could have done it easily because it wasn't even in pen; it was in pencil. But I decided, nah, I can't do this.' I think that speaks to his integrity as much as anything."

With Desin's opportunity at Cal gone, Davey tried to arrange for Desin to play for Bud Presley at Menlo College, where Davey thought Desin would benefit from Presley's nationally-acknowledged ability to teach defense. But Desin instead decided to play at West Valley College in nearby Saratoga, where he immediately enhanced his major-college credentials. He led the team in scoring, rebounding and assists over the first 19 games, 17 of which West Valley won.

However ...

"I was such a screwup," he said later. "We were the No. 2-ranked (community college) team in the state; only Compton was ahead of us. But Jody stopped going to class and Jody flunked out. I was so stupid; I didn't even know what the consequences (of skipping classes) would be. I let the whole team down, and it finished 20-9 and didn't even make the postseason. Totally my fault. It was bad ... I was like 'basketball isn't for me.' I went to work with my dad, and I sat out the next season working.

"But then Coach Davey talked to David Brown, the coach at Yavapai (a community college in Prescott, Ariz.). He needed a point guard, and Coach Davey told him he should try to talk me into giving basketball another shot. They called, I went down there, and it was a very high caliber of junior college basketball ... they had guys from places like Indiana and Louisville who couldn't get (into those schools) because of grades. I had a good year there, and a lot of Division I schools recruited me, especially San Diego State. But (under NCAA rules) I would only have one year of eligibility at a D-I school. I wanted to play in the NBA, and I thought I needed two (four-year college) years to be ready to do that."

Desin that summer had worked out with a number of NBA players in Phoenix – "Paul Westphal, Curtis Perry and I never lost a 3-on-3 game that summer," Desin recalled – and Bob Bass, who had been the coach and general manager of the ABA's San Antonio Spurs, recommended him to Oklahoma Baptist, an NAIA school where Bass once had coached. (The NAIA, unlike NCAA Division I, allows transfers to play immediately instead of requiring them to sit out a redshirt year.) He played well there, but his team struggled, and toward the end of the year, he aggravated a knee injury originally suffered at West Valley.

"I was operated on by the same guy who fixed Joe Namath's knees," Desin said, "and he said that when he got me under, my knee just moved from side to side … it just collapsed. He said I had no cartilage left, and that I already had 70-year-old knees because arthritis had already started. They still bother me; I've been putting off knee-replacement surgery. So I knew basketball was over for me. I came up here (Montana), got married, and started working. I always stayed in touch with Coach Davey, and when Steve Nash was a senior (in November 1995) I took my whole family out to Hawaii for the Maui Classic.

"My kids all will tell you to this day that the best coach ever is Coach Davey, and all they have to go on was how he treated them and what I had said about him and what he said to them about me. That's one thing that's so great about him … the way he remembers people and always acknowledges them. And after I started my family, I coached my kids in basketball and baseball through eighth grade. I had a lot of success, and with a lot of the philosophies I've used with younger kids, the biggest inspiration was him. Even just playing seven or so games for him affected the way I taught and the way I looked at the game.

"I think you could take him and replace any coach, even somebody like a Coach K (Duke coach Mike Krzyzewski), in the country with him, and if he had the same players, he'd win at least as many games – anywhere. I honestly believe that. I'll always be grateful to him for what he did for me."

But even with Desin in 1972, the Chargers were unable to duplicate their Final Four showing of the year before. The team was better than it had been the previous season, especially after Desin was added, but it wasn't better than what many considered the most imposing collection of raw basketball talent ever assembled in the CCS up to that time.

When Silver Creek High on San Jose's southeast side opened, the coaches there inherited an unusual bounty of athletes. That was partly because of their quality (track sprinter Millard Hampton, a 1974 graduate, won a gold medal in the 400-meter relay in the 1976 Olympics) but mostly because almost all of them were black.

The black community always has been small, by U.S. metropolitan standards, in the Santa Clara Valley. Blacks made up only 2.8 percent of the county's population in 2005, and from 1990 to 2000, while Santa Clara County continued its exponential growth, the African-American community in the county decreased in size from 52,860 residents to 44,475. Even at Silver Creek, enrollment in 2005 was only 5 percent black, while Asians accounted for 56 percent ... but in 1972, the school's black enrollment was one of the most sizable in the county. The team Gervasoni put together that year had five black junior starters, including guard Vester Robinson, a prized Santa Clara recruit who had a Baron Davis type of game and seemingly could take over a contest whenever the impulse seized him. Silver Creek also had forward Warren Jackson, who later played at De Anza and at Cal State Bakersfield.

A few CCS members, particularly the three San Francisco private schools (Riordan, St. Ignatius and Sacred Heart) in the West Catholic Athletic League and some public schools in northern San Mateo County, routinely featured black players, but they had been rarities in the Santa Clara Valley through the 1950s and 1960s. The prevailing basketball protocol at that time was a measured, structured power game, and many teams were dumbstruck by Silver Creek's speed and the ability of the Raiders' players to hoist and make shots like featherweight boxers flinging punches. (Silver Creek went 23-0 the following year, 1972-73, before being upset by Woodside, featuring future Santa Clara player Myrt Easley, in the CCS semifinals.)

Del Mar under Morgan was an up-tempo team, but in a first-round playoff matchup against Silver Creek, the Dons had the ball stolen in the backcourt on eight straight second-quarter possessions. Silver Creek converted each of those steals into layups, transforming an eight-point deficit into an eight-point lead, and went on to win 84-68. In what turned out to be Davey's last game as Leland coach – although he had no way of knowing that at the time – the Chargers responded better than Del Mar to Silver Creek's quickness, but lost anyway, 70-65. (Silver Creek then lost to eventual champion Sacred Heart – with yet another Santa Clara recruit, Glen Hubbard – in the CCS semifinals.)

"They were a great team," Desin said of Silver Creek, "and I think some teams in our area were intimidated by them, because you just didn't see many blacks playing there then. But we could have played with them. I was trying to be unselfish, almost to an extreme. If I'd tried to take over the game a little more, I think we would have done better."

Davey at this point had not yet turned 30, yet he already had a program that had evolved into a year-in-and-year-out sectional championship contender. Leland was located in a major growth area, was buoyed by a good junior high feeder system, and had an affluent, goal-oriented student body from which to draw players who would respond to Davey and his *modus operandi*. He was a popular teacher and coach, had the full support of his administration, and had formed the type of strong and enduring relationships with Desin and his other players that would characterize him throughout the rest of his career, and beyond.

"I really liked what I did," Davey said. "I always had a little ambition to get to the next level, but if that (coaching at Leland) had turned out to be my lot in life, that would have been fine. I enjoyed the kids, and the reason they were so successful after only three or four years, in every sport, was the quality of people they had out there. Fun guys to be around … I get together with those (Leland) guys every year still."

But a phone call from Dick Edwards later that spring changed all that permanently. That call beckoned Davey to the college coaching ranks, where he was to stay for the next three decades.

Three of the four coaching positions Dick Davey accepted
during his 40-year career were destinations. Although he
didn't know it at the time, the other – at the University of
California, Berkeley – was a stop.

"Dick Edwards had just become head coach at Cal, and
he knew me because I played a year for him at UOP,"
Davey said. "I didn't quite understand the circumstances
of coaching opportunities; I was just eager to take the
job because I wanted to coach at the college level. What
I didn't realize was that I wouldn't have much input into
what was done as far as the coaching and teaching. I really
like working individually with kids, and I didn't have the
opportunity to do that. Dick was kind of a hands-on guy.
In some programs, the head coach does everything; in
others, the assistants are more involved. (Edwards) didn't
let you get involved as much because he did everything
himself. He wanted his assistants scouting, and (as an
assistant coach under him) you couldn't get as involved
as you could with Carroll and (later) with me.

"It was a different experience. Jeanne and I lived in Walnut
Creek and we loved it there, and Bill Berry and I had a good
relationship and became good friends. (Berry, the other
paid assistant, went from Cal to Michigan State, where he
was an assistant on the Magic Johnson-led 1979 NCAA title

team. He was the head coach at San Jose State for 10 years after that, and in 1994 and 1995 was an assistant with the Houston Rockets when they won NBA titles.)

"It just wasn't as good a coaching situation as far as getting an opportunity to coach, and truthfully, after five years I was looking to get out."

After Davey graduated from UOP, Edwards made the Tigers' program a national power and morphed venerable 2,901-seat Stockton Civic Auditorium into the Winchester Mystery House of college basketball in the late 1960s and early 1970s. His teams won 39 consecutive games at the Civic (the streak was extended to 45 games under Stan Morrison, who succeeded Edwards in 1972-73), including an upset win over Jerry Tarkanian's No. 3-ranked Long Beach State team in 1972.

Cal's program, meanwhile, had shuddered and staggered for more than a decade after Pete Newell resigned in 1960, after leading the Bears to the NCAA title in 1959 and a runnerup finish the following year. Rene Herrerias, Newell's assistant, had assumed the head-coaching duties after Newell stepped down, but the combination of the carryover expectations from the Newell era, the campus unrest that diluted sports interest at Cal during the early and mid-1960s, and the emergence of John Wooden's UCLA colossus eventually doomed Herrerias. Jim Padgett, his successor, recruited electric and eclectic players like Phil Chenier, Charlie Johnson and Russ Critchfield, but the team always amounted to less than the sum of its parts. Cal officials thought Edwards' success at a private school like UOP, where he had employed some of the same formulae popularized by Newell, might be translatable to the high expectations and rigorous academic standards at Cal.

Padgett had been long on recruiting skill, but short in terms of teaching and game management. Edwards, as it turned out, was long on teaching and game management, but short of players at a time when what was then the Pacific-8 Conference was the strongest in the country. While UCLA was No. 1 in the country throughout its NCAA-record 88-game winning streak from 1971-74, USC more than once was ranked No. 2, and Oregon, Oregon State and Washington State also were nationally competitive. Against that backdrop, Cal was 62-69 overall and never finished above a fourth-place tie in the Pac-8 during the five seasons Davey served on Edwards' staff. The Bears, in fact, did not place a single player on the Pac-8/Pac-10 all-conference team from 1972-80.

Little about the five years he spent in Berkeley is luminescent in Davey's mind, although he still keeps in touch with Gene Ransom, a 5-foot-8 human waterbug from Berkeley High who played there from 1976-78 and remained among Cal's top 20 career scorers three decades later. "Tremendous player," Davey said of Ransom, who in 2007 was running a recreation program in Berkeley. "His physical skills and his talent were unique. I once saw him make an incredible play on the jump ball at the beginning of a game ... as he's diving out of bounds with his body parallel to the floor, he caught the ball with one hand, ripped it without any vision to the other end of the court to one of our other guys, who went in and scored on a layup. Gene (made the 60-foot pass while parallel to the floor and falling out of bounds even though he) never saw the guy."

Stan Morrison thinks Davey benefited from his time under Edwards, both as a player and as a coach, even though Davey and Edwards didn't agree on Davey's coaching role at Cal.

"He is an immense competitor," Morrison said. "He played for a great competitor, Dick Edwards, at UOP. Small, quiet and very determined. It was 'my way or the highway' with Dick Edwards. I saw a little of that in Dick Davey too. He didn't care what your reputation was or how big you were or what the name on the front of your jersey said. You had to deal with the truth, as he knew it, between the lines in front of him and the crowd. That was the ultimate truth to Coach Davey. Can you block off and get a rebound or can't you? Can you take the charge or can't you? Can you hit the open jump shot from 15 feet or can't you? Black and white. No gray."

Even so, Davey didn't like the big picture at Cal, and at the end of the 1976-77 season, he began circulating his resume. (Edwards was on his way out too; he was fired after the following season, and took a job at Montana State, where he coached only two years before his death of a heart attack in 1980 at age 50.)

"I wanted to coach (in a more hands-on manner)," he said. "Dick (Edwards) was an excellent coach, but it was time for him to make changes on his staff too. Bill (Berry) left at about the same time (to go to Michigan State)."

After his experience as an underused underling at Cal, his initial thought was that he wanted to return to the high school ranks and be in control of his own program, as he had been at Leland. It might have worked out that way if Davey hadn't made the determination that among the keys to his eventual success were the keys – as many as he thought he needed – to the gym at San Ramon Valley High in Danville, about 20 miles south of Berkeley.

San Ramon Valley was much like Leland in that it served a rapidly-growing, upscale area, and the Wolves traditionally have been strong in almost every sport. Major league baseball player Randy Winn, who went to Santa Clara and played basketball for Williams and Davey as well as baseball, and Mark Madsen, later a star at Stanford and an established NBA player by 2007, were among the athletes who would have played for Davey if he had gotten the San Ramon Valley job and stayed for the duration of his career.

As it was …

"A frat brother of mine in college, Jim Henderson, had become principal at San Ramon High," Davey said. "I applied for the job and got an interview, and I think I probably would have gotten the job if I hadn't said, 'I have a couple of requests, and one is the keys to both gyms for my players and myself.' There were probably a dozen or so people on the interview committee, and after we finished, Henderson says to me, 'Why did you say that? That's gonna kill us as far as trying to get you on here, because the women's programs (which were far more established than they had been at Leland) aren't going to like that.'"

Sure enough, Davey didn't get the San Ramon Valley job, and that left him, briefly, at loose professional ends. Fortunately, Carroll Williams was looking for him, even though Williams didn't have a paid position to offer him at Santa Clara. Andy Locatelli, who had left Willow Glen to become what now would be called a graduate or limited-earnings assistant at Santa Clara, had resigned that position to take the job as SCU facilities director, and his spot was open – *if* Davey could find a way to make financial ends meet as essentially a volunteer assistant.

"I'd known Carroll through camps and clinics, but Fitz was the only paid assistant, and that first year I made my salary by selling radio ads and running clinics and camps for the high school coaches in the area," Davey said. "At that time there was really a bonding between the Santa Clara Valley and Santa Clara … we got Kurt Rambis, we got Mark McNamara, and we got a lot of other local guys. It would have been a really good group if it had stayed intact."

At the time he accepted Williams' offer, Davey had no way of knowing whether his new situation would be any more secure than the one he had just left, because there was no certainty that Williams himself would be at Santa Clara indefinitely.

Williams, who had played with Stu Inman and was a classmate of Hall of Fame football coach Bill Walsh at San Jose State, never played in the NBA in the 1950s, but he was better than a lot of people who did. Although he was barely 6-foot and not imposing in stature, he could and did guard much bigger, stronger players because of his ferocity and his uncanny ability to beat penetrating opponents to a spot, and he had few peers from the standpoint of worming his way inside and cashing in on free-throw opportunities. (As of 2007, he still held the San Jose State career records for most free throws attempted and made.)

In 1962-63, his first year as a Santa Clara assistant after serving an Army hitch, he met an Army assistant coach in Provo, Utah while both were scouting a Brigham Young game. The two struck up a conversation that continued into that night – "over Cokes," Williams said later – and the two established a close friendship that endured over four decades.

"Later, we began talking fishing, because he's a black-bass guy," Williams said of Bob Knight, who soon after meeting Williams became Army's head coach, beginning a career that was to yield more wins than that of any other Division I coach. "He used to flail at the fish. He'd attack them as if they were the competition."

Williams also became good friends with Hubie Brown, later a longtime NBA and ABA coach, while both were in the Army. Brown several times tried unsuccessfully to pry Williams from his Santa Clara job with an offer of an assistant's position with whatever pro team he was running at the time. In 1985, when Brown was head coach of the New York Knicks, he made a special trip to Los Angeles, at Williams' behest, to see the Broncos play against Loyola Marymount – and with Brown watching, Santa Clara center Nick Vanos ensured his NBA future by going for a career-high 44 points.

In 1960, while still in the Army, Williams made the gold medal-winning Olympic team as an alternate. Many still consider that squad to be the best amateur team ever assembled in the U.S.; its coach was Pete Newell, and its roster included transcendent names like Oscar Robertson, Jerry West and Jerry Lucas along with Terry Dischinger, Darrall Imhoff, Walt Bellamy, Bob Boozer and Adrian Smith, all of whom had productive NBA careers. Soon after, Williams joined the Santa Clara staff as an assistant to Dick Garibaldi, and was a critical component as the Broncos became national title contenders.

Garibaldi, whose nephew was Santa Clara baseball great Bob Garibaldi, took Santa Clara to three straight NCAA tournaments from 1968-70, when the event included just 16 teams and only conference champions were eligible. In 1968-69, with future NBA players Ralph and Bud Ogden and Dennis Awtrey on the front line and future major league baseball player Bruce Bochte coming off the bench, Santa Clara was ranked No. 2 in the country most of the season, and finished third in the final Associated Press poll behind only UCLA and LaSalle. Bud Ogden's photo was on a *Sports Illustrated* cover early in 1969. Aside from a double-overtime loss to San Jose State, the Broncos' only defeat was against UCLA, 90-52, in the Western Regional title game.

(Santa Clara has reached the Final Four only once, in 1952, when it lost to eventual champion Kansas in the national semifinals despite the presence of All-America forward Kenny Sears, who later starred for many years with the New York Knicks. The Broncos came close to reaching the Final Four each of the next two seasons, losing to Washington in 1953 and in double overtime to USC in 1954 in the West Regional title games.)

The NCAA during the Awtrey-Ogden years did not seed its tournament, and conducted its regionals strictly along geographical lines. Both of those practices were changed two years later, and Awtrey thinks that if that had happened during his Santa Clara career, the Broncos might have reached the Final Four at least once, and possibly played UCLA for a national championship.

"We wouldn't have had to play UCLA on their home court, anyway (as they did in the 1969 regional final)," Awtrey said. "They said, 'Why not send them down there to play the big guy (Alcindor) on his home court?' Gee, thanks. Maybe Santa Clara getting to the Final Four or playing for a national championship might have made it a Villanova-type program. Who knows?"

(Villanova, also a Catholic school, got to the NCAA finals in 1971 before losing 68-62 to UCLA, and has been a national power ever since.)

"I don't know how much longer Dick (Garibaldi) could have kept it going," Awtrey said, "but I do know we had a bunch of guys who were willing to sacrifice their individual games, and we had guys who would run through the wall for Dick. My junior year, we won the Rainbow Classic in Hawaii, and in that tournament we played Columbia with (future NBA star) Jim McMillian. We were up big early but we were hanging on by our fingernails when Dick calls a timeout with about a minute and a half to play and tells us we're going to go into a weave, which was our stall offense.

"We'd lost a game to USF the year before because we went into a weave with a lead and it didn't work, and when Dick told us we were going to run it again, Joe Diffley (a Santa Clara reserve from 1966-69) gave just a little, almost imperceptible, shake of his head. Dick saw him, grabbed him and lifted him out of his chair. I think he wanted to swim back to the mainland right then, but Dick knew how to motivate guys."

Santa Clara won 64-58.

Another distinction, of which Santa Clara people are less proud, was the fact that those SCU teams may have been the last great all-white squads in college basketball.

Garibaldi, unlike UCLA, USF and other West Coast basketball powers of the time, never recruited a black player during his eight-year stint as head coach, and while athletic integration and civil rights weren't flashpoints at Santa Clara to the degree that they were at large public universities like Cal, the fact big-time college basketball was becoming predominantly black may have been a factor – along with Garibaldi's general aloofness and sometimes-acerbic relations with alumni, his superiors at Santa Clara, and media members – in his decision to retire from coaching after the 1969-70 season.

Williams inherited the job, the expectations and the baggage from the Garibaldi years, but he didn't inherit many of the same players, and in his early years, many believed he wasn't up to the mandate.

One of his first moves was to recruit and sign Santa Clara's first black player, Mike Stewart, who was a standout during the early 1970s, and he never hesitated to bring in African-Americans subsequently. But as with Davey three decades later, having a clean program that graduated its players, won more than it lost and took on the nation's best teams every year wasn't enough for some Santa Clara boosters. Williams' record as head coach at the time he hired Davey was 93-91 with no WCAC titles, and in an effort to improve that mark, he brought in some players with whom he never could establish rapport – most notably Londale Theus, who in 2007 remained Santa Clara's No. 6 career scorer even though he didn't complete his senior season in 1980 because he was kicked off the team by Williams after a series of clashes between the two.

Williams had the full backing of Santa Clara's longtime athletic director, Pat Malley, and the school administration, so he was able to withstand the criticism. In fact, Williams lasted 23 seasons before retiring in September 1992 to accept the athletic directorship at Santa Clara, and he retired with a legacy at which his won-lost record only whispers.

His final record , 344-274, was good but hardly imposing, and Santa Clara never won a WCAC/WCC regular-season championship during his tenure. The Broncos reached only one NCAA tournament during that span – in 1987, when the Broncos, seeded fifth in the first-ever WCAC postseason tournament, beat Pepperdine in the championship game. They subsequently were waxed 99-76 by Iowa in the first round of the NCAA tournament and finished the season 18-14; wryly, Williams later got hold of a photo of the scoreboard at the University of Arizona's McKale Center, taken when Santa Clara led that game 4-0, and kept it on the wall in his office.

The fact Williams finally received an opportunity to coach in the NCAA tournament, though, prompted his players and assistants to reflect on what he had meant to them … and 20 years later, they were still saying the same things, both about Williams and about Davey.

"It was the most emotional moment of my life," Matt Wilgenbush, who was diagnosed with leukemia soon thereafter, told the *Peninsula Times Tribune* before the Iowa game. "I was thinking about how he must feel, as if a giant weight had been lifted. The reason all of us felt so much joy was we knew how much joy he was feeling. He has helped me more as a coach than any coach I've ever had, and he's the best teacher I've had here. But the greatest thing he did for me was to make me feel good about myself. He talks about basketball as a stepping-stone to making you a better person.

"If he gets a bad progress report from a teacher, he'll sit you down and tell you that basketball is nothing compared to the education you're getting, and if you can't get that education then you won't play basketball here. He told me that, and now that my knees are bad and I can't play anymore, I realize how important my education here is."

Larry Hauser had come to Santa Clara the year before as Williams' No. 2 assistant after a number of coaching stops, most of them in the Midwest. Although he stayed at Santa Clara for a decade, it took him some time to adapt to the Santa Clara program because he had worked in environments where nothing mattered except winning.

"Being from Chicago, I've spent most of my life around people who motivate through fear and intimidation, not through honest concern and integrity," Hauser said. "Carroll's concern for individuals motivates his players to discipline themselves. That's what I've learned from him – that you can *do* that."

Twenty years later, after his own retirement, Davey reflected in similar terms.

"I like to think a lot of things I've done came from my father, but some obviously came from Carroll," he said.

"Dan Coonan came down one summer when he was still at Cal, and he saw me teaching and working with some of our big kids, and he was amazed that a head coach on the Division I level would spend time (personally) working with kids in basketball camp or in the summertime individually. Carroll was that way ... he'd step right in. It helped guys like Fitz and I have a better appreciation for the time and energy you have to put into what you're doing.

"To Carroll, nobody was so little or so small that they can't be helped. I remember Carroll working with guys who had no chance to be any good at anything in basketball, and spend an hour teaching a kid to dribble a ball. He was just that way. He's my mentor ... other than my dad, he's a guy I look up to in this profession, and so do a lot of other people. You're talking to somebody (in college coaching) and they say, 'Jeez, you work for the best guy.' They have an appreciation for him and immediately think somebody from Santa Clara is going to be like that until proven differently."

Williams' hands-on involvement with his athletes, both on and off the floor, was the salient reason Davey made what at the time was a risky career move, and it was why he was willing to work a full-time schedule for nary a Santa Clara penny throughout the 1977-78 season. He became Williams' top sidekick after Fitzgerald took the Gonzaga job the following year, and although they differed on some basketball matters – and by doing so complemented each other – they never lost their mutual admiration and respect. Davey knew almost from the time he took the job that he had found both his mentor and an individual who respected him and would let him do what he did best.

Three days into his new assignment, he knew Santa Clara wouldn't be like Cal or UOP or Leland or anywhere else in his previous travels. The first hint was the beer-soaked seminar with Fitzgerald; the second came a couple of days later, when it fell to him to dissuade the program's best-ever player – both statistically and in terms of NBA championship rings won – from walking away from Santa Clara and perhaps basketball for good.

"It was my third day at Santa Clara," he said. "Rambis was a sophomore … he had a bad practice, and afterward he threw his gear into the locker room, said he was quitting, and left. I was the new guy on the block, so (Williams and Fitzgerald) decided I would be the guy to sit in his dorm room and talk to him about staying around. He was our franchise player.

"I remember going into his room … he was in his bed reading. I spent about two hours, maybe three, talking to him. I said, 'Hey, I've seen Oscar Robertson make mistakes in games … it's not the end of the world.' He was such a deranged, determined human being in terms of how good he wanted to be and how hard he worked that sometimes he'd get upset if things didn't work out the right way. We talked and he came back, thank God, and we had some pretty good teams during that time.

"He came in kind of moody and temperamental or whatever you want to call it ... kind of his own man. But he surely developed personality as he went along."

Those who remember Kurt Rambis from his days in the Los Angeles Lakers' percussion section during the Magic Johnson years – he was on four of the Lakers' five NBA title teams in the 1980s – might be surprised to learn that physically he was all arms, legs, elbows and glasses as a high school player and early in his Santa Clara career. In contrast to his garbageman role with the Lakers, he was a low-post scorer of considerable distinction, and could wander outside to score on the perimeter when defenses clogged the middle against him. He once scored 50 points in a playoff game against Ravenswood of East Palo Alto while leading Cupertino High to Central Coast Section titles in 1975 and 1976. In addition to his octopus-like capability as a rebounder, he was a skilled passer on a Cupertino team that included three other starters – Steve Rodgers, who played four seasons at UC Irvine; and Ken Sayre and Greg Rasmussen, who played at De Anza – who moved on to the college level.

Rambis, an excellent student, initially had hoped to play for Stanford, but the Cardinal's coach at the time, Dick DiBiaso, expressed only perfunctory interest even though Stanford was the worst program in the Pacific-8 Conference at the time (and remained so until after DiBiaso was fired after the 1981-82 season and replaced by Tom Davis). Santa Clara, conversely, courted him ardently, and the fact the Broncos ultimately signed him may have helped Williams fend off his critics, who were numerous after the Broncos went 10-16 in 1975-76, the year before Rambis joined the program.

At Santa Clara, he added some of the bulk and muscle that distinguished him as a pro without losing any of the offensive tools he happily shelved after joining the Lakers. More than a quarter-century after his graduation from Santa Clara in 1980, Rambis was still the school's career scoring leader, was second in rebounds, and was in the top nine in seven other offensive categories. He led his team in scoring three times and in rebounding four times during his four-season career. He was one of only three players in the WCC's first 50 years to rank in the conference's top 20 in career scoring and rebounding.

Rambis' impact was immediate, as the Broncos improved from 10-16 to 17-10 during his freshman season and in 1977-78 – Davey's first year at Santa Clara – gave Williams his best season to that point, 21-8. But the team slumped to 13-14 and 15-12 the next two seasons, partly because of internal discord that prompted Londale Theus and Mark McNamara, two other build-around players, to leave the program before their eligibility had expired. McNamara – a unabashed spirit who kept snakes in his dorm room, among other idiosyncrasies – and Rambis never meshed, on or off the court, and many believe that was a major factor in McNamara's decision to transfer to Cal after the 1978-79 season.

Even so, Santa Clara established a reputation as a team not to be played without seat belts fastened. Greg Newell, Pete's son and a guard for WCAC rival Pepperdine from

1977-79, remembered his introduction to the Santa Clara approach during the Rambis years.

"I got clocked by (Mark) Bruening and Rambis after chasing (Santa Clara point guard) Eddie Joe Chavez around on defense," Newell said, "and he ran me right smack into Mr. Bruening's right elbow and big-ass shoulder. Rambis just came over and finished me off, as I was knocked out on my freaking feet. Then Rambis put his 'touch' by his right elbow (on me) for good measure, knocking my wobbly ass right into the Santa Clara cheerleaders as Eddie Joe received a pass on the other side, wide open, and buried a 15-foot jumper and Toso Pavilion went wild and I thought I got jumped in the parking lot. I was never more happy to get substituted in my freaking life than when (Pepperdine coach Gary) Colson took me out of that game … immediately after I came to, after going through 15 tabs of smelling salts."

Bruening, who had played for Dave Morgan at Del Mar, was 6-8 and nicknamed "Bruiser," and not only because of his last name. He and Davey were together for only his senior season, but he authored one of Davey's incandescent Santa Clara moments.

"My first year at Santa Clara (on January 17, 1978) we played Cal in Berkeley and I remember being in the huddle during a timeout," Davey said. "There was a second or two left in the game, we were tied, and Bruiser was going to the line to shoot two free throws. Obviously when you've just been to a place (as a coach) and you go back there with someone else, it's going to carry a certain amount of significance. I guess I must have looked worried, because Bruiser just winks at me and says, 'Don't worry, coach … I got it.'"

Bruening was a prototypical low-post player who rarely ventured beyond 10 feet from the basket, and he wasn't known for his proficiency from the foul line. But he made both free throws, and Santa Clara escaped Harmon Gym with a 63-61 victory.

Davey's influence on Bruening, both as a player and his subsequent successful career in real estate, was evidenced by the fact he was at Davey's 65th-birthday party almost three decades after he graduated. Rambis also has stayed close to the program. In 2007, when he was a Lakers' assistant coach under Phil Jackson, Rambis was mentioned as a possible successor to Davey, although he soon removed himself from consideration for the position that eventually was given to UCLA assistant Kerry Keating.

Because of his work with Rambis, Bruening, McNamara, Korky Nelson (a 6-11 center who later played professionally in Israel for many years) and others, Davey quickly established a reputation in coaching circles as an expert in the care and feeding of big men. He isn't sure exactly when or why that reputation was bestowed on him, but it was one he quickly embraced, and to him, it is as important a part of his coaching portfolio as his notoriety as the man who groomed Steve Nash or the man who orchestrated perhaps the most shocking upset in the history of the NCAA tournament.

Long before he supplanted Williams as the Santa Clara head coach, Davey had established a post-player summer camp similar in some ways – but different in most – to the operation that Pete Newell began in the late 1970s (when NBA player Kermit Washington came to him looking for a post-play primer) and continued to run 30 years later. Davey, like Newell, was in demand as a camp speaker and lecturer on the subject of pivot-play proficiency even after he retired.

A month after his retirement, during a talk in the living room of his Saratoga home, Davey immersed himself in the subject that he considers, along with the bonds he has had with his former players, his basketball *nom de guerre*.

"I don't really know how it (his reputation for improving post players) transpired … I guess because I had a few in high school and in my early stages at Santa Clara I enjoyed working with," said Davey, who was a guard throughout his playing career. "I went to some clinics, especially this one at Santa Barbara … Bob Hamilton (a longtime coach at Division II UC Davis), Rick Majerus, Dan Hayes (who in 2007 completed his 24th year as head coach at Oklahoma Christian), Jim Thrash (a former Purdue and Fresno State assistant who in 2007 was a scout for the Golden State Warriors) … about half a dozen of us would get together at night after the clinics and talk Xs and Os. I started learning things from other people and started developing my own ideas about footwork and posting.

"I liked working with big guys, and I started developing my philosophy and terminology and kind of took on that role a little bit more as I moved through different coaching phases. Kurt helped it ... I did some footwork things with him. One thing he could do that was amazing for his size and (limited) jumping ability was this little specific drill I had come up with. The footwork is easy to show on the floor but hard to describe ... I ask guys to try to touch the net (from a standing position), touch the rim, dunk a tennis ball and then dunk a basketball (from an unaccustomed stance). Not a lot of guys can do it, but Rambis could dunk the basketball because he had such great thrust and balance. It's a move that requires you to move, step, move, step, and score by being able to extend yourself. To me, it kind of became a barometer when I was visiting with other big kids to see where they were (developmentally)."

Newell's camps and teachings usually emphasize footwork and, according to Davey, are tailored primarily for players whose main function is to barge inside from a facing-the-basket station on the low post. Davey, on the other hand, promulgated the idea that back-to-the-basket and high-post players can become accomplished inside scorers and rebounders.

"(Inside play is) a lot more than just footwork ... it's also about the ability to anticipate," Davey said. "Something that used to be a dominating thing to say to big kids was 'Never put the ball on the floor and keep the ball high.' You can't always do that today because the way the game is played now won't allow it. We've dealt with cliches that may have been in vogue 30 years ago that aren't in vogue today. The quickness, athleticism and brutality (of the contemporary game) require that the ball may have to come down for you to get it out of the way (of the defender). We tend as coaches to talk about 'never do this, never do that,' but those things don't always apply, or they may apply to one guy and not another, and you don't always want to use the same techniques with all players. You don't want to get out of their ability range.

"It just depends on the player and who you're playing. You might have to force this guy to front you and (allow the entry passer to) get it over the top because you can't score on a guy if he's behind you. I'm familiar with what he (Newell) does and we do some of the same things, but most of what we do is trying to create opportunities for players to play with their back to the basket when catching the ball. Footwork is a part of it, but a part that maybe gets underestimated by some people is creating opportunity to catch the ball by your posting technique."

At this point, Davey seemed to forget he was in a living room, and one expected him to spring to his feet and demonstrate his postulates at any moment. His second-favorite – and sometimes his favorite – language is basketball-speak, and while he never was a self-promoter and always tried to steer praise away from himself and toward his players, his face and his voice mirrored his passion for helping players connect their fundamental dots.

"How do you post? Do you go down and spread out and post? That may work against one guy, but against the next guy, you may have to make it look like you're gonna screen and then post. With the next guy, you may have to walk away, (at which point) he'll relax and then you flash back while he's not ready. Next guy you might have to circle-post him because he's really over you on one side and you have to get your feet around to the other side. Next guy, you really want to work on transition postups because if you beat him up the court, you might be able to seal him and get the post.

"Now there's the ability of the passer to get the ball to you over the top, his ability to ball-fake and then get the ball to you, his ability to use one dribble to get a better angle to make the entry pass, his ability to look off a defender so that the defender relaxes and then you look back and get it in. (He tasks players with) all the different techniques of being able to get the ball. I've never seen a guy who can score a basket without the ball … you can get some rebounds and score that way, but if you can't catch it on the block and figure out a way to get open and if you can't pass it to the post, you've got some problems trying to score down there."

Davey can turn evangelist when he's talking about defense as well, but his approach to that phase of the game is less position-specific than his teachings about offensive post play. Santa Clara almost never played zone defense while Davey was there, and he says he benefited from sessions with Bud Presley, who was and still is considered an oracle on the subject of man-to-man defense, while Davey was still at Leland.

Even though George "Bud" Presley died in 2002, and hadn't been active in basketball for a decade or so before that because of declining health, the mere mention of his name invigorates any conversation involving long-time basketball people. Bob Knight once called Presley the best defensive coach who ever lived, even though he never was a head coach at a four-year college, and UNLV's emergence as a perennial national-championship contender coincided with the two years Presley spent in Las Vegas in the early 1980s as an assistant coach whose main duty was to teach Jerry Tarkanian how to teach defense. (He also had a masters degree in English, and was known to critique both the language and the content of stories by reporters he liked. Some remember him as a better editor than some of the people at their papers who were paid to streamline and scrutinize copy.)

Memories of his eccentricities parallel remembrances of all that he did for the coaching profession. A favorite "Bud story" involves the time his Menlo College team was playing archrival Skyline College, and one of Presley's players was beaten to the baseline – an outright sin for anyone connected with a Presley program. He ran out onto the court while the game was in progress, grabbed the offending player, dragged him to a corner of the gym and began berating him almost molar to molar. The referees were so conscious of Presley's volcanic temper (although he seldom if ever unleashed his wrath at officials) that they bade the game go on, so Menlo played several minutes with only four players. Yet it went on to win the game.

Davey smiles at the memory of the time he found himself playing the Sidney Poitier role in the Bud Presley production of "Guess Who's Coming to Dinner."

"I remember the first time I ever went to his house," Davey said. "I was still at Leland, he was at Menlo (then a two-year junior college, but by 2007 an NCAA Division III member) and I'd known him for a couple of months. He always referred to you as 'kid' … I don't think he remembered names very well, even though he was one of the most brilliant guys I've ever met. Anyway, we're about two months into our season … he had heard through the grapevine that I was really into the defensive end of the game, so he invited Jeanne and I to his house for dinner. His wife's name was Gloria but he called her 'Bear' … 'Come on over and have dinner with Bear and me, OK kid?' My wife had never met Bud or Gloria, and I'm not sure Gloria even knew we were coming for dinner. We get there about 5, have a beer, eat dinner about 6:30, and at about 7:15 Bud says, 'Kid, come on in here,' and he takes me off to this little room off to the side, kind of a small bedroom, puts a reel of film on a projector and shuts the lights off. He starts the film and we start watching a presentation on defense by Bud. We were in there until 12:30, maybe a quarter to 1 in the morning.

"(Meanwhile) I left my wife with Gloria … she was a very gracious person, but when you haven't met someone before, you don't have a lot in common to start with. They were both teachers, so maybe they talked about that. Finally Bud gets done with the presentation, and on the way home Jeanne said, 'I like Gloria, but really ... five hours in a film room with somebody you'd never met?'

"Bud surely had an influence on my life and my coaching. People have talked about him being in a restaurant and getting up on a table to demonstrate a defensive technique, and putting out cigarettes in places you shouldn't put cigarettes out in. He'd go right out on the floor during games to instruct, but what I remember as much as anything was the fact in the 10 or so games I saw his (Menlo) teams play, never once did I see him yell at an official. He never communicated negatively with officials, and that's something I was always into with our kids: Don't show facial expressions, don't make it look like you're accusing the official of anything, don't let it (officiating) enter into your play. Like my dad always said, keep your mouth shut and play hard. Don't make it about someone else. It's about you and your team, not about the officials."

Davey carried that approach over to his deportment on the bench – unlike Williams, who had a spiky relationship with several WCC officials.

"I think I had only a half-dozen or so Ts (during his 15 years as Santa Clara's head coach)," Davey said. "Occasionally, everybody goes off a little bit, and maybe there were a couple in there that were strategic (to bestir his players), but officials have a horrible job. I often thought, if I were doing the game, how would I be able to do it? And honestly, I think it's almost impossible to officiate."

After he became the head coach at Santa Clara, Davey showed his appreciation for the early insights by making Presley an honorary coach for a game against San Francisco in 1994 and giving him a seat on the Santa Clara bench. "Same old Bud," Davey said, grinning. "We go out on the court and he's smoking a cigarette and he puts it out right there on the floor."

By the early 1980s, with the help of Presley, Williams and others, Davey had established himself as a coach on the rise within the profession, but he rarely if ever cast even a glance at openings elsewhere because he knew he wanted to stay at Santa Clara. He never interviewed for another position during his 30-year Santa Clara stay, and he said after his retirement that he seriously considered only two outside jobs – at UOP and San Jose State, both in the late 1980s. (In the mid-1990s, after he had taken Santa Clara to three NCAA tournaments in four years as head coach, officials at Cal and Oregon State made overtures, but Davey quickly removed himself from consideration for those posts.)

Despite the permanence of his situation, though, Davey wanted to be part of a winning program, and the upward thrust Santa Clara had made during Rambis' first two years there had dissipated, largely because of the Theus and McNamara controversies and the fact several other players were reluctant to relinquish their personal agendas in favor of the team quest. Although Davey said he and Williams never etched in their minds the idea that Santa Clara should define character over raw talent as its No. 1 recruiting prerequisite, the fact was that the

Broncos' top players in the early 1980s were individuals who were lightly recruited, yet brought Santa Clara its longest sustained run of success since the Awtrey/Ogden years.

And so began the era that brought Davey many of the fondest memories and most epochal victories of his 40 years in coaching.

Chapter 7
'THEY REALLY, REALLY LIKED EACH OTHER'

Santa Clara's last team during the Kurt Rambis era started three seniors and two juniors, yet went only 15-12 amid a series of conflicts between the coaches and players. McNamara and Theus weren't the only unhappy campers – Myrt Easley, Tony Gower and Vester Robinson were other highly-touted recruits who had left the program early – and it was after that 1979-80 season that Williams and Davey began to change their recruiting priorities, even though Davey said they didn't do so as part of a proclaimed manifesto.

Passing on great athletes whose academic and character qualifications were questionable wasn't an easy thing to do in the WCAC of the late 1970s and early 1980s, because the league had more than its share of "bandit" programs that were enjoying success and getting away with their transgressions.

San Francisco, which often was nationally ranked during those years and was the No. 1-ranked team in the country throughout an undefeated 1976-77 regular season, was notorious for its post-office-wall makeup, which was to result in the program being dropped for three seasons starting in 1982. Santa Clara couldn't beat the Dons in the middle and late 1970s, losing all 13 of the acrimonious rivals' meetings between 1974 and 1979. (One loss was post-scripted by a fight between Williams and USF coach Bob Gaillard.) The closest SCU came was in 1977, when the Broncos led the entire game at Toso Pavilion only to lose 71-70 on a 30-footer by Chubby Cox at the final buzzer, enabling USF to preserve its No. 1 ranking.

Seattle University, which was in the league until 1980 when it dropped out of the WCAC and NCAA in the aftermath of widespread recruiting and eligibility violations, was another program with no qualms about bringing in players with dubious backgrounds and academic qualifications. Ditto UNLV, which was a WCAC member from 1969-75. Pepperdine, Nevada and St. Mary's also had talented teams consisting primarily of players Santa Clara couldn't even consider recruiting.

Many of those programs were rife with transfers from other schools. Santa Clara rarely accepted transfers, so it was ironic that one of the first players brought in to help define Santa Clara as a character-first program had begun his college career elsewhere.

After an all-conquering high school career at Damien High in LaVerne, Calif., Bill Duffy had accepted a scholarship offer from the University of Minnesota, but transferred to Santa Clara for his final two college seasons, 1980-81 and '81-82, and led the Broncos in scoring with a 15.2 average as a senior.

"Santa Clara had recruited me hard out of high school," Duffy said. "I'm Catholic, I came out of a Catholic high school, and my dad had been inspector-general of the Presidio (a military base in San Francisco), so I knew the Bay Area. Dan Fitzgerald was one of the first in my house (during the recruiting process) ... he was a high-energy guy, and my mom and him hit it off right away.

"But I was one of the top 15 or 20 recruits in the country, and I wanted to play at a bigger program. UCLA recruited me, and I would have gone there if John Wooden hadn't retired. Gene Bartow (Wooden's successor) talked with me after that, and my reaction was, 'Wow, this sure isn't John Wooden.'"

Duffy was an on-court success at Minnesota, but the program was in the midst of the first of several internal conflagrations that were to land it in the NCAA's doghouse often over the next quarter-century. Duffy decided to transfer after the 1978-79 season when the Gophers were placed on NCAA probation, and Carroll Williams was one of the first coaches he called.

"He said, 'Good, let's stay in touch,'" Duffy said. "That summer I was working at the Superstars Camp in San Diego, and I was scrimmaging with some of the guys on the (then-San Diego) Clippers ... Bill Walton, World B. Free, Marvin Barnes. I was scoring 15, 20 points a game in those scrimmages, and all of a sudden I heard from it seemed like 50 schools in a couple of days.

"I was going to go to Hawaii ... I'm a beach guy and I liked it there. But my dad said, 'Your ass is going to Santa Clara.' (He made sure) I understood the importance of education … it was 50-50 if I was going to play pro basketball, but I wanted to go to a place where there wouldn't be any politics. (Santa Clara) had had some issues with guys in the program not being focused, and I remember that there was a mandate (at the time he arrived) that anybody they recruited had to have good character."

It was during the Superstars Camp that Duffy first met Davey – at which point Davey used the same recruiting entrée, almost word for word, that in the spring of 1992 was to help him bring Steve Nash to Santa Clara.

"Bill Berry had recruited me for Cal when he and Dick were the assistants there," Duffy said. "I didn't visit Cal, because I didn't think it was really a basketball school. I didn't talk to Dick then. First time I met him was at the Superstars Camp, after one of those scrimmages. I was feeling about as good about myself as I had ever felt as a basketball player, and he comes up to me and says, 'You know what? You might be the worst defensive player I've ever seen.'

"It woke me up a little. My first reaction was, 'Forget you.' It may have been a little bit of an overstatement, but (he later realized) it wasn't really that far from the truth."

Duffy subsequently decided, as Nash did later, that he needed coaches who would challenge him and who emphasized education and work ethic and winning the right way, and he signed with Santa Clara.

Although Duffy and Davey had a good relationship from the beginning, Duffy wasn't sure during his first season at Santa Clara whether he had made the right decision.

"I didn't think I was being used the way I thought I should be used, or playing the way I thought I should be playing," he said. "After my junior year, I thought about going to play professionally in Europe (and foregoing his senior season). But my dad told me that I had to buckle down and think about my education rather than about playing pro basketball. He told me, 'You have to buy into your coaches. They're the bosses.' From then on, I totally embraced the culture, and Dick had a lot to do with that. He was a straight-laced, hard-nosed, tough guy. He pushes you, and he teaches you to push yourself, and after I was done playing, I became even more fond of him as a man and as a mentor and as a friend.

"I love Dick Davey. He's about as good a man as anybody I've ever met."

Even before he graduated in 1982 – he was a fourth-round draft choice of the Denver Nuggets that year – and for some time thereafter, Duffy trumpeted the Santa Clara program to recruits and helped the coaches bring in many of the players who were to lead the Broncos to three straight seasons of 20 or more wins from 1982-85.

"I helped recruit that (1984-85) class," he said. "Michael Norman had been at the Superstars camp, so I played against him. Two or three weeks later, I show up at Santa Clara and I asked the coaches who they were recruiting. They mentioned Michael, but they said they were pretty sure he was going to Stanford or Washington. So I go up to St. Francis (in nearby Mountain View, where Norman was a senior) and I told him, 'Let's go have dinner and work out.' We went one-on-one going up to 11 points a game, and I beat him 11-0, 11-0, 11-1. Then I told him, 'I know about (big-time) college basketball. I played at the University of Minnesota, and I'm telling you not to get caught up in the hype. You need to go to a program where you're going to have coaches who are teachers, where you'll get a chance to play and improve, where you're in a program that will be part of you for the rest of your life.'

"He signed with Santa Clara the next day."

After Duffy's playing career ended, he went into the sports-representation business, eventually forming BDA Sports, which by 2007 was representing more than 50 clients – including Carmelo Anthony, Yao Ming, Antonio Davis, Raja Bell, Tayshaun Prince, Leandro Barbosa and Drew Gooden. Five of the top 23 selections in the 2002 NBA draft were BDA sports clients.

Another was Steve Nash.

"Frankly, Dick was instrumental in my relationship with Steve Nash," Duffy said. "He told Steve what he thought about me and my character, and of course Steve knew

I was a Santa Clara guy. And there's a lot that I learned from Dick that applies to my work now.

"Dick and Santa Clara have a kind of holistic approach that I try to use in my business, and I try to maintain the same kind of rapport with my clients, during their career and beyond, that Dick does. A good person, when they become wealthy, is going to be even more humble and more generous than he was before, and we seek out those kind of people."

Another arrival at Santa Clara during that period was 6-8 center Dan Larson, whose style reminded many of the demolition-derby players of the Awtrey/Ogden and Rambis/Bruening years. Larson was far more of a complementary player, concentrating primarily on rebounding and defense, and his career appeared over in December 1981 when he suffered a knee injury that required more extensive surgery than was readily performed at that time.

The anterior cruciate ligament in Larson's right knee not only was torn, but was shredded to such an extent that it couldn't be repaired through the surgical means available in 1981. It was almost identical to the injury that in 1980 effectively ended San Francisco 49ers running back Paul Hofer's career, but neither Larson nor Dr. Michael Dillingham were willing to accept the career-ending prognosis.

Dillingham became the 49ers' team physician in 1983, and it was his surgical work that later enabled running back Garrison Hearst to play again after suffering a knee injury so severe that doctors almost were forced to amputate his leg. Dillingham also was Santa Clara's team orthopedist during most of the years he worked for the 49ers, and was willing to do the research and push the envelope of convention with Larson.

In what was believed to be the first such procedure attempted on an athlete, Dillingham reconstructed Larson's knee ligament using almost five feet of carbon-fiber material to replace the irreparable fibrous tissue of the ligament. Within a couple of months of the surgery, he could be found at Toso Pavilion shooting free throws, with his wife Elaine (a volleyball player at Santa Clara) rebounding for him. And he was the Broncos' starting center as a senior in 1982-83, the year of the breakthrough that defined the Santa Clara program for the next quarter century.

Davey, the big man's tutor, had many pupils who were more skillful than Larson, but few if any maximized their skill set the way Larson did.

"He was a real stoic, hardworking, no-nonsense, absolutely super stick-to-the-game and work-your-ass-off type guy," Davey said of Larson, who was nicknamed "Uncle Dan" by his teammates because he looked and acted so much older than his teammates. "He has a son we almost recruited (two years before his retirement) … his kid was 6-7, 6-8, more of a skill guy and not quite as tough as Danny. He wound up somewhere else (Northern Arizona) … Danny wanted him to come here but it wasn't in the cards."

The player in question was Nick Larson, who is named after Nick Vanos.

While Dan Larson did enough as a player to certify himself as a major contributor to Santa Clara's early-1980s revival, his enduring gift to the program was the impact he had on Vanos, the 7-foot-1 center who had that size, a pair of feathery hands, and not a whole lot else going for him when Davey first recruited him for Santa Clara during his senior season (1980-81) at Hillsdale High in San Mateo, about 30 miles north of Santa Clara on the San Francisco Peninsula.

"When we were making our home (recruiting) visit, I remember saying 'You must not like your teammates very much,'" Davey said. "Nick asked why. I said, 'Because a lot of times when you're on the offensive end, you won't come down and join them on the defensive end.' I told him, '(Given his lack of conditioning), you will not make it through our first practice.' Carroll told him he (Williams) liked only one thing about him: that he was 7 feet tall."

Indeed, Vanos – the first 7-footer ever to play for Santa Clara – played much smaller than his size in high school. Bill Wilkin, who coached at Hillsdale for more than 30 years and in 1997 had a team that was 31-1 and reached the Division III state finals, gave him a solid grounding in low-post fundamentals. But he could hardly leave his feet and thus had almost no impact above the rim, and he had no carnivorous instincts on the floor. The only other major-college player in Hillsdale's league was San Mateo High's Paul Pickett, who later played for St. Mary's, and even though Pickett was a foot shorter than Vanos, he pestered him to distraction, and San Mateo had the better of Hillsdale in most of the crosstown rivals' meetings.

Several programs more prominent than Santa Clara, including Cal and Oregon State, recruited Vanos, but most college coaches saw him as a stock low-post player whose job it would be to stand under the basket and be big. But Vanos' availability coincided with Davey's emerging vision of a high-post center around whom a team could run a rotational offense. He and Williams also saw a young man with inner fire, even though one had to look beyond the veneer of introspection to see the flame at the time Vanos was at Hillsdale.

Vanos, whose given first name was Nicholaas, was the son of Dutch immigrants. His father Peter had come to the U.S. in 1957 virtually without financial resources, and built a thriving nursery business. Although his wife Josie is an irrepressible extrovert, Peter is far more reserved; because of that and the fact Nick was self-conscious about his size, Nick rarely spoke unless addressed before (and for a while after) his arrival at Santa Clara in the fall of 1981. When attention was bestowed upon him, he erected a fortress of silence. When he smiled, it was without mirth.

Despite that, and despite the fact he seemed incurably soft as a player, the Santa Clara coaches remained piqued by Vanos' possibilities.

"I still see us sitting in the living room," said Josie Vanos. "They were the first school that came to us very serious about Nick. He didn't like Berkeley at all but we all liked Santa Clara right away. Coach Williams not only became his coach but a friend of the family. We had to remind Nick that basketball wasn't the only thing in life. It was the right place for him."

Vanos wasn't so sure after his first college practice. Larson pummeled, pushed and prodded him from the time he stepped onto the court, and that practice, Davey remembers, ended with Vanos violently ill under the stands at Toso. It wasn't the last time he ended a practice on all fours, but his game – and the young man within – began to emerge during his first two seasons, even though he was an infrequent starter during those years because of Larson's presence.

"I remember Dan would stand on his crutches (after his knee surgery) and hit Nick with them from behind the basket when he didn't do something," Davey said. "But Danny loved Nick, and Nick loved Danny. I don't think I've ever seen as big a change in a person in four years as the one Nick made. He went from really a head-down, very self-conscious guy to a guy who walked out of there with cowboy boots and a cowboy hat, and standing tall."

His height notwithstanding, the first on-court quality Davey saw in Vanos was his deftness while handling and distributing the basketball. It was the first time in his coaching career that Davey had had a center who was probably his team's best passer and had the vision of a point guard, and Davey threw himself into the task of stoking Vanos' competitive embers and molding him into a center who could be an offensive force from anywhere in the forecourt.

Dick Davey, to a large extent, made Nick Vanos … and Nick Vanos, to a large extent, made Dick Davey. Although he already had a reputation for sculpting post players in a way other coaches couldn't, the fact he hardened Vanos into an NBA player was and remained his defining pre-Steve Nash achievement in many minds.

The promise was glimpsed in Vanos' first college game, when he scored 10 points, gathered 10 rebounds and blocked six shots in a win over UC Davis. But the first real breakthrough came during his sophomore year, in a home game against Pepperdine. Sports information director Mike McNulty, teasing Vanos before the game about playing soft, told him that he, McNulty, would quit smoking if Vanos were ever to dunk in traffic. Vanos did just that, with virtually the entire Pepperdine team draped on him, late in the game to lock up an important win.

After the game, Vanos emerged from the Broncos' dressing room with only one thing in mind: Tracking down McNulty, which he quickly did. Vanos extended his hand. McNulty gave him his pack of cigarettes, which Vanos proceeded to shred and then fling into the air as if he were tossing rice at a wedding.

Vanos had his detractors. After Santa Clara beat Oklahoma City early in Vanos' senior season, OCU coach

Abe Lemons said of Vanos: "Every time that 7-foot clown touched the ball and pivoted, he walked. If he could turn around without walking, I would buy you a Cadillac. Every time he stood in the middle of the court and caught the ball, he walked. Clyde Beatty couldn't train him."

But Davey could.

After his breakthrough against Pepperdine, Vanos erased almost all memories of his high school and early college years. After Santa Clara reached the NIT during his junior season, he outplayed Oregon's Blair Rasmussen, who later logged eight years in the NBA, in the Broncos' first-round upset at McArthur Court. The 44-point game against Loyola Marymount the following year, and a strong showing against future NBA center Dave Hoppen of Nebraska earlier that season, sealed his status as a player with NBA potential, and the Phoenix Suns made him their second-round choice in the 1985 draft.

While Vanos was refining and deciding his game under Davey's tutelage, his personality was beginning to emerge as well.

The Santa Clara teams that were to reach the 20-victory mark three times and play in two NITs in the early 1980s were made up primarily of athletes whose personalities were as garrulous as Vanos' was restrained. In particular, he fell in with Scott Lamson (his roommate) and Steve Kenilvort, whose prodding – sometimes gentle, sometimes pointed – and unconditional friendship helped him work through his insecurities and self-consciousness.

He filtered gradually into the social life at Santa Clara, found he could make friends because of his warmth and his generosity and the quality of his mind, and before long came to see himself – as his teammates had already seen him – as far more than a 7-foot basketball player.

For those who followed the Santa Clara program on a daily basis and traveled regularly with the team, the anecdote that perhaps best illustrated Vanos' metamorphosis involved a team flight to Southern California for WCAC games against Loyola Marymount and Pepperdine during Vanos' junior year. As the flight attendant began her pre-takeoff spiel, Vanos, at a prearranged signal, stepped into the aisle, and as the attendant went through the seat-belt-and-oxygen-mask presentation, Vanos mimed her, adding some of his own subtle flourishes to the performance.

The Santa Clara players, and all the passengers, howled hysterically at the sight of a 7-foot would-be airline steward ... but while they were laughing, those who knew Vanos well also exchanged looks that told you they knew that the Nick Vanos of two or three years before probably would have dissolved into a puddle of introversion if the stewardess had even spoken to him.

Another time, late in Vanos' Santa Clara career, he, a couple of teammates and a reporter were in a hotel elevator during a road trip when an elderly woman boarded. Apparently taken aback after seeing a 7-footer up close for perhaps the first time in her life, she examined him from head to toe, as if he were a mink stole in a display window. Finally, she asked, "Are you a basketball player?" Nick looked down at her and rejoined, "Are you?"

"Nick was always special to me among the big guys I've had," Davey said. "Obviously, the tragedy makes it even more apparent, but he's always had a special place in my heart for all the changes he made. He was starting to prove himself at the pro level ... he started 11 of their (the Suns') last 12 games, and they won 11 of them. He was all set to take off as a (pro) player. Boy, he had hands ... he could pass, had a nice (shooting) touch, and it was just a case of (Vanos gaining) confidence at that (NBA) level, which he was starting to get. He had some major, major games with us."

On August 16, 1987, when he boarded Northwest Airlines Flight 255 in Detroit, Vanos had completed a two-year apprenticeship with the Suns, who had demonstrated their trust in him as veteran center Alvan Adams' replacement by signing him to a long-term contract. He also was engaged to his girlfriend, Carolyn Cohen, and had traveled to Plymouth, Mich., to meet her parents for the first time. Flight 255 to Phoenix was to be their return trip.

The flight ended before it began, rolling 35 degrees in each direction on its initial climb with the left wing striking light poles about a half-mile from the end of the runway, and then hitting other light poles, the roof of a car rental building, and finally the ground. At 8:46 p.m., the plane skidded across the ground on the runway centerline near Interstate 94.

The official cause of the accident, the Federal Aviation Administration later determined, was "pilot error." The pilot had failed to make sure the flaps and slats were extended for takeoff. Only one of the 155 people on board, a 4-year-old girl, survived.

Twenty years later, Davey's eyes glistened as he remembered that day, and the kid who had become a 24-year-old man with only happiness and success beckoning to him. When he talked about Vanos and his life and death, the words came in streams of consciousness rather in a narrative form, because it still was difficult for Davey to distill the events of that day, and immediately thereafter.

"Scott Lamson had called me … he had heard the news coming home from a Giants game that night," Davey said. "He said, 'I don't want to alarm you, but did you hear about that plane crash in Detroit? I think that was the plane Nick was on.'

"It's the worst thing that can ever happen to anyone who's been a parent, having a child go before you, and having him go in that manner was even worse. It was kind of like what happened (when Kathleen Davey was stricken) … you think it had to be a bad dream or something. I think we all were kind of numb … it's still hard to believe something like that happening to someone you know so well. You can't visualize anything like that … you think it can't happen, but can or can't, it did."

Vic Couch, one of Vanos' Santa Clara teammates, was coaching at Kennedy High in Fremont when he found out.

"I got a phone call early in the morning and decided to just run," he said. "It was a run from reality. Running wasn't my thing but I went about four miles just to get away. I was never able to get away from the truth and it hit us all very hard."

When Harold Keeling heard of the crash, he remembered the Aloha Classic, an all-star game for the nation's best players after their senior season. Vanos and Keeling were in the waters of Waikiki Beach with the tide pulling the pair out into the ocean. Keeling told Vanos he thought they had gone too far, but Nick assured him they were fine because his feet were still touching the ground. "That's the first time I realized how tall he was," Keeling said. "The tide pulled us again even deeper and the next thing I know, I'm coughing up sand and ocean water after he dragged me back in. I could have drowned, and I thought I should have been on that plane to save his life to return the favor. Logically, that didn't make any sense, but that was running through my mind at the time."

"Whenever you heard about big crashes, you think about whether you know anyone from that area, and where the flight was going," Kenilvort said. "I didn't know he'd gone to Detroit that week, so I didn't give it a lot of thought. But when I went to bed that night, I was just a little bit uneasy. About 2 in the morning, the phone rang, and as soon as

I heard it, I knew Nick was dead. It was (teammate) Terry Davis, who said he'd heard it on the news.

"You can't even describe the feeling, even after 20 years. I remember Nick so much more as a person than as a player. He was one of the sweetest human beings you could ever come across … you knew he would be there at the start and he would be there at the end. He was a guy you would be friends with forever."

The funeral service, at which Lamson gave the eulogy, was at the Santa Clara Mission, around which the campus originally was built in 1851. Several NBA players showed up; so did several of Vanos' Little League coaches.

"I've only seen that place overflowing twice," Davey said. "Once for (beloved football coach and athletic director) Pat Malley's funeral (in 1985), and the second time for Nick's service. And this was in the middle of summer when nobody was on campus.

"You kind of knew what you were getting when you got to know the rest of the family. They (Vanos' parents) still come to a lot of events on campus, Josie still comes to a few games a year, and we go to lunch once or twice a year. They're just good people, and they've helped a lot of former players by making loans at certain percentage rates to (recently graduated) guys to buy homes."

Lamson's eulogy was to the point and to the heart. "He was always there with me to share the bad times and celebrate the good," he said in conclusion. "He was the best friend I ever could have had."

One reporter who had a close friendship with Vanos put his feelings this way: "How Nick died Sunday, and why, are questions that only cause more hurt when pondered. I prefer (to reflect on) how he lived and what he made of himself. I think of the little girl who survived the crash because her mother shielded her from the flames. There's no question in my mind that Nick's last thought also was of trying to do something to help, to save someone else. No question whatsoever."

After the service, Kenilvort, Lamson and several others in or close to the program who knew Vanos best assembled for their own tribute.

"Nick certainly wouldn't want people to sit and cry over him," Kenilvort said. "We played cards, dice, drank beer ... that's the celebration (of his life) he would have wanted. The golf tournament we've had (in his honor) ever since is a great opportunity for his friends and family to salute and recognize him.

"He impacted all of our lives. He's one of those people you don't forget about."

Lamson and Larson both named their oldest sons after Vanos. Through them, the golf tournament, and in many other ways, he lived on more than 20 years after he was gone. Unfortunately, so did the memories of that August day in 1987.

"I never flew a Northwest plane for maybe 15 years after that, and even then I was forced into it (because no other flights to his destination were available, and it was too far away to drive)," Davey said. "I didn't want to fly it. It was pilot error that caused this whole thing to happen … you don't want to be closely associated with Northwest, or at least I didn't.

"I remember one time when my dad had Nick and Scott (Lamson) up to his cabin for two days of fishing. My dad was a unique fisherman … he took both of them out on his boat, and my dad caught something like 17 fishes and Nick caught one. The kidding that went back and forth that night … my dad was teasing him about how you had to make the bait smell a certain way or you have to twitch your right eye at a certain moment to get the fish's attention. My dad was that way, but Nick knew he was kidding him, and they just went back and forth all night.

"He was quite a guy, God dang it."

He wasn't the only one … and though Davey can tell you something intimate and personal about almost every athlete who ever played for him, he probably can tell you more about Steve Kenilvort and Harold Keeling than most of the others.

Kenilvort came to Santa Clara in the fall of 1982 from Drake High in San Anselmo, an affluent town in Marin County, on the opposite side of the Golden Gate Bridge from San Francisco. Keeling had arrived the year before after graduating from Lincoln High in one of the rougher neighborhoods of San Francisco. Kenilvort never had to be introduced to anyone, because he would introduce himself, and you didn't have to wait long to see his friendliness away from the floor or his competitive zeal while on it. Keeling was almost as quiet as Vanos when he first arrived at Santa Clara, but had a sort of Joe Dumars dignity to him, and when he spoke, it was with feeling and sincerity and grace and sensitivity that told you he wanted people to know through his words not only what he thought, but who he was.

Kenilvort went into real estate and then the mortgage business after graduation and was an unbridled success in both endeavors. Keeling, after a 20-game stay with the NBA's Dallas Mavericks in 1985-86, was as successful as Kenilvort in a divergent career. In 2007, he was running a center for underprivileged youth in Atlanta.

"I think what I learned from Dick and Carroll and Santa Clara that competing in athletics has a direct parallel to what I do every day competing in the business world," Kenilvort said. "Losing teaches you as much as winning does ... how to bounce back from disappointment or a loss, personal or professional. Life is not fair. I'd say I've learned from Dick my entire (adult) life, but as much as anything, I've learned from the way I've seen him handling this (his firing) with such dignity and grace. How to take the high road on stuff like that ... it's been amazing the way he's handled himself."

Together, Kenilvort and Keeling brought a human element to a program that, for all its emphasis on attracting and nurturing true student-athletes, seemed like a feature-less aqueduct to many who didn't have long-standing Santa Clara ties. In the early 1980s, Kenilvort was the Broncos' raging rapids, Keeling their shimmering mountain stream, and they were the primary conduits as Santa Clara regained some of the national basketball stature it had enjoyed in the 1950s and 1960s.

"That group was a special group from my standpoint," Davey said. "They were hard workers, tough-minded kids who really stuck to business. They loved the game, they wanted to win, they had all the attributes you look for in a team, and they really, really liked each other."

Davey was primarily responsible for bringing both Kenilvort and Keeling to Santa Clara, and his first memories of the two players are among his most poignant.

Kenilvort, at 6-foot-5, was a center on a Drake team that won 56 straight games and a state Division II championship, even though it wasn't nearly as athletically endowed as many other Bay Area programs at that time. As a senior, he scored 35 points and snared 16 rebounds in the Pirates' victory in the state title game over Banning of Wilmington, which had a veritable cornucopia of college-level athletes. His inner drive was a dynamo, but it appeared unlikely he would get a chance to play major-college basketball because he didn't project into any specific position in the eyes of evaluators who were looking for pieces that would fit smoothly into holes dictated by basketball dogma.

Davey was the only recruiter who saw Kenilvort as a central, if unconventional, fragment in a team mosaic.

"I probably saw him play 15 times his senior year, because we really wanted him," Davey said. "In games, he was always down around the basket so we really couldn't see him do anything (that could relate to Santa Clara's needs). So I'd always go early and watch him in warmups, and I could see then that he could shoot the ball on the perimeter. Warmups are important to evaluate, and after I saw him some, I hoped he'd be a point guard, but I knew he'd (be able to) play for us somewhere."

"During my first phone conversation with him, he asked me who else was recruiting me," Kenilvort said. "I told him one of the schools was Cal, and he said, 'Do you really think you can play at Cal?' I said, yeah, I think I can, but I was pretty puzzled by the question (which was intended, as with Davey's introductory comments to Duffy, Nash and others, to determine his level of determination and self-confidence). I thought 'What do you mean?' Is Cal harder to play at than Santa Clara?' What was interesting was that we played Cal after I went to Santa Clara and beat them, and I hit the winning shot. But that was the first of many (conversations we had) in the recruiting process.

"Dick used to drive up to our Drake games; it seemed he was there every other game. I don't know what he picked up during those warmups, but I had played power forward at Drake and he recruited me as an off-guard.

Harold was playing point, but after a few games we flip-flopped and it stayed that way for three years."

Kenilvort, for his part, was won over by Davey when they went to lunch during a recruiting trip. Davey ordered a full meal, while Kenilvort ordered a soft drink that cost exactly 86 cents. College coaches, of course, are prohibited by NCAA rules from making any sort of purchase for a recruit, but Kenilvort had received enough recruiting attention to know that the rule was conspicuous more in the breach than in the observance.

Except by Davey, who made Kenilvort pay the 86 cents for his beverage.

"One thing about Dick, and anybody who knows him will tell you the same thing ... he's got so much credibility," Kenilvort said. "He's a straight shooter, and he takes an interest and really cares about the people around him. He was really the reason I wound up going to Santa Clara. He was very much a father figure, and over the years, he developed into a friend."

"I felt close to Steve because he'd lost his dad when he was very young," Davey said. "He is the epitome of what a student-athlete should be. He's held a special place for me, although I could probably tell you stories about (incidents that reflected the character of) 90 percent of our players."

Kenilvort didn't begin the 1982-83 season as a starter, but an incident after the Broncos' 79-68 to USC at the

Los Angeles Sports Arena early in the season illuminated him in the eyes of his coaches.

"I remember Vanos had about 10 shots blocked in that game," Davey said. "After we lost, one of our (upperclassman) players was laughing as he talked to some friends of his as he walked off the floor. Steve gets inside the locker room, picks up this guy – he was about 6-8 – off the floor, shoved him against the lockers and told him that if he ever laughed again after a loss, he'd beat the living you-know-what out of him. That's the kind of competitor he was … is."

Asked in 2007 about the incident, Kenilvort laughed.

"Carroll and Dick tell that story over and over, and it kind of gets bigger with time," he said. "I don't remember the actual incident … I was probably red-lining at the time. It was the second or third game of the year and SC was just taking it to us. They had a little point guard (Jacque Hill) who kept running at me off Nick, and in transition Nick was a little slow setting picks. I think I just asked Nick to not let that happen anymore … not in so many words, but the story grows and grows.

"You have to remember at that point I hadn't lost at all. We were 36-0 my senior year (at Drake), and losing was very unfamiliar to me. Right or wrong, I always believed we could win every game. I didn't know how to handle it … I guess I learned over the years, but I was emotional when I played."

Kenilvort was promoted to the starting point-guard slot soon after that USC game, thus beginning his three-year backcourt partnership with Keeling, who was moved from point to shooting guard. The Broncos were squashed 84-56 at home by seventh-ranked Louisville in their next game, but then won 13 of their next 15 games, with one of the losses coming against 17th-ranked North Carolina in Chapel Hill.

Before Santa Clara's game with Loyola Marymount in Los Angeles later that season, Williams assigned another player to guard LMU's Greg Goorjian, who previously had played at Arizona State and UNLV, and as a high school senior had set a national single-season scoring record with a 43.2 average. (Goorjian, who later flourished in the booming Las Vegas real estate market and won four straight Nevada 2A state championships as a coach at The Meadows School, finished that 1982-83 season as the nation's fourth-leading scorer with a 26-point average.)

Kenilvort took immediate umbrage. "What do you *mean* I can't guard Goorjian?" he asked Williams, who decided to test his freshman by giving him the assignment.

Goorjian scored 33 points in the game, but needed 36 shots (22 of which he missed) to reach that total, and Santa Clara won 87-83. By the end of the season, Williams had so much confidence in Kenilvort that he wound up averaging almost 35 minutes per game down the stretch.

USF, which had made the WCAC its fiefdom throughout the previous decade, was no longer a concern, because the school had shut down its program (a hiatus that lasted three years) in the aftermath of a succession of scandals that culminated with accusations of sexual assault against Dons star Quintin Dailey. As the 1982-83 season began, the Broncos were favored by most to win the WCAC's automatic NCAA tournament bid for the first time since 1970 by capturing the league championship – the conference didn't have a postseason tournament then – but the Broncos' 9-3 league record left them one game behind Pepperdine, and Santa Clara was snubbed both by the NCAA tournament committee and by the NIT.

Keeling, who led the team in scoring with a 14.9-point average in 1982-83 and was the WCC steals leader for the first of two times, was a first-team all-conference selection that season, and earned that distinction at the end of each of the next two seasons as well. He scored at a 19.8-point clip as a senior, and in 2007 remained No. 2 on Santa Clara's career scoring list with 1,731 points, second only to Rambis' 1,736. (Brian Jones, who played from 1996-2001, was third with 1,722 points, followed by Steve Nash with 1,689 and Dennis Awtrey with 1,675.)

As with Kenilvort, Davey saw something in Keeling's game and in his temperament that other coaches either failed to see, or ignored. As one reporter put it, Keeling in high school was "a scoring champion in the madcap (San Francisco) Academic Athletic Association, where defense is about as welcome as smallpox."

"I went to watch him play at Lincoln one time, and I walked out of the game (before its conclusion)," Davey said. "He had a great high school career, but in that game he finished with two points and two rebounds. Terry Malley (a former Santa Clara quarterback who later become head football coach, replacing his father Pat) had gone up with me to see a football player. We walked out, and Terry asked me, 'Well, what do you think?' I said. 'He can't play.' Thank God we recruited him anyway.

"He wore a tie to class every day he was at Santa Clara, and he ended up being a good student (even though his academic credentials even in high school were marginal, and he struggled with the demanding Santa Clara curriculum for some time). He was the kind of guy who never gave up on anything.

"I spent an evening with him and Vic Couch (who played for Santa Clara from 1983-85, and later coached there, at Minnesota and at Long Beach State) in Atlanta during the (2007) Final Four. I have a letter that he wrote me (two months earlier, after his "retirement" had been announced) that I think shows how deep and aware he is."

The letter, in part, reads: "I am writing you to say thank you on behalf of all the student-athletes whose lives you have touched along the way. You should hear the way that people talk about you, people like Duff (Bill Duffy), Vic, Steve (Kenilvort). Man, coach Davey, people love you! I hear your career is coming to an end … Please know that you helped so many of us along the way in basketball and life.

"There are family members of yours throughout the years who have had to share you with 'us' whom I need to thank as well. For so many years they sacrificed in different ways so you could spend countless hours preparing the team for a game or the season. It's not like there was a vote and I was selected to write this letter but I wouldn't be able to sleep at night without reminding you how much of a difference maker you have been. It's not like it would be inappropriate, because how many nights have you gone without sleep worrying about us?"

"We had Sean Denison (the WCC co-Player of the Year as a senior in 2006-07) back in Atlanta for an all-star game during the Final Four," Davey said. "Harold met him the day before the game. He introduced himself by saying, 'Hi, I'm Harold Keeling, and I'm the second-leading scorer in the history of Santa Clara.' Now some might misconstrue that, but you have to understand that this is maybe the most polite human being I've ever met. Somebody's immediate reaction might be that he's not humble at all, but it's the opposite. He's so humble and proud, and he wants to you know how much he thinks about Santa Clara and how proud he is to be part of the history there."

Even though Santa Clara didn't qualify for the NCAA tournament during any of the three seasons Kenilvort, Keeling and Vanos were together, they added some history of their own to Santa Clara's proud basketball heritage during the 1983-84 and 1984-85 seasons.

Chapter 8
ECSTASY AND AGONY

At the start of the 1983-84 season, Williams and Davey were cautiously optimistic that they had a team capable of winning a conference title and challenging even the best teams on a brutal schedule.

Larson had graduated, but Vanos was ready to step in as the starting center, and Michael Norman, a 6-7 graduate of nearby St. Francis High who could play both silky and swarthy underneath and could make opposing big men follow him outside because of his middle-distance shooting accuracy, was in his fourth year as a starter. Scott Lamson stepped into the small-forward vacancy created by the graduation of Gary Hopkins, the Broncos' second-leading scorer the previous season.

Vic Couch, a junior college transfer from Iowa who wrote poetry in his spare time, yet played with a ferocity on defense that Williams said matched that of any player he had coached, gave the Broncos a troubleshooter off the bench. Senior Terry Davis was a dependable point-guard reserve, although Santa Clara's depth at other positions was to become an issue later in the season. All five of the starters were obliged to play heavy minutes in most games, and the Broncos' energy tank ran low more than once when they could least afford it.

The Broncos began their season by beating New Mexico and losing to defending national champion North Carolina State 78-75 (despite Vanos' 25 points and 12 rebounds) and Oklahoma 91-77 in the Great Alaska Shootout in Anchorage. They won four straight home games – including a 74-54 rout of USC – before losing 60-53 to Princeton in the Kettle Classic in Houston, then enhanced their national credentials by winning their Cable Car Classic with a 71-69 victory over a Ohio State team led by Tony Campbell, who averaged 11.6 points per game over 11 NBA seasons and won a title ring with the Lakers in 1988.

That victory was perhaps the Broncos' most significant since the Awtrey/Ogden years, save an upset of then-No. 2-ranked Providence in 1972, but it also was a portent of difficulties to come. Santa Clara led 63-47 with 3:20 to play before the Buckeyes' defensive pressure began to exact its toll, and Ohio State could have forced overtime with a 20-foot jumper that missed at the buzzer.

Then began a WCAC season that was at once exhilarating, exasperating and – for Davey in particular – exhausting. Davey virtually had two fulltime jobs for the next two months. In addition to his conventional coaching duties, he was Santa Clara's fulltime sentinel on the Craig McMillan Watch.

McMillan was a 6-foot-6 senior point guard from Cloverdale, a town of perhaps 4,000 people that straddled U.S. 101 about 150 miles north of Santa Clara. While relatively proximate to the Bay Area, Cloverdale was distinctly rural. Most of the downtown buildings looked as if Model Ts ought to be parked in front of them, the 101 freeway narrowed into Main Street when it hit the town limits, and the high school housed only about 325 students.

Davey made the trip to Cloverdale, and to even more remote hamlets like Kelseyville – the "Pear Capital of the West" – and Clearlake and Upper Lake and Lower Lake, at least once almost every week during McMillan's senior season. No Santa Clara player during the Davey era was recruited so widely and vigorously ... and no player, not even Steve Nash or Kurt Rambis in their high school years, loomed as such an obvious difference-maker for a program like Santa Clara's.

More than 100 colleges, from Notre Dame to Kentucky to UCLA, wanted McMillan enough to offer him a scholarship, and the *Long Beach Press-Telegram* – the most reliable recruiting barometer on the West Coast at that time – anointed him the best guard in the state of California after he had played well in a summer league that included nationally-ranked Southern California teams like Mater Dei and Crenshaw. Even at 6-6, he was a ghost ship when he ran the Cloverdale fast break, and he used the ball like a conductor's baton while making no-look passes of the type more commonly associated with Magic Johnson. He had 3-point shooting range even though the 3-point arc didn't exist in the California Interscholastic Federation (or the NCAA) then, and he was a 6-9 high jumper during track season.

Better yet from Santa Clara's standpoint, he was no pampered prodigy; his father John was one of the most respected high school coaches in Northern California, having had only two losing seasons in the 23 years before Craig was a senior. He made sure Craig always respected the integrity of the game and the sanctity of the team and the fundamentals, and he made sure his son maintained excellent grades and study habits. Some of the people within the Santa Clara program who had met the quiet but articulate, blond-haired, blue-eyed McMillan referred to him as Prince Valiant, and they did so without sarcasm.

He was the type of player Santa Clara usually never even considered recruiting because it couldn't compete, in terms of resources and exposure, with the teams that were on national TV as a matter of course. (Santa Clara at the time didn't even have an off-campus radio contract.) But he had gone to Santa Clara's summer basketball camp annually as a kid, and had struck up a friendship with Garry Mendenhall, one of the other Santa Clara assistant coaches, during that time. He loved the environment, and the passion and the personalities of the 1983-84 Santa Clara players and coaches. In January 1984 he announced that Santa Clara was among the four finalists for his college services, along with Arizona, UCLA and Stanford.

McMillan deferred his college choice until after he had led Cloverdale to its second straight state championship. In due course, he picked Arizona – a choice that turned out to be propitious both for him and for the Wildcats.

He was a four-year starter, and helped Arizona reach the 1988 Final Four as part of a backcourt triumvirate that also included Steve Kerr and Kenny Lofton.

The determining factors in his final decision, he said in 2007, were the fact Santa Clara didn't have a physical education major – even then, he knew he wanted to follow his father into coaching – and Santa Clara's relatively low basketball profile. Even at that, he said, he came close to shrugging those considerations off and going to Santa Clara anyway.

"I would have gone to Santa Clara if I hadn't gone to Arizona," McMillan said. "If Santa Clara had been in the Pac-10, I definitely would have gone there. They're not as worried about selling and the business end ... they're about ethics. I appreciated the way they recruited me ... they didn't send me 10 stacks of recruiting material and all that other BS. It was more personal."

Even during his Arizona career, McMillan often asked Bay Area reporters about the goings-on at Santa Clara, and he stayed in touch with Davey, Williams and some of the Santa Clara players. More than 20 years later, his friendship with Davey continued.

"I love Craig," Davey said. "I definitely think of him that way (as a sort of honorary Bronco)."

After he graduated from Arizona, McMillan was an assistant coach at Marquette, Tennessee and Arizona before becoming head coach at Santa Rosa Junior College near his hometown in 2000. McMillan's Santa Rosa teams had a three-year run during which they went 82-17 and won two conference championships, and 14 of his players during his first seven seasons – including eight on the Division I level – went on to four-year programs. More than 90 percent of his two-year players had graduated as of 2007 – an almost unheard-of figure for a junior college.

In the spring of 2007, one of McMillan's players, point guard Zac Tiedemann, signed with Santa Clara, which almost never pursues juco players because their courses usually aren't transferable under the school's academic restrictions.

"The funny thing about Zac was that he's like me … he wants to be a high school basketball coach after he graduates, and he was concerned about Santa Clara not having a P.E. major," McMillan said. "I told him not to worry about it … you don't have to be a P.E. major to be a coach.

"Dick said the only thing that bothered him about taking Zac was that he didn't want to take him away from me after only one year. How many college coaches are you going to see who are worried about something like that? And when all that (the controversy surrounding his departure) was happening, Dick called me and said he still wanted Zac to go to Santa Clara, that it was a great school and it would be a great fit for Zac."

(In fact, Davey made similar calls to all four of the players he had signed during the previous recruiting period, and all four maintained their commitment to Santa Clara despite the coaching change.)

"He did that even after he got shafted," McMillan said. "He could have sabotaged that program if he'd wanted to. I have so much respect for Dick Davey and Carroll Williams, and I try to run my program the way Dick ran his … get good guys, play unselfishly, graduate your players. I try to prepare my players for the recruiting process, and how brutal it can be and how you can't always rely on what some people tell you. With Dick, his word is as good as gold. A lot of coaches leave (potentially negative) stuff out when they're talking to kids. He never did."

Whether McMillan could have been Santa Clara's Richie Frahm – the first nationally-renowned player of the later Gonzaga monarchy, followed by exemplars like Adam Morrison, Ronny Turiaf, Dan Dickau and Matt Santangelo – is only conjecture. But if McMillan had gone to Santa Clara, he would have been teamed as a freshman with Vanos, Keeling, Kenilvort and Lamson, and at the very least, the Broncos would noy have had the dearth of depth that ultimately undermined their NCAA tournament hopes on several occasions during the 1980s.

"We had a shot at him," Davey said after his retirement. "I can't honestly tell you (what sort of impact McMillan might have had at Santa Clara). Sometimes a guy who goes to a bigger school might not have quite the impact that he might have had at a smaller school. At the same time, sometimes a guy can go to a bigger school (as McMillan did) and have a big impact, or go to a smaller school and just not fit with that group. He can't get the ball where he needs it. (With McMillan) he was a good shooter, but you needed to set screens for him. Trying to analyze a guy and saying he would be 100 percent super, I don't know, but I don't think he would have been anything less than a very good player. Would he have meant an extra win or two (as a freshman)? Probably, and maybe then we're an NCAA team and not an NIT team.

"That's what Gonzaga has done: Get the first guy and then keep it going. We didn't, and maybe that's one of the areas I was discouraged with (late in his tenure as head coach). We didn't get enough to keep us better. I don't belittle coaching, but as I've always said, you gotta have players."

While the McMillan recruiting regatta proceeded, so did Santa Clara's 1983-84 season.

After opening their WCAC season with home wins over Pepperdine and Loyola Marymount, the Broncos withered against a quicker St. Mary's team in an 81-64 loss, and then played tired again in a 69-61 defeat at San Diego two nights later. Three weeks after that, Santa Clara again faded late in road losses to Gonzaga (with John Stockton, who scored 21 points in the game) and Portland, and a 63-61 home loss to eventual champion San Diego ended the Broncos' hopes for a WCAC title and an NCAA tournament bid. At that time, the conference, minus USF, was at one of its lowest-ever ebbs, and San Diego was relegated to a play-in game against Princeton when the 53-team NCAA field was announced.

(Princeton won.) Unlike the previous year, nobody from Santa Clara seriously expected to be invited to the NCAA tournament unless the Broncos got the WCAC's automatic bid.

The Broncos finished the regular season with three wins to improve their record to 20-9 and earn a second-place tie in the WCAC, but many believed Stanford (19-12) had a better shot at an NIT bid – even though Santa Clara had beaten Stanford in a non-league game, and had played a much harder non-conference schedule – because of Stanford's superior name recognition and drawing power. The NIT in those years determined its field and pairings largely on the basis of finances, and it was routine for middle-of-the-road schools from top-shelf conferences to "buy" as many as three NIT home games. (The Broncos, despite their success, averaged only 3,180 spectators per home game in 1983-84, and had sold out only two, against St. Mary's and Stanford.) The Cardinal also had a "name" coach – Tom Davis, who had left Boston College in 1982 to resuscitate the lifeless Stanford program.

That's why Santa Clara's inclusion in – and Stanford's exclusion from – the NIT field came as something of a surprise. But the NIT didn't do the Broncos any favors; their first assignment was against Oregon and Blair Rasmussen at McArthur Court in Eugene. And the WCAC season had taken its toll on several players. Lamson had a bruised shoulder, Couch was limping because of a strained patella tendon in his knee, and Norman had a "turf toe." But Vanos, who had been yearning for an opportunity to prove himself against one of the nation's best centers, was ready to take up any necessary slack.

"He might not talk about it," Lamson said before the game, "but don't let him fool you. He's thinking about it. He wants to prove he can play with the best."

"We'll find out which of us is better, I guess," Vanos said. "He was better three years ago when we were both at Superstars Camp. It'll be interesting, I know that."

With Vanos leading the way, Santa Clara registered two victories that to a large extent elevated the Santa Clara program to the point where it could expect to approach the 20-win mark, play in the postseason and get "in the door" with recruits, like McMillan, other schools coveted.

During Davey's 30 years at Santa Clara, the Broncos won only two WCAC or WCC regular-season titles (the conference lost its 'A,' so to speak, in 1989), and those came in 1995 and 1996, Steve Nash's junior and senior seasons. One reason for the dearth of championship banners was the fact the conference during those years had several teams that made a significant dent in the national basketball consciousness – Pepperdine under Jim Harrick through the 1980s, Loyola Marymount with Hank Gathers and Bo Kimble and its record-shattering offensive wherewithal in the late 1980s and early 1990s, and Gonzaga in the 2000s.

San Diego and St. Mary's almost always had fierce, well-coached, talented teams in the late 1980s and 1990s.

USF had its moments after it restored its program in 1986, although the Dons no longer were the leviathans they had been before the shutdown. Portland was the conference's only oasis during most of that period. And until San Diego and Gonzaga opened new arenas during Davey's final five seasons at Santa Clara, every gym in the league was a cauldron boiling over with ravenous, frighteningly proximate crowds. The fact the WCAC/WCC hasn't changed its membership since 1980 (aside from the three years San Francisco was idle) made every game a rivalry game, and the league often played an energy-draining Friday-Saturday schedule, so every road win was a heirloom.

Despite all those factors, Santa Clara as of 2007 had lost more than 16 games only once since 1982-83 – in 1989-90, when the Broncos went 9-19 – while annually playing some of the nation's highest-ranked teams. Santa Clara had eight seasons during which it won 20 or more games during that span, including Davey's final year, which was highlighted by the victory that ended Gonzaga's 50-game home winning streak.

"There are a lot of great memories," Davey said. "We beat Georgia Tech (in 1995-96) when they had (Stephon) Marbury, we beat (North) Carolina the year they won the national championship (2004-05, at the start of the season when the Tar Heels were ranked No. 4), and Maryland (91-79 in the 1995-96 NCAA tournament) was a big win. We've had an opportunity to play a number of different teams and coaches over the year, like Syracuse, UCLA, Indiana, North Carolina, Kentucky ... we've pretty much run the gamut over the past 30 years, most of the time at their places."

While the win with which Davey and Santa Clara will be identified most in retrospect was against Arizona in 1993, that wasn't the only pedestal win the Broncos achieved during Davey's 30 years at Santa Clara. The Broncos won at UCLA and beat Nebraska and Cincinnati in 1984-85, and lost by only five points at Louisville. In 1987-88, Santa Clara beat Seton Hall (which advanced to the national championship game the following season) and won at Stanford. Other subsequent Santa Clara upset victims during the Davey years included Utah, Charlotte and 17th-ranked St. Mary's (1988-89); Oregon and California with Jason Kidd (1993-94); UCLA, Michigan State and Oregon State (1995-96); Marquette and Alabama (1996-97); Oregon (1997-98); Southern Illinois and Butler (1999-2000); Stanford (2004-05) and Bucknell (2005-06).

All those benchmark wins notwithstanding, though, Santa Clara's reputation as an ambush specialist began in 1984 with its NIT victories at Oregon and Lamar on two of the most daunting home courts in the country at the time.

After Santa Clara beat Stanford during the regular season, Stanford coach Tom Davis rationalized the defeat by saying the game "was more important to them than it was to us." That might also have been the case with Oregon, another Pac-10 school, but it shouldn't have been, because the Ducks hadn't been to the NCAA tournament since 1961 and wouldn't compete in another until 1995. Six straight losing seasons had cost former coach Jim Haney his job, and the program seemed to be on the verge of a revival under first-year coach Don Monson, who had been hired after a successful run at Idaho.

Davey didn't know Monson before that night in Eugene, and their introduction was less than cordial, although they later became friendly.

"I remember Carroll telling me Monson was tough-minded and he'd get on the officials, especially with their crowd at their place," Davey said. "Here I was, just a little assistant, and sure enough, during a timeout, Monson is all over the officials. Carroll says, 'Go over there (so that Monson couldn't try to manipulate the officials).' So I stand there while he's talking to them … I (came to) like Don (in later years), but he's talking to the officials and I'm standing right there, and he says to me, 'What the fuck are you doing here? Go sit your ass down.' So I sat my ass down.'"

Scott Lamson remembers other details of that confrontation.

"We were supposed to get killed," Lamson said. "But Nick was up against Blair Rasmussen, who was an All-America, and Nick just killed him. Their fans were right on top of the court screaming and yelling, and Don Monson is screaming at the refs the entire game. Finally Carroll tells Dick, 'It's your job to get on him. You don't let him get on the refs. I've got to coach and it's pissing me off what he's doing. Your job is to get on him and don't let him get the best of the officials.' So we're up eight or nine and he's screaming at the refs, so Dick yells at him, 'Get back on your spot.' So Monson looks down and says, 'What the fuck are *you* doing here? You're not even the head coach. Do you know where you are?' So Dick says, 'Yeah, I know where we are. We're at The Pit and we're kicking your ass.'"

The game started at 9 p.m. because Mac Court already was booked for a high school game earlier in the evening, and high school basketball is of such importance in Oregon that university officials couldn't afford the public-relations negativity that would result from moving the prep game. The late starting time may have reduced the size of the crowd, but the wedding-cake decks that overlook the floor in the arena, one of college basketball's oldest, were close to full when the two teams took the court.

The Oregon fans never were able to make themselves a factor in the game. The Broncos never trailed in a 66-53 victory, and gave Rasmussen and the other Ducks a primer on power basketball. Vanos scored 18 points and snared nine rebounds; Rasmussen also had 18, but he was able to pluck only a single rebound. Fourteen of Santa Clara's 27 field goals came from 4 feet or closer to the basket.

"That was a game where we went on the road, to a Pac-10 school, and we truly expected to win that game," Kenilvort said. "We were so prepared for that game. We were in a very hostile environment, but we had matured to the point we actually enjoyed that environment. You hear athletes talk about liking to close out (playoff) series on the road, and that's because it's actually more of a reward to silence a crazy crowd like that.

"The Pac-10 had a reputation of being superior to our conference. We had a point to prove, and I think we actually dominated that game."

Kenilvort said the degree to which the team was prepared enhanced the Santa Clara players' confidence.

"That game said a lot about the coaches' preparation," he said. "As a player, it was a nightmare, but in this game it made a difference because I think we knew their offense as well as they did. (Davey) was so detailed … in high school we did no preparation (involving) our opponents; it was 100 percent preparing ourselves. So it was a little bit of a culture shock, doing so much studying of our opponents and getting to know their tendencies and stuff. But certainly it helped us succeed and win games.

"Dick literally would spend the whole night in the film room. We'd show up in the morning and you could just tell he had been there the whole night preparing 10 minutes of clips that might give us an advantage. That one tendency or play-call or inbound play or a 'special' that they ran, or the tendencies of a certain player … those are little things that differentiate him from many coaches. He never let those details slip, neither he nor Carroll. They were both *maniacs* when it came to detail."

The victory earned Santa Clara a trip to an even more hostile clime than Mac Court – Beaumont, Texas, to play Lamar, which had just had its 80-game home winning streak terminated in the Southland Conference tournament the previous week. The Cardinals had begun to establish a strong basketball dossier under Billy Tubbs in the late 1970s, and after Tubbs left for Oklahoma in 1980, assistant coach Pat Foster took over and won 70 games, including two NCAA tournament contests, in his first three seasons.

In 1983-84, Lamar brought a 26-4 record into the Santa Clara game, but a loss to Louisiana Tech in the Southland championship game had cost the Cardinals not only their 80-game home winning streak – seventh-longest in NCAA history as of 2007 – but an NCAA tournament bid as well. Lamar was denied an at-large berth because of its soft schedule, within which the most difficult opponent was Utah State. But the Cardinals had won their NIT opener, 64-61, at New Mexico's dreaded "Pit," and were prohibitive favorites at home over the Broncos.

The game was played in the Beaumont Civic Center, which Lamar would leave after that season to take up residence in a 10,000-seat arena on campus. The Civic Center, into which a basketball floor fit only awkwardly, had the same shape, size and meat-locker ambiance of Stanford's Maples Pavilion, but the fans were far more surly than those at Stanford – or, perhaps, anywhere else Santa Clara played during the Davey era.

In the first half, the Broncos couldn't find an answer for Lamar guard Tom Sewell, and the Cardinals led 47-37 at the intermission. But Keeling, who finished with 26 points while Sewell had 32, was in his element in the up-tempo game that Lamar dictated. The Broncos rallied, with Vanos taking advantage of Lamar's lack of size to forage inside for 16 points, and had forged a 74-74 tie when a Lamar turnover in the final minute enabled the Broncos to play for the final shot of the game. Norman posted up, wheeled and attempted a lean-in shot that missed ... but he was fouled as the final buzzer sounded, earning him a trip to the free-throw line for two shots with the clock showing 0:00.

Norman wasn't much better than an average free-throw shooter, but Davey's mind immediately reverted to something Norman had said to him at breakfast that morning. "He said, 'Coach, I had a dream last night. I was shooting a free throw to win the game at the very end ... and I made it.'"

With the lane cleared of players because time had run out, Norman made the first free throw with the Lamar fans screaming as if being examined by proctologists with hangnails. He added the anticlimactic second free throw amid library-like silence, and Santa Clara escaped with a 76-74 victory.

"We were down 10 at half, and they were very athletic," Kenilvort recalled. "I remember going in at halftime. Their place was going crazy, and as we went into our locker room under the bleachers, their fans were pouring beer and soft drinks on us and saying 'You guys don't belong here' and a lot worse. Well, at halftime Carroll used some of the same words. He said, 'If you think we aren't going to win this game, don't go back on the court.'"

Said Lamson: "Beaumont was like Stockton on steroids. Just a cow town. We walk in this gym and there were 10 or so Santa Clara parents behind us on the bench, and everyone else was from Beaumont. We went in there and just played our ass off. After we won the game, I remember people throwing beers on us as we were walking out. Terry Davis yells up at them, 'Pour more. You won't be back. Your season's over.'"

Santa Clara's improbable run ended three days later, when the Broncos were crushed 97-76 at Southwestern Louisiana (now Louisiana-Lafayette), but the springboard effect of the two NIT victories did not subside – at least not for long – for the remainder of Davey's Santa Clara career. (Lamar, interestingly, was never the same after that loss. Foster left after the 1985-86 season to replace Guy Lewis at Houston, and concluded his coaching career at Nevada in 2000. The Cardinals beat Houston in the first round of the 1984-85 NIT, and as of 2007 hadn't won another postseason game even though the school went through seven coaches, including Tubbs again, during that period.)

The following year was supposed to be the Broncos' cash-in season, with Lamson, Vanos and Keeling poised for their senior years, Kenilvort entrenched at point guard, and freshman Dan Weiss from San Jose's Independence High sharing some of the inside burden with Vanos. Couch, who played almost as much as Weiss, also returned. Guard Kenny Mulkey gave Santa Clara a wraithlike defensive and penetration presence off the bench, and Tony Vukelich was a sturdy type who could play small forward, power forward, or even center in a pinch. Sophomore Matt Wilgenbush was expected to be an interior enforcer as well, although a back injury hampered his work during pre-season drills.

The Broncos won at UCLA (which was at its lowest ebb since the pre-John Wooden years) in their season opener, beat Nebraska and Cincinnati in the Cable Car Classic, and brought an 11-5 non-league record into WCAC play. But the Broncos were blasted 89-61 by Weber State in their next game after beating UCLA, and that set a one-step-forward, one-step-back pattern that prevailed throughout the season.

Vanos at times appeared worn down from more than a year of almost-continuous play – he had tried out for the U.S. Olympic team, holding his own against future pros Wayman Tisdale and Jon Koncak, during the off-season – and he endured a season of nagging injuries. Kenilvort was benched briefly for ineffective play. Keeling was the 1929 Dow Jones Industrial Average: 33 points, including two Richter-scale dunks, in a win over Nevada, then two points in a loss to Hofstra. Wilgenbush's injury never healed sufficiently for him to contribute much, and the rest of the Santa Clara bench proved inconsistent.

The Broncos' 53-52 home loss to Pepperdine, during which Santa Clara was held scoreless over the final 4:14 while squandering a seven-point lead, permanently compromised the team's position in the WCAC standings. Another home loss, 60-57 to San Diego, put the Broncos in a win-or-else predicament entering the Pepperdine rematch in Malibu, and the Waves secured the conference title with a 97-90 victory – relegating Santa Clara to its third straight second-place finish.

Santa Clara finished the regular season 20-8 and again was selected for the NIT, but again, the Broncos were sent to a treacherous destination – Fresno's 10,132-seat Selland Arena, home of the Fresno State Bulldogs and the Red Wave fan base that made Selland perhaps the loudest basketball building in America at that time. The Red Wave, a carryover from Fresno State's NIT championship run the previous season, was so devoted that it traveled to other Pacific Coast Athletic Association destinations *en masse* and more often than not outnumbered the fans at the home school. Against Santa Clara, the Fresno fans played a role in a game that would have been incandescent to the participants whether it had been for an NCAA title or for the next game at the local YMCA.

The final game of the Vanos-Keeling-Lamson era was in many ways a reflection of the previous 115, 79 of which Santa Clara won. Fresno State's team had been constructed using blueprints similar to those used by Williams and Davey. The Bulldogs were coached by Boyd Grant, who recruited along the same character-based lines as Santa Clara and whose team was among the national defensive leaders virtually every year he was there (and, subsequently, during his tenure at Colorado State). One of the few differences between the teams was the Red Wave, which only got louder even after the Broncos bolted to a 15-2 lead.

Fresno quickly dissipated the deficit. Through the first half, through the second half, through one overtime and then two, this game for the ages continued to nudge each team to the brink of its endurance and wherewithal. Santa Clara got 24 points and 13 rebounds from Vanos, 24 points from Keeling and 15 from Lamson, and a career-high 12 assists from Kenilvort. But two missed free throws and a wayward 12-footer cost the Broncos four points at the end of regulation. Turnovers wrenched away last-shot opportunities at the end of the first two overtimes. With 16 seconds left in the third OT and Santa Clara up 76-75, Vanos thwarted a drive by a Fresno player – only to have the blocked shot carom directly to the Bulldogs' Mitch Arnold, who made an 18-footer to give Fresno State the lead. The Bulldogs won 79-76.

"The only good thing right now is that I know everybody in this locker room will always be my friend," Keeling said after the game.

With one of the most memorable periods and groups in Santa Clara's basketball history consigned to memory, it was time for Williams and Davey to begin anew.

And begin anew they did … albeit painfully, at first.

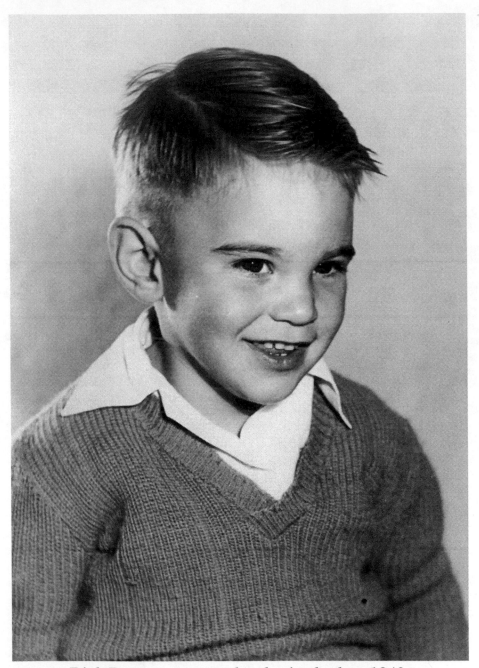

Dick Davey as a pre-schooler in the late 1940s

The 1964 Decatur Commodores. Davey is the first player
from the left in the second row from the top.
(Photo courtesy of Scott Finch)

Dick and Jeanne Davey on their wedding day in 1965

Davey coaching his Leland High team in the
Central Coast Section playoff semifinals at Stanford in
1971. It was the first time Davey coached on an NCAA
Division I floor, but it hardly would be the last

Davey during his early years as a Santa Clara assistant

Davey and Carroll Williams

Williams and Davey hold the 1987 West Coast
Conference tournament championship trophy

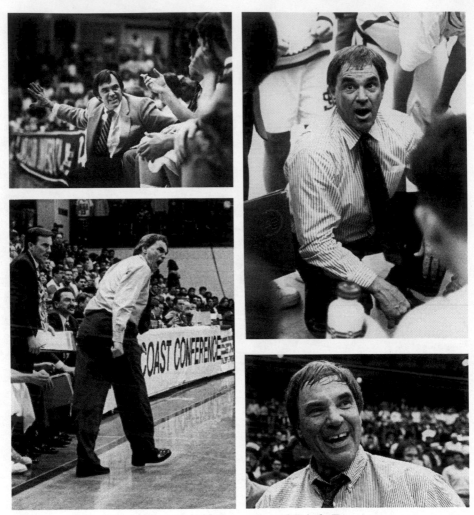

The mercurial moods of Dick Davey

Sartorial splendor: Davey in the argyle sweaters that became his trademark

Davey surrounded by assistants Larry Hauser (left),
Steve Seandel and Scott Gradin.

Davey and Steve Nash during a game in 1995

Davey confers with Jason Sedlock during the 1992-93 season,
his first as Santa Clara head coach

Davey during a timeout late in the Broncos' 64-61 upset
of Arizona in the first round of the NCAA tournament.
Seated, from left, are Phil Von Buchwaldt, DeWayne Lewis
and Pete Eisenrich

Jeanne and Dick Davey before Santa Clara's victory over
Maryland in the first round of the 1996 NCAA tournament

The Broncos' starters after the Maryland win in the
1996 NCAA tournament

Davey instructs guard Brian Jones during a game in 1998.
Davey describes Jones, who recovered from a career-
threatening knee injury while at Santa Clara, as perhaps the
toughest player he coached during his 30-year career

Davey addressing his team in 2003

Mike and Kathleen Davey

Mike Davey with his two daughters, Rachie (left) and Samie

Kim Davey performing as a soloist with the Pacific
Northwest Ballet Company in Seattle

Jeanne Davey with the Santa Clara mascot

Jeanne and Dick Davey in 2007 after his final home game as Santa Clara coach

Dick and Jeanne Davey with Scott Dougherty, one of the stars of Davey's last team

With his top three scorers and rebounders from 1984-85 lost to graduation, Williams had to be flexible during the transitional season that followed. He had the right offense – one of his own invention – to do so, and he and Davey knew that they would have to convince their 1985-86 players to trust the flex offense to create shots for them instead of attempting to manufacture offense individually.

Within the coaching profession, Williams is known as the man who invented the flex offense. The scheme was described this way by former New Mexico, St. John's and Manhattan coach Fran Fraschilla, who became an ESPN commentator after he left coaching: "A continuity (or pattern) man-to-man offense where all five players are interchangeable. It involves constant reversal of the ball from one side of the court to the other. It can also be described as a structured form of 'motion offense.' And, with patient ball movement and good screening, it can keep a defense on its toes for the entire 35-second shot clock."

Williams first conceived the offense in the early 1970s, long before the shot clock became part of the college game, and it was brought from Santa Clara to Gonzaga by Dan Fitzgerald, who had helped Williams design it.

The Bulldogs under Mark Few still used it during their ascent to the basketball heights after 1999, with some variations. Maryland coach Gary Williams also installed the flex as his team's base offense, and many other coaches on the college and high school level have implemented elements of it.

Greg Newell, who played for Pepperdine in the late 1970s, remembers preparing for the flex – and the emphatic way the Broncos played it.

"About the only thing I remember about preparing for an opponent, my entire career, was Santa Clara," he said. "The only thing I remember about our preparation had probably more to do with what happened to me on that play (described in Chapter 4) where I got knocked into Oakland by Bruening and Rambis. (Pepperdine coach Gary) Colson described Santa Clara's penchant for 'picking the picker,' meaning they would *always* hard-screen the screener. They doubled up on a single screen, to get a scorer the ball on a pop out around the perimeter. I got nailed hard by the 'pickee' and the 'picker.'

"As far as the flex goes, that was the 'hip' offense being run by a lot of coaches. We used to run the flex as our secondary offense."

Most basketball people, and even many coaches, think the flex was so named because of the type of motion it included. Davey, though, said the name was short for "flexible" and wasn't intended to describe any written-in-stone patterns. He and Williams tweaked it often while they were working together, and Davey ran his own version of it after he became head coach.

"I don't know if Carroll actually invented it," Davey said. "He invented the intricacies of it, but there was an offense called 'spots' in the late 1930s that was similar. I don't think Carroll got it from that, though. He and Dan developed their own process of running flex (before Davey came to Santa Clara), and he (Williams) is considered the inventor in modern-day basketball. It really had a tremendous influence on basketball for about 20 years. It's not as popular now (in 2007) as it was then … it'll come back and be in vogue again, but right now it's out of vogue a little.

"It's a screening, moving offense that basically allows players who aren't quite as good (as most of their opponents) to create shots for themselves. 'We're not going to be very good this year, so let's come up with something so we can monitor when and where shots will come from and give us a chance to be successful.' Before I came, they got off to a really good start with it one year, and then they expanded it a little in terms of where guys could shoot the ball. It was more flexible … hence 'flex.' It was a pretty good offense that really involved everyone. The only negative about it was that you had to have a big man who could pass the ball (because the center assumed a passing position within the context of the offense instead of anchoring himself at the block and awaiting service)."

Interestingly, the first in-print mention of the flex offense in the *Peninsula Times Tribune,* a now-defunct Palo Alto paper that covered Santa Clara more extensively than any other Bay Area media outlet throughout the 1980s, was before the 1985-86 season. Santa Clara had run it long and often before that, of course, but 1985-86 apparently was the first season during which the Broncos had to depend on it because they simply were outmanned by most of their foes.

Under a different set of circumstances, that might not have been the case.

In 1984, while he was in the midst of the quest for Craig McMillan, Davey had another recruiting epiphany that might have had a monumental impact on the Santa Clara program had it translated into a signature on a letter of intent. It was during a trip to Mount Diablo High in the East Bay city of Concord to see a junior who at that point was little more than a tiny blip on the recruiting radar, and about whom Davey knew little himself.

"I got there late, just before the end of the half," Davey said in 1989, "and 10 seconds after I walked in, I saw this kid get a rebound, turn and throw a pass left-handed the length of the court for a layup at the end of the half. I said to myself, 'Dang, I didn't know the kid was left-handed.' Then at the start of the second half, he comes out shooting jumpers right-handed. Now I'm saying to myself, 'I *know* I saw him throw that pass left-handed.'

"I was willing to give him a scholarship after seeing him play for five minutes. Without knowing anything about his character, I sensed he was the kind of player coaches dream of having. In terms of agility, knowing the game, and enthusiasm, he was as good as I've ever seen. The greatest pleasure of my career was coaching Kurt Rambis, and one reason for that was that he was deranged about the game. He wanted to play it 365 days a year. It seems to me Todd is the same way."

"Todd" was Todd Lichti, and although Davey was the first major-college coach to see him and appraise his talent, he didn't have Lichti to himself for long. By the end of his senior year at Mount Diablo, Lichti was getting almost as much recruiting attention as McMillan had received, and unlike McMillan, Lichti made it clear early on that he would only consider high-profile-conference programs. Consequently, Davey reluctantly stopped recruiting him.

Lichti wound up signing with Tom Davis at Stanford, where he remained the career scoring leader as of 2007, and as a senior in 1988-89, he led Stanford to its first NCAA appearance in 47 years. The Denver Nuggets took Lichti with the 15th pick in the 1989 NBA draft, and he appeared on his way to stardom before suffering near-fatal injuries in an auto accident that killed his fiancée early in his second season. Lichti was never the same after that, although he wound up playing five NBA seasons with four teams and then had a long career in Europe.

If Lichti *and* McMillan had signed with Santa Clara – and if the Broncos had gotten McMillan, they very well might have had a realistic shot at Lichti – the two would have been together for three seasons, from 1985-86 through

1987-88. The 1987-88 Broncos went 20-11 while starting Osei Appiah and Chris Lane, two of the program's best all-around athletes of the 1980s, in the backcourt. Both could run and defend and score at a high level, but neither was suited by skills or temperament to play point guard. The Broncos' starting frontline that season usually consisted of 6-9 tenderizer Dan Weiss, fluid 6-9 forward Jens Gordon, and 6-4 Roland H'orvath, a Lamson type whose most frequent contributions were on defense.

"Jens Gordon was probably one of the best big players we had at Santa Clara," Davey said of Gordon, who was still playing and coaching professionally in Germany more than a decade after he left Santa Clara. "Tremendously capable scorer, athletic. He could shoot a 15-footer, go get rebounds, run the court. He was still a young pup when he played for us, but a really good player."

"Weiss was a footwork guy. A little slow, but very intelligent and really knew how to use his feet and his body to get where he needed to be to have a chance to score. He went to Japan after he graduated; then he went to work for a shoe company, and he still lives there and has a good position there."

With McMillan and Lichti also in the equation, Santa Clara would have had a point guard who could score and create on the fly, and a small forward who could score in virtually any imaginable matchup and at any tempo – two of the few elements the '87-88 team didn't have. Appiah or Lane, or both, could have provided instant energy off the bench, and H'orvath could have done likewise on defense. Mitch Burley, who in 2007 remained second on the Santa Clara career-leader lists in games played, sixth in 3-pointers and ninth in assists, also was on hand in 1987-88 and could have been used as a zone-buster when defenses sagged inside. Six-11 Karl Larson and 6-10 Nils Becker provided shot-blocking and ballast.

The '87-88 Broncos were coming off an NCAA tournament appearance the previous season. They lost only two games by more than nine points, beat Lichti-led Stanford, and reached the WCAC tournament finals and the NIT.

Could Lichti and McMillan, or even either one of them, have made the difference between a 20-win season and a level of achievement that would have continued to resonate, just as Gonzaga's Elite Eight season in 1999 began a stretch of NCAA tournament appearances that stood at nine straight at the end of the 2006-07 season?

Nobody will ever know. As it was, Santa Clara had neither Lichti nor McMillan when the 1985-86 season started, and it also had lost four of the five starters from the last Vanos-Keeling-Lamson team. The only returning starter was Kenilvort, and if it hadn't been for him, the Broncos – who had only one other senior on the roster – might well have had their worst season since the 1963-64 team went 6-20.

Despite a knee in which cartilage was torn and that late in the season audibly creaked when he ran, Kenilvort led Santa Clara in scoring (16.5), rebounding (6.1), free-throw percentage (.833), assists (3.9), and minutes played (35.8). Considering the inexperience of the players surrounding him, it might have been the most all-encompassing season ever compiled by a Santa Clara player during Davey's years there. Davey called him "a poor man's Larry Bird," and predicted that he would be taken in the NBA draft – which he was, by the Golden State Warriors in the eighth round.

Santa Clara lurched to a 6-14 start, with three of the wins coming over Division II teams and another against then-Division I member Brooklyn College, which dropped its entire athletic program in 1992 and later resurfaced in Division III. The Broncos' 84-56 loss to Purdue in the Cable Car Classic matched the program's worst-ever home defeat up to that point.

But Kenilvort wouldn't let the Broncos disintegrate, and they won six of their last eight games – including their only two road wins of the season, against rivals St. Mary's and USF – to finish 12-16.

"I logged a lot of minutes there," Kenilvort said. "My senior year, there weren't a lot of guys who had any experience, but as the season progressed, a lot of guys were getting experience and playing better and better. I think we were confident we could beat anybody, and it's too bad the league didn't have a tournament that year.

"I'd actually had knee surgery at the end of the season. The Warriors drafted me anyway, and I went to camp with them, but I blew out the knee again at the end of camp.

I think George Karl (the Warriors' coach at the time) took a liking to me because I was the same kind of player he had been, and he invited me back to veterans camp in the fall, but when I went in (for a medical opinion after hurting the knee a second time) I knew I was done; there was no more cartilage left.

"I had a clean cut away from basketball; I didn't have to chase Europe or try to get into the CBA or whatever. I ended up going to work (after getting his Santa Clara degree)."

Thanks largely to Kenilvort, the 1985-86 season was not a precipice. Instead, it turned into a bridge to a period during which Santa Clara reached the postseason three straight times for the first – and, as of 2007, only – time since the late 1960s. During those three seasons, Santa Clara won 58 games, and was denied greater glory only by the presence of Loyola Marymount teams that shattered most NCAA scoring records while turning every court on which they played into a dragstrip.

This was the "Loyola Merriment" team, led by Hank Gathers and Bo Kimble, that in 1989 beat U.S. International 181-150 as the teams set a still-standing NCAA record for most points scored by two squads in a game. The 1987-88 and '88-89 teams that beat Santa Clara in the WCAC/WCC title games weren't as prolific as the 1989-90 unit that averaged an NCAA-record 122.4 points per game, set another NCAA record by scoring 100 or more points in 28 games, and reached the NCAA West Region title game (losing to eventual national champion UNLV) after the death of Gathers from heart failure during a game against Portland in the 1990 WCC tournament. But they were prolific enough to dominate their conference, and the Broncos lost all six of their games against the Lions during those two years (and eight in a row, counting two losses in 1989-90 when the teams were less evenly matched).

Davey acknowledges that the style and, to a lesser extent, the composition of those Loyola teams – which included a number of transfers and some players with dubious academic credentials – made those defeats particularly maddening.

"We were very good during the Loyola years," Davey said. "There was a little frustration, but you never know how things happen on those deals. We weren't sure if they (the rumors about LMU not adhering to recruiting and eligibility rules) were true, so to us it was mainly preparing for games against an awfully good team. We were one of the few teams that would try to tempo them, keep it at a pace where we had a chance, but they were always just a little better and we couldn't get over the hump with them.

"They were awfully good and awfully hard to play against … (in 1990) if they hadn't run into UNLV, that team was good enough (to win the NCAA title). (Coach Paul) Westhead did a good job of doing what he did with the people he had. It was annoying to me (philosophically) that they'd just give you baskets to keep the game at a fast tempo. You could come down and a lot of the time, if you made a basket you'd be giving them a layup because they didn't want to stay down there (on defense) any longer than a few seconds. They were frustrating from that standpoint ... you have to make (unusual) decisions. If it's a good shot, do I take it, or do I wait (to keep the tempo under control)? You'd get a lot of good shots against them, but if they don't go in, look out."

The year before the Loyola Marymount program began to wreak havoc on the NCAA record book, though, was the year Santa Clara returned to the NCAA tournament for the first time in 17 years.

The WCAC, mindful of the much-needed national television window a conference tournament would provide, instituted the event for the 1986-87 season, and San Francisco's Memorial Gym was chosen as the venue for the semifinals and finals (the first round was played at home sites). Memorial Gym, of course, had been Santa Clara's Bates Motel almost from the time it opened in 1958, and the Broncos didn't appear poised to change that pattern in 1987 as the four semifinalists converged on San Francisco.

Santa Clara had shown promise during a 9-5 non-conference slate, particularly in a 60-55 Cable Car Classic win over Wake Forest – the program's first victory ever against an Atlantic Coast Conference opponent – in which Chris Lane dominated his matchup against Tyrone "Muggsy" Bogues, the 5-foot-3 guard whose name was one of the most-voiced in college basketball at the time. Lane, who had come to Santa Clara two years earlier as a walk-on freshman from the tiny and impoverished Northern California mill town of Weed, was such a gifted athlete that the NFL's Dallas Cowboys later expressed interest in him even though he hadn't played football since high school. Bogues had 15 points in the game, but 10 of those came in the final 3:08 after Santa Clara had built a 51-35 lead.

However, the WCAC regular season was San Diego's fiefdom. The Toreros, led by 7-foot center Scott Thompson, beat Santa Clara 80-61 and 71-53 and went on to a 13-1 league mark. Because of San Diego's 23-4 overall record, most people figured – correctly as it turned out – that the Toreros already were in the NCAA tournament regardless of how they fared at San Francisco. Santa Clara, plagued by injuries to key players such as Lane, Matt Wilgenbush, Dan Weiss and Craig McPherson, finished in a three-way tie for fourth at 6-8 in league (15-13 overall) and was relegated to the No. 5 seed, sending Santa Clara to Portland for a first-round game. The Broncos usually had owned the Pilots since Portland came into the league in 1976, but Portland had beaten Santa Clara twice during the 1986-87 regular season, and had a future NBA guard in Greg Anthony, who played his freshman season at Portland before transferring to UNLV and helping the Runnin' Rebels win the national championship in 1990.

Santa Clara was not playing particularly well going into the postseason, winning only three of its final six games, but Weiss, who had been hobbled by a bad ankle, scored a career-high 23 points, Lane – who led the league in steals that season – held Anthony to 11 points, and Santa Clara routed Portland 91-60 to reach the semifinals at USF.

The Broncos beat third-seeded St. Mary's 55-50 to reach the championship game, where San Diego did *not* await. Seventh-seeded Pepperdine, which was 10-17 during the regular season after winning five of the six previous WCAC titles under Jim Harrick, stunned the Toreros 64-63 in the other semifinal. In the final, Santa Clara built a 37-18 lead and held off the Waves 77-65 to reach the NCAA tournament for the first time since Williams had taken over as head coach.

The afterglow of that victory didn't last long, as the Broncos drew the 15th seed in the West Regional, obliging them to face second-seeded and nationally sixth-ranked Iowa – coached by former Stanford head man Tom Davis – in the first round in Tucson, Ariz. The locale was to prove ironic six years later when the Broncos got another 15 seed, against Arizona, after another unexpected WCC tournament championship, but it wasn't much help to the Broncos in 1987. After Santa Clara scored the first four points of the game, Iowa scored the next 22, and the Hawkeyes led by as many as 37 points on their way to a 99-76 romp.

Despite the severity of the loss, though, the players and coaches looked upon it as the beginning of the next season, because their four leading scorers – Jens Gordon, Dan Weiss, Chris Lane and Mitch Burley – all returned. The Broncos also had Osei Appiah, who with Lane gave the Broncos the quickest guard combination in the league. Sophomore swingman Jeffty Connelly, a transfer from USC, was expected to give the Broncos another outside marksman in concert with Burley, along with a fearless penetrator.

Weiss made two free throws with two seconds left to give Santa Clara a 72-71 victory at Stanford, and the Broncos beat Seton Hall and St. Joseph's during an 11-1 stretch that included the start of the WCAC season. Everybody in the league knew that Loyola Marymount, with Kimble and Gathers and a flotilla of international recruits, would be improved over the team that had finished dead last the previous season and had had only one winning season in the previous 13. But the Lions were far better than anyone expected. They upset Marquette in Milwaukee in December, then won their first seven league games before back-to-back games against Santa Clara Feb. 6 at Santa Clara and Feb. 12 in Los Angeles. Santa Clara was 6-1 in league, but the Broncos had just lost Chris Lane for the season with an Achilles' tendon injury, and the coaches knew his athleticism would be missed, particularly against Loyola Marymount.

What followed was the start of the continuum of frustration that was to bedevil Santa Clara for the next two seasons.

At Toso Pavilion before a shrieking full house, Santa Clara took a 50-36 lead with 12:36 remaining in the game. Without Lane, the Broncos were on their way to a school-record total of 28 turnovers, but it didn't seem to matter at that point, not with Gathers and Kimble saddled with four fouls each. Dan Weiss was on his way to a 33-point, 12-rebound game, and Santa Clara shot 63 percent from the field for the game compared to LMU's 41 percent.

With 4:50 left, Santa Clara still had an 89-81 lead – at which point the Lions pieced together a 12-0 run to take a four-point advantage. Santa Clara's riposte was a pair of baskets, by Weiss and Burley, to tie the game at 93-93 with 39 seconds to go, whereupon Loyola Marymount sequestered the ball for the final shot. (The NCAA had instituted a shot clock that season, but it was a 45-second shot clock and not the 35-second clock that was implemented in 1993-94.)

Though it may have been the first time all season that Loyola Marymount actually *tried* to maintain a possession for 39 seconds, the Lions did just that. Mike Yoest took the shot with five seconds to play. It missed, and Weiss seized the rebound and turned to call for a timeout before the final buzzer sounded.

The problem was that Yoest and Santa Clara's Jens Gordon had become entangled while going after the rebound, and the officials had called a loose-ball foul on Gordon. The decibel level was so high that nobody heard the whistle. When the officials finally clarified the situation, the game was held up for several minutes as the Santa Clara coaches and players protested to a degree that would have resulted in multiple technical fouls under almost any other circumstances, and the Santa Clara fans reacted as if they were in the galleries for the 1968 Democratic National Convention.

The protests were to no avail. Yoest was waved to the foul line, and with :02 on the clock, he defied the crowd noise and made the front end of a one-and-one. Gathers was called for a lane violation on the second shot, giving Santa Clara one last desperation possession, but the Broncos couldn't get off a shot and lost 94-93.

Loyola Marymount beat Santa Clara again the following week in Los Angeles, 108-89, and went on to complete a perfect league season. Santa Clara tied for second at 9-5 with St. Mary's, and dispatched the Gaels 69-62 in the tournament semifinals to earn a third shot at Loyola Marymount. But 12-for-26 free-throw shooting in the second half doomed the Broncos to a 104-96 loss, and although they were chosen for the NIT, Oregon beat the Broncos 81-65 in a rematch of the teams' 1983 NIT meeting on the same McArthur Court floor.

It was as that 1987-88 season was drawing to an end that Davey was presented with his first serious temptation to leave Santa Clara for a Division I head coaching job elsewhere. Pacific, his alma mater, had just fired Tom O'Neill – a close friend of Davey's – in the midst of what became a 5-21 season, and the school sent Davey and other coaches on its "short list" a questionnaire regarding their interest in the jobs and their assessments of what they might do in O'Neill's place.

Davey later acknowledged that he had some interest in the job, but he eventually sent the questionnaire back, saying he didn't intend to apply. He made more than a token inquiry into only one other head-coaching opportunity while he was working under Williams. That was after the 1988-89 season, when his friend and former Cal coaching contemporary, Bill Berry, was fired at San Jose State in the aftermath of a player revolt that obliged the Spartans to finish the season with a team comprised mainly of football players and volunteers from the student body. But Davey never formally applied for that job, which eventually went to former UOP and USC coach Stan Morrison.

In both cases, Davey said he was happy at Santa Clara, and he was, but he said much later that a major factor in his reluctance to make a move was the fact Ronnie Reis had signed a letter of intent to play basketball at Santa Clara starting in the fall of 1988. Reis, Davey felt at the time, had the potential to reach the NBA, just as three of his previous bigs (McNamara, Rambis and Vanos) already had done.

Anybody who was around the program in the late 1980s and early 1990s has to work to suppress a smile when the subject of Ronnie Reis – or, as he was later known during his World Wrestling Federation gig, the "Vanilla Gorilla" – is broached. He was the second 7-footer ever to enter the program, after Nick Vanos, but that was about the only thing they had in common as freshmen at Santa Clara.

Vanos, as earlier noted, was almost painfully introverted and self-conscious as a college freshman. Ronnie Reis arrived, literally, on a skateboard. Not only was he not self-conscious about his unusual frame – he weighed 275 pounds and was built like an Olympic power lifter, with stubby legs and a massive torso – or anything else about himself, but the effervescence of his personality seemed to pollinate the practice floor and the locker room.

"You could write a story a day about Ronnie, just about," Davey said. "They told me one of the funniest things was the time we were in Ireland on a summer tour – I wasn't there – and he tried to get in position to kiss the Blarney Stone."

The sacred site of Irish folklore is said to endow the gift of eloquence upon those who kiss it, and if there was anything that Reis lacked, it wasn't eloquence. But he kissed it anyway, which may have been the most memorable physical feat of his Santa Clara career. Originally, pilgrims were hung by their heels over the edge of a parapet – a technique that was abandoned after someone fell to his death after his friends failed to hang on to him. Since that time, the stone has been kissed by another method. First, you sit with your back toward the stone and then someone sits upon your legs or firmly holds your feet. Next, leaning far back and downward into the abyss while grasping the iron rails, you lower yourself until your head is even with the stone.

"I don't know how he got in position to do it," Davey said, "but everyone who saw it said it was the funniest thing they'd ever seen.

"He's so unique. Every time he comes out here (from the Atlanta area, where he moved after his basketball and wrestling careers were over, for a golf tournament or an alumni function) he always makes it a point of sneaking up from behind and lifting me off the ground with a bearhug. I know as soon as I get picked up, it's him, because very few guys are big enough to lift me off the ground. Ronnie, he just *crushes* you.

"Ronnie was Ronnie … you never knew each day what to expect. He had a Mohawk (haircut) one day and a shaved head the next day, or he'd dye his hair (long before that became fashionable among teens). I can still see him with (guard) Melvin Chinn, skateboarding into the gym … I was afraid the two of them were going to kill themselves on one of those things. Nick, when he first came here, was friendly, but he left here wearing cowboy boots. Ronnie came in wearing the cowboy boots.

"Ronnie was one of the few guys I've been around, and I don't mean this in a negative way, who wasn't subservient to his coaches. He'd joke with them, he had the ability to talk with them and be involved with them and kid with them."

Reis set the tone for his stay at the start of his freshman year, during Santa Clara's trip to Bloomington, Ind., to play in Indiana's tournament. The team had a long layover at O'Hare airport in Chicago on the trip home, and to while away both the time and his considerable appetite, Reis had a pizza delivered and proceeded to devour the entire thing. When the team's flight home finally got airborne, and the flight attendants began passing out peanuts and soft drinks, Reis ate a bag of peanuts, then turned to the person sitting next to him. "Don't tell the coaches I ate those peanuts," he said. "They're fattening."

Earlier, during preseason practice, he had spotted Davey and a reporter talking in the locker room. "I want to ask you a question," he said to the writer. "This guy keeps telling me I'm the worst basketball player he's ever seen. Now don't you think, if this guy recruited the worst basketball player he's ever seen, wouldn't that make him the worst recruiter?"

Other Quotations from Chairman Ronnie, all uttered before he ever played a college game:

On how he lost 35 pounds after weighing 310 pounds during his senior year in high school: "The food here is terrible. You kind of worry when the guy who runs the dining room is at the SPCA the night before."

On how he expected the Broncos to do during his upcoming freshman season: "Somebody said something about an 18-10 season. If we lose 10 games, it's going to cost my roommate a $250 fine for littering because I'm throwing myself out the window." (The Broncos went 20-11, but Reis contended that the Broncos' two postseason losses didn't count in his calculations, and both he and his roommate's budget were unscathed.)

On Ray Snyder, who retired from coaching the year after Reis graduated from Monta Vista: "Coach was a great influence on me. He invented the jump shot (which was popularized in the early 1940s), so there isn't too much he hasn't seen."

Of course, much as Davey and the other coaches loved Reis' spontaneity, they might have looked upon it far less favorably if Reis didn't also have equal passion for basketball and a yearning to become a better player. As offbeat as he could be away from the floor, he had been schooled by Snyder to be decidedly on-beat once practices or games began.

"We played St. Mary's here his senior year … we lost, and they cut down the nets in our own gym," Davey said. "So we get on the bus to go to St. Mary's for our game there, and he's got Army fatigues on, and he's wearing a helmet and he's carrying this crescent wrench. He tells me he's going to take down their *rims* when we beat them – which we did (but he didn't). That was Ronnie … he *hates* St. Mary's, and every year before we play them, I get his call and here's this voice saying, 'Coachhhhh, if we don't kick their ass, I'm coming out there to kick *your* ass.'"

At the start of his freshman season, Reis was an understudy to 6-10 junior Nils Becker and 6-8 Jens Gordon, and the threesome gave the Broncos inside leverage to complement the Broncos' three-man backcourt – Jeffty Connelly, Osei Appiah and Mitch Burley. Burley was 6-6, Connelly was 6-5 and Appiah was 6-3, so the Broncos had unusually strong rebounding from their guards. That was expected to be valuable against Loyola Marymount, which hoisted 3-pointers – with resultant long rebounds – whenever it couldn't turn a fast break into a layup or a dunk. Melvin Chinn, a freshman guard and Reis' usual on-campus sidekick, was available off the bench to append quickness and defensive energy.

Most of the excitement surrounding Bay Area college basketball in the fall of 1988 involved Stanford, which had Todd Lichti and four other starting seniors and was ranked 20th in the nation in the preseason Associated Press poll – the first time Stanford had been in the national rankings since the early 1960s. Santa Clara and Stanford didn't play each other that season because of a scheduling conflict that was resolved the following season, and the Broncos' December schedule wasn't as strong as in previous or subsequent years. Still, Santa Clara went 11-2 during its non-conference season, including a win at Boise State at a time when that arena was one of the country's toughest for visitors – whereupon Santa Clara proceeded to excavate a hole from which the Broncos never emerged, losing their first three WCAC games to Pepperdine, Loyola Marymount and St. Mary's.

Santa Clara finished 7-7 in league play and was the fifth seed in the conference tournament, while St. Mary's, which had climbed to 17th in the national rankings with a 24-3 record entering the tournament, had the top seed. (The Gaels made the NCAA field as an at-large team.) But Santa Clara, after knocking off USF in the first round of the tournament at Memorial Gym, shocked St. Mary's 63-61 in the semifinals to earn a title-game rematch with Loyola Marymount.

In many ways, the Broncos' 75-70 overtime loss to the Lions was the most galling of all the defeats administered by the Gathers-Kimble teams, and one of the most galling of Davey's career, because Santa Clara did everything the coaches felt it needed to do to have a chance against a team that was averaging 115 points per game. In fact, many felt this game was Williams' pre-eminent coaching masterwork. Loyola Marymount, which hadn't scored fewer than 79 points previously that season, shot only 33 percent. LMU coach Paul Westhead's stated goal during the Loyola Merriment years was to hoist 100 shots per game, but in this contest, the Lions managed only 72, even though they had the extra five overtime minutes with which to work.

The fork-in-the-road play of the game came early in overtime, after the teams had exchanged baskets. Santa Clara's Jeffty Connelly dispossessed Kimble at midcourt and appeared to have a breakaway. Gathers ran him down and blocked the shot from behind, but the Santa Clara coaches and players felt he touched the ball on or near the rim. No goaltending call was made. The Lions quickly advanced the ball into their forecourt, and LMU's Jeff Fryer made a 3-pointer on the other end to put the Lions ahead to stay. The defeat effectively ended Santa Clara's season; the Broncos were invited to the NIT, but were listless in a 91-76 first-round defeat at New Mexico.

For the 1989-90 season, the Broncos figured to revert to the hammer-on-anvil style that so often had been their *nom de guerre* in the past. Williams and Davey moved 6-10 senior Nils Becker from center to forward and installed Reis in the pivot, and with 6-7 Rhea Taylor, a Stacey Augmon type whose length enabled him to escape entanglements inside and grab long rebounds, the Broncos had one of the biggest front lines on the West Coast. Connelly led the team with a 16.2-point average, and Chinn was a disruptive influence on opponents' backcourts.

However, the Broncos lacked depth and experience, suffering through a 1-9 stretch that included the first two games of league play. They steadied somewhat, finishing 6-8 in league play, but lost 65-62 to Portland at Loyola Marymount in the first round of the WCC tournament, which was cancelled the following night when Gathers collapsed and died during a semifinal game against Portland.

Loyola Marymount dominated league play even more resoundingly than it had the previous two seasons, beating Santa Clara 117-81 and 113-100. In the latter game, though, Reis had probably the best game of his Santa Clara career, outscoring Gathers – who was averaging a national-best 37.4 points per game at the time – by 30-22 on 12-of-14 shooting. Reis also grabbed 10 rebounds, and committed only two fouls and one turnover in 34 minutes.

"I can't believe how much better that guy is," Gathers said after the game. "Last year the guy struggled to make a layup. Now, if he gets the ball under there, it's *two*. He's got a big body that he uses well. I've got to take my hat off to the big fella. He's improved immensely."

"As soon as he gets better defensively, we can talk about him being a player," Williams said. "But I'll tell you this: Nobody in the gym tonight has worked harder over the past year to improve than Ron Reis."

Reis finished with averages of 12.4 points and 6.9 rebounds that season. Rambis, by comparison, averaged 13.7 and 8.5 as a sophomore for a much better team, while Vanos wasn't even a fulltime starter as a sophomore. The following year, Reis hiked his numbers to 15.2 points and a WCC-best 11 rebounds, and as the WCC tournament approached, NBA scouts were beginning to eyeball him in earnest.

In the first round of the 1991 tournament, at Santa Clara, the Broncos faced rival St. Mary's, whose fans, never known for their magnanimity toward any or all things Santa Clara, trained their invective solely on Reis. They started with the chant "freak of nature" and worked their way south from the standpoint of delicacy, and while Reis never indicated that the abuse from the stands distracted him, the fact was that all the confidence and wherewithal Davey had helped him build over the previous three seasons disappeared in the final 10:40 of the game, and never fully returned again.

Reis had a presentable 65 percent free-throw shooting figure during the regular season, but his touch deserted him in this game, and St. Mary's began to foul him every time he had the ball and sometimes when he didn't. In that fateful 10:40, he attempted 14 free throws, and missed 12 of them, including three air balls. He was 2 for 15 for the game, and Santa Clara lost 79-74 after leading by nine points at halftime. It was the Broncos' third loss that season against St. Mary's – the first time that had ever happened in a rivalry that began in 1910.

The Broncos ended the 1990-91 season 16-13, and although they'd begun the season with a win over Loyola Marymount in the Maui Classic (ending an eight-game losing streak against the Lions) and beat Iowa State two nights later in the same tournament, they didn't beat anybody else they weren't expected to beat. The pattern continued through the 1991-92 season, during which Santa Clara went 14-15 and lost 54-51 to Gonzaga in the WCC tournament semifinals in what turned out to be Carroll Williams' last game as Santa Clara head coach.

Reis' numbers dropped to 13.0 points and 8.8 rebounds during his senior season, and although he was a first-team all-conference selection for the second straight year, the promise of the previous three seasons largely went unrequited. He fell off the NBA radar, and soon thereafter received the offer from what was then called the World Wrestling Federation, in which he was the "Vanilla Gorilla" for several years before moving to the Atlanta area and going into private business.

"He had such good hands and he could do a lot of things you wouldn't think he could do just by looking at his frame," Davey said. "He couldn't shoot a free throw in that (St. Mary's) game, and you think about his career and you think maybe he could have done more. But what did he average, 14 points and 10 rebounds over four years? That's a pretty good college career … you'd like to have your big guy do that every year."

Some felt the St. Mary's trauma cost eroded Reis' confidence to such an extent that his NBA possibilities were extinguished. But Davey says that for all his size, strength and competitive zeal, Reis would have had difficulty making an NBA team even if the St. Mary's game hadn't blown up in his face.

"I kind of doubt it," he said. "Running up and down the court, he was fine, and strength-wise he was fine. But he was not flexible … he couldn't manipulate his body or change (his stride) to get from one place to the other. But Ronnie was a rebounder. He did a great job for our program rebounding the ball and scoring around the basket, and yet he got criticized because everybody expects a 7-2 guy to do more."

The Broncos started four seniors, including Reis, during most of the 1991-92 season, and while Santa Clara had developed some depth with sophomores Pete Eisenrich and DeWayne Lewis at the forwards and one-time walk-on Mark Schmitz and defensive specialist John Woolery in the backcourt, Williams and Davey knew entering the summer of 1992 that newcomers would be the keys to their next season. They recruited what they thought was a solid class, but it didn't include any players for whom other schools clamored.

Moreover, the program, though hardly destitute, was flagging. The results over the past three years had not met expectations, and attendance – 2,536 per game in 1990-91 and 2,713 the following season – was at its lowest level since the Broncos had moved into Toso Pavilion in 1975. (Prior to that, they had played most of their home games at 2,412-seat San Jose Civic Auditorium, sharing that venerable building with San Jose State.) Nobody blamed Williams, whose integrity and coaching acumen were unchallenged, and whose teams continued to be hard-working on the court and serious about academics and citizenship off it. There was little outside pressure on him to step down, but one reason for that may have been that comparatively few people outside the Santa Clara inner circle were particularly interested in Santa Clara basketball at that point.

The NHL's San Jose Sharks had just taken up residence at the brand-new 18,000-seat San Jose Arena, giving San Jose its first major league professional sports team. The Golden State Warriors were at the tail end of the "Run TMC" period during which they were NBA playoff participants almost every year. Stanford and Cal had become consistent NCAA tournament contenders, and more often than not, one or both of them were in the national rankings. Consequently, Santa Clara basketball usually was an afterthought among casual Bay Area sports fans, and in the eyes of most decision-makers in the Bay Area media. The national-championship contenders of the late 1960s, and even the Vanos-Keeling-Kenilvort years and accomplishments, were beginning to look hazy in the rear-view mirror.

Unbeknownst to Davey, events behind the scenes and in offices to which he was not privy were churning … and the result, somewhat to his surprise given the timing, would be that at age 50, he got his chance to be a college head coach at long last.

Chapter 10
AT LONG LAST

As the 1992-93 school year began at Santa Clara, Dick Davey had settled into his usual work routine – a routine of the sort that would have extinguished the passion of many 50-year-old college assistant coaches who had never had more than a fleeting sniff of a head-coaching job.

"This (his time as an assistant coach) was a tough time for my family and for Jeanne," he said. "I don't think I'm exaggerating this ... from the time I got the assistant job at Santa Clara going maybe into the early 1990s, I would spend three, sometimes four or five nights a week in the office until 10 or 11 at night. I was trying to do everything ... scouting, recruiting, planning. This was when you didn't have (as many) coaches and people around a program as you do today. Sunday, Tuesday, Wednesday, Thursday ... I was in the office from 7:30 in the morning till 11 at night. That was just the way it was during the season.

"I didn't have any confidence in anyone else doing the scouting report, even though it (the other assistants' work) might have been better than anything I could have put together. I wanted to make sure everything got done the way I thought it should be done."

Even so, continuing that regimen, and remaining an assistant coach indefinitely, represented an acceptable career path for Davey as the 1992-93 school year began. He hadn't pursued the UOP job, although he said later he likely would have accepted it if it had been offered, and he had no real desire to go to San Jose State at the time Bill Berry's firing created an opening there.

At the same time …

"I loved Santa Clara, and I wanted to stay," he said. "I know Carroll had given some thought to retiring, and obviously he was going to retire someday, but there was no guarantee that I would get the job at that point. I was 50 years old and it was getting close to the point where you either do it (seek a head-coaching position) or you're never going to do it."

Williams had not indicated publicly that he had any thoughts of resigning after the 1991-92 season, and he was still attending to his duties as usual as the 1992-93 school year began. In September, though, the wheels of officialdom began to spin like the spools of a slot machine.

A case can be made that a doomed football program was the single most salient factor in the chain of events that resulted in Davey being handed the reins of a basketball program for the first time since he had left Leland High in 1972.

Santa Clara often was called the Notre Dame of the West during the 1930s and 1940s, when it won two Sugar Bowls and one Orange Bowl while playing its home football games at San Francisco's 60,000-seat Kezar

Stadium. The arrival of the San Francisco 49ers, who began play in the All-America Football Conference in 1946 and joined the NFL in 1950, dovetailed with the spiraling costs of maintaining a major-college program as two-platoon football became the norm after World War II. St. Mary's dropped football in 1950 and USF the year after, and with its two chief rivals dormant, Santa Clara accepted the inevitable and dissolved its program after the 1952 season.

It returned on a club level seven years later under Pat Malley, who had played for Santa Clara in 1950-51, and whose father George had played for the Broncos in 1925-26. Malley, who also was the Santa Clara athletic director, was a revered figure who buffered his coaches from overzealous boosters – he fired only one coach, and then only after the coach disobeyed a direct order and left the area to coach in a summer league – and made it a point to know everyone connected with Santa Clara, from the 8-year-olds at the school's summer coaching camps to the loftiest alumni, many of whom held high positions in local government and industry during the Malley years.

Eventually, Santa Clara attained College Division (now Division II) status in football, and when Malley – who went 142-100-3 as the Broncos' coach from 1959-84 – died of cancer in 1985, control of the program passed to his son Terry, who'd been an assistant coach and before that a quarterback under his father. The school produced a number of high-profile NFL players under the Malleys, most notably Brent Jones and Dan Pastorini, but the

251

program rarely made money or created a splash on the national level, and a new NCAA rule that was passed early in 1992 forced Santa Clara to rethink its football priorities.

The rule essentially prohibited schools from participating at the Division II level in football while maintaining Division I status in basketball and other sports. That left Santa Clara with limited options, none of them particularly palatable.

The school could have upgraded the football program to Division I-AA, but it probably would have had to follow the example of the University of San Diego – which by 2007 was the only WCC school that still had a football team – and join a limited-scholarship league in the Midwest, with the attendant increase in travel costs and without any proximate rivals to jack up attendance and interest. Or Santa Clara could have challenged schools from leagues like the Big Sky Conference, whose members gave up to 70 football scholarships while Santa Clara was giving only about 20. There were even some discussions among alumni regarding the feasibility of trying to return to big-time college football, although that idea never was seriously considered by the school.

After Pat Malley died, the athletic-director vacancy was filled on an interim basis by assistant AD Dan Curry, who tried to carry on Malley's policies and shared his priorities. But Curry didn't get the permanent job, which instead went to Tom O'Connor, who had a long-term vision for Santa Clara athletics that was not shared by those who supported the Division II football program and still pined for the days when Santa Clara was front and center on the national football platform.

O'Connor, by most accounts, wasn't anti-football, but he had come to Santa Clara from Loyola University of Maryland, which didn't have football, and he saw immediately upon his arrival that the Santa Clara Valley was one of the nation's soccer incubators. (The San Jose Earthquakes had been one of the North American Soccer League's most successful franchises, and actually continued to operate as an independent team after the NASL folded in 1984.) With so much recruitable talent nearby, O'Connor reasoned, Santa Clara could do in soccer what it had once done in football, but only if the school adjusted its list of priorities accordingly.

O'Connor was right about Santa Clara's soccer possibilities. As of 2007, the women's team had appeared in 18 straight NCAA tournaments, winning the championship in 2001 and getting to the Final Four on nine other occasions. In June 2007, coach Jerry Smith was given a seven-year contract extension carrying through the 2013 season. Next to Steve Nash, Santa Clara's most renowned athlete as the 21st century turned probably was Brandi Chastain, who converted the match-winning penalty kick in the women's World Cup final against China in 1999 (and pulled off her jersey in celebration), and was an assistant women's coach at Santa Clara before and after that. The men's program shared the national championship with Indiana in 1989, appeared in four other Final Fours, and made the postseason in 14 of 18 seasons from 1989-2006.

Butmostofthelongtimesupportersof Santa Clara's athletic programs – especially the people who attended Santa Clara when college soccer didn't exist on the West Coast – looked upon Santa Clara's soccer emergence with singular indifference. Some even considered soccer to be a threat to a football program that was underfunded and rapidly becoming orphaned on the West Coast, where six of the 13 schools Santa Clara scheduled during its final three football seasons (1990-92) subsequently dropped football themselves.

Those boosters also thought the basketball program, which had been to only one NCAA tournament since 1970, should be given a financial booster shot with the money that instead was being pumped into soccer. But university president Paul Locatelli and some other Santa Clara officials with policy-making power were in agreement with O'Connor that the school would be better served if it redirected some of its resources toward soccer and away from football.

O'Connor never said publicly that he thought Santa Clara football ought to be dropped – some, in fact, say he went above and beyond his job description to try to save it – but many believe the decision to do so already had been made by the time he resigned in September 1992 to take the athletic directorship at St. Bonaventure. (He left there after two years to become the AD at George Mason, and by 2007 was head of the NCAA Division I basketball tournament selection committee.) Some believe part of O'Connor's motivation for making a parallel, or even downward, career move was his knowledge that the decision by Santa Clara to drop football was imminent, although it wasn't announced until the following February, and that it would be unpopular and make fund-raising difficult.

At that point, Locatelli and other Santa Clara officials knew their new AD would need credibility in the Santa Clara community, along with the ability to deflect the outrage that everyone knew would result from the decision to drop football. Only one man had those qualities, and that man was Carroll Williams.

And given the fact the start of preseason basketball practice was only about a month away, Davey was not only the logical man to assume Williams' basketball position, he was the only quality candidate available at that late date. Williams knew he had the administration in a tenuous position. He leveraged that power to ensure that Davey would become Santa Clara's next head basketball coach, even if he wasn't Locatelli's first choice.

"I don't think they wanted to do it that way," Williams said, "but when they agreed, I opened the job search up to anyone on campus, which meant there was no choice (besides Davey) at all. I didn't think the dean of arts and sciences had the experience. I think it took 30 seconds to do."

"My recollection was that when Carroll talked to Locatelli, he indicated that he would not take the athletic-director job unless I was named head coach," Davey said. "Paul didn't want me to become head coach. He wanted to go out and find somebody else."

But Locatelli had limited options at that point, so Davey got the job. Larry Hauser, who had been at Santa Clara since 1984, was elevated to the No. 1 assistant position, and to fill the other vacancy, Davey hired Steve Seandel, who had been an assistant at Stanford and, like Davey, had begun his coaching career at Leland High. Seandel became the top assistant when Hauser left in 1997 to accept the head coaching position at Cal State Dominguez Hills, and he remained at that post throughout the remainder of Davey's tenure.

Hauser, from the Chicago area, gave the Broncos a recruiting presence elsewhere in the country, particularly in the Midwest, and had been a sort of defensive coordinator, overseeing the installation of the matchup zone defense Santa Clara sometimes used during Williams' tenure (but almost never under Davey, a man-to-man advocate). Of Seandel, Davey was to say later, "In my opinion, there is no better basketball mind in the game than Steve's," and because of the quality of his assistants and the immediately-apparent need to oversee the program rather than micro-managing it, Davey actually cut back on his office hours and became more comfortable delegating authority than he had been as an assistant. Nobody was more pleased by this than Jeanne Davey, who had her husband for a dinner companion almost every night for the first time in many years.

"(By the end of his head-coaching tenure) my confidence level in my assistant coaches was so high," Davey said.

Perhaps because he had held more responsibility under Williams than most assistants are given, Davey was able to anticipate some of the transitional pratfalls every first-time college head coach encounters. At the same time, he also knew his vantage point would be entirely different than the one from which he had viewed his teams over the previous two decades. That, he said, was the most difficult element of his transition period.

"Whether coaches are willing to admit it or not, when you go home as an assistant after a game which you've lost and you look in that mirror, the first response from most guys, no matter how good the relationship (with the head coach), is 'If I'm the head coach, maybe I would have done it this way,'" he said. "I'd always make suggestions (as an assistant), but unless you're the one calling the shots, it doesn't work that way. As a head coach, you look in the mirror and you say to yourself, 'Hey buddy, it was you. It wasn't somebody else who made the call; it was you.'

"Assistants will make suggestions during a game, and sometimes I used them, but it doesn't make any difference in the final analysis. You're the guy who's held accountable. How much does coaching enter into the winning or losing equation? A small portion, but a portion, so don't start putting blame on somebody else when you're responsible. That's where the difference lies ... you're held accountable."

Davey and Williams had been equally involved in assembling the incoming recruiting class, which included

Kevin Dunne, a 6-5 forward from San Ramon Valley High who could penetrate, shoot, rebound and defend. "Kevin Dunne was the best 6-5 rebounder who could not jump I've ever been around," Davey said. "And smart? Defensively, it was embarrassing, he was so smart. He knew exactly what to do all the time."

Other newcomers to the program included Drew Zurek, a 6-9 senior with good post moves and the same hockey-player ferocity that had characterized the program more than a decade before; and Jason Sedlock, who was a somewhat less burly Scott Lamson because his ability to dredge up "hustle points" and defend the other team's top offensive threat made him valuable even though he wasn't a prolific scorer.

Brendan Graves, a 6-10 center who was to become the WCC's Academic Player of the Year in addition to earning first-team all-league honors on the floor later in his career, came from Canada. So, as the Broncos' last scholarship recipient the previous spring, did a skinny, bookish-looking, perennially-smiling point guard from Victoria, B.C., who was better known there as a soccer goalkeeper and had received no other Division I basketball offers.

In fact, Steve Nash wasn't even a starter as the 1992-93 season started ... and while Davey was optimistic about his team's chances of improving on its 14-15 showing of the previous year, nobody on the team emerged as a follow-me force as preseason practice progressed and the season opener against San Jose State approached.

"We had a pretty good class coming in, and that was encouraging," Davey said. "Both Carroll and I had recruited that class. But (Davey didn't initially think) it was that special. I liked them; it was a good solid group, but not anything super special. Steve kind of took the bull by the horns for that group. He was a guy who would stay after practice and then come back to the gym at night. He was the Pied Piper of that group, and they all kind of connected."

It didn't happen immediately – and it happened more slowly for Nash than for most of his teammates.

"I remember Steve, about a month into his freshman year, sitting in the bleachers (upset) because he couldn't get the ball up to halfcourt in practice," Davey said. "He was telling me, 'I don't know if I can play college basketball.' He was frustrated, and the reason for that was John Woolery. Woolery will go down as maybe the best defensive point guard we've ever had at Santa Clara. Eddie Joe Chavez was there a year or two before I got there, but John was the best I had. He didn't make mistakes and he could *really* defend."

Woolery, in fact, was a starter most of that 1992-93 season, with Nash – who throughout his Santa Clara career wore No. 11, not No. 13 as he did in the NBA – spelling both Woolery, a 6-1 junior, and 6-4 senior shooting guard Mark Schmitz, a onetime walk-on who had overcome chronic knee problems to emerge as a starter. Six-9 junior Pete Eisenrich, who was a hybrid power/finesse player, and 6-5 junior DeWayne Lewis, who could slash

259

productively but was erratic as a perimeter shooter, were the forwards, and 6-8 senior Kevin Fitzwilson was the starting center because of the bulk he provided. Davey usually went with a smaller lineup as Nash, Sedlock, Zurek, Graves, Dunne, Adam Anderson and Andy Karich all worked their way into the rotation at various junctures.

Eisenrich (14.4), Schmitz (13.0) and Lewis (12.9) were the team's leading scorers, but none of them were force fields of the sort that for so long had given Santa Clara its reputation for being the bumper-car ride at the WCC county fair. On the other hand, Davey's first Santa Clara team had more fluidity and depth than most of its predecessors, even though Schmitz was the only senior who played much. Davey also sensed early in the preseason that his charges had some qualities he didn't want to muzzle – comradeship, a zest for the game, an understanding of basketball geometry, and the do-the-right-thing-without-thinking instincts that the new players brought to Santa Clara from high school programs where the means were just as important as the end.

So despite – and maybe even because – of his team's youth, Davey removed some of the pages from the previous playbook, and committed to his players' intuition to a greater extent than Santa Clara had seen in many years.

"The one thing I decided that was maybe a shade different, and I think Steve Seandel had something to do with it … we stayed with the flex, with some alterations, but because of the nature of the team, we became a little more flexible again, allowing them more freedom," Davey said. "I don't think Carroll restricted guys, but it (the system Davey inherited) was a little more regimented than we wanted it to be. We wanted them to come off a screen and *know* they were open and feel comfortable shooting it instead of thinking they had to make three or four more passes.

"That was the biggest difference. Initially there was kind of a mirror process that took place … however well or not so good you play, the one thing that always sticks out is that you could have done better, that you could have won another game and been a little more efficient. It was a young team, a nice team but not quite mature enough, but by the end of the year, with the veterans and the younger kids, we had some maturity.

"We didn't have a real center, but we had a good enough group with enough depth that we could sneak a Nash or a Dunne in early, and by the end of the year they were playing a lot and other guys were starting to fill roles and play more. Sedlock ended up playing quite a bit … (by the end of the season) we had 12 guys who could play a minute or two here and there."

Davey played a broader rotation than Williams had, with 15 players logging minutes during his first season. Davey also changed the Santa Clara approach to the concept of the 3-point shot, which had been introduced by the NCAA in 1987, along with the 45-second shot clock. Williams had been an outspoken opponent of both rule changes, and the only 3-point practitioner who had the freedom to fire when ready had been Mitch Burley, who attempted 357 treys during his career and made 137. (Nash, by contrast, finished his Santa Clara career with 656 attempts and 263 makes from beyond the 19-foot, 9-inch arc.)

"I was never a big advocate of the 3-point shot except for the fact we won some games using it," Davey said, smiling. "If I had my druthers, I still don't like it that much, but it's part of the game now. I also thought shortening the game (in the pre-shot clock years) had worked to our advantage, and I'd still like to have 45 seconds (instead of the 35-second limit). But I think we might have had a little effect on that (when the rule was changed during the summer of 1993). Inferior talent sometimes can beat superior talent if they do things right."

Santa Clara only periodically did multiple things right during the first six weeks of the 1992-93 season as Davey tinkered with his starting lineup and his substitution rotation. The Broncos played well in losses to No. 16 UCLA and No. 25 Cal with Jason Kidd, and were competitive in defeats against Southeastern Conference members Alabama and Georgia. But Minnesota crushed them 87-63 at Toso Pavilion in a game for which attendance was only 1,438 – an indication of the degree to which public interest in the program had waned – and Stanford, which was in the midst of a 7-23 season, handed Santa Clara a 66-35 spanking at Maples Pavilion just before the start of WCC play. The Broncos were only 3-4 in league and 9-10 overall at the halfway point of the conference season.

But Nash had shown a glimmer of what was to come in the Minnesota game, during which he scored 15 points and grabbed six rebounds in 27 minutes against the defense of Voshon Lenard, a future NBA player. The Broncos won six of their final seven conference games, giving them the No. 3 seed in the WCC tournament at USF, and Davey and the team were optimistic about their chances. This was partly because they were playing the best basketball in the league, and partly because Memorial Gym, where Santa Clara teams had come to grief so often before USF dropped basketball in 1982, had actually become a welcoming nest. Since USF returned to basketball in 1986, Santa Clara had won 10 of its 12 games at Memorial Gym, including the semifinals and finals of the 1987 conference tournament.

"We started off real shaky," Davey said. "We got it going (to the point where) we were playing decent, and we were at our best at the end of the year."

After dispatching sixth-seeded St. Mary's in the first round, Santa Clara edged second-seeded Gonzaga 53-51, moving the Broncos into the final against top-seeded Pepperdine, which finished that season 23-8 and had beaten the Broncos twice during the regular season. Santa Clara made all nine 3-pointers it attempted in the second half to complete the 73-63 upset and secure only its second NCAA trip in 23 years, but virtually everybody figured the postseason excursion, like that of 1987, would be a short one. The Broncos (18-11) were given a 15 seed in the West Regional, and their first game would be against second-seeded and nationally sixth-ranked

Arizona on March 18, 1993 at the Huntsman Center in Salt Lake City.

The players and coaches, though, didn't share that fatalism.

"We were kind of fired up about (merely) going initially," Davey said, "but then you want more out of it, and our reaction (to the news they would be facing Arizona) was pretty good. We'd watched them on tape and kind of prepared for what we thought we were going to get. Our extra week (after the WCC title game and before Selection Sunday) was not completely wasted on no opponent; we had an opponent in mind (from the broad preparation standpoint). We had three more tapes on them within a day (after the tournament pairings were announced) and we knew what kind of team they were going to be, so in a roundabout way we were able to prepare for them.

"We knew we would have to rebound because they were leading the nation in rebounding margin, and we knew we would have to be able to handle pressure, so we put an extra guy on the floor (on defense) for all our offensive drills. We emphasized blocking out as best we could with our limited capability. I really felt we had a chance to win, more because of my kids than theirs.

"It was a kind of team that kind of developed little by little … Mark Schmitz, DeWayne Lewis, Pete Eisenrich, Nash, all of them were gaining momentum individually. Their shooting percentage kept going up, little by little, from

37 percent to 39 to 41 to 42. We grew during the year offensively, and against Pepperdine, we just couldn't miss."

Nevada oddsmakers weren't impressed, and made Arizona a 20-point favorite. Arizona, the Pacific-10 Conference champion, had qualified for every NCAA tournament since 1985, Lute Olson's second season as coach, and the Wildcats had reached the Final Four with Craig McMillan, Sean Elliott, Kenny Lofton and Steve Kerr in 1988.

Entering the 1993 NCAA tournament, Arizona was 24-3, and guards Khalid Reeves and Damon Stoudamire constituted arguably the most combustible backcourt in the country. Reeves, a junior, was chosen by the Miami Heat in the first round of the 1994 NBA draft, after leading Arizona to the Final Four that spring, and Stoudamire, a sophomore, in 1995 became the expansion Toronto Raptors' first-ever first-round draft selection. Senior forward Chris Mills, the team's scoring leader with a 20.4 average, was a first-round draft pick of the Cleveland Cavaliers in 1993, and teammate Ed Stokes, a 7-foot center, was taken in the second round of the same draft by Miami. (Three other players on the roster that season – Joseph Blair, Ben Davis and Reggie Geary – were second-round NBA draft picks in 1996, and starting center Ray Owes also played briefly in the NBA.)

Santa Clara? The Broncos were described in a *St. Louis Post-Dispatch* preview story as "a motley jumble of eggheads, surfers and imports."

Actually, the only "imports" – a.k.a., players born outside the U.S. – were Nash and Graves, both Canadians, and the only "surfer" was Andy Karich, whose floppy blond hairdo made him look as if he'd just been on a date with Annette Funicello. Karich, from Southern California, actually *was* a surfer, but Davey described him as perhaps the most intellectually brilliant individual he'd ever coached. Karich was a bright prospect who'd started as a freshman before his career was sidetracked and eventually ended by a chronic back injury. He became a doctor after graduating from Santa Clara.

There were some pregame considerations that seemed in retrospect to point toward a competitive game, including Santa Clara's nine wins in its previous 10 games, the fact the Broncos had made 34 of 59 3-point tries (57.6 percent) in their four games prior to the Arizona contest, and the fact Arizona had won only three tournament games in the previous three years. The Wildcats were blown out 77-55 by Alabama in the second round in 1990, dropped an 81-77 decision to Seton Hall in the 1991 Sweet 16, and as the No. 3 seed in 1992, were bushwhacked 87-80 by 14th-seeded East Tennessee State in the first round – a game that may have subjected the 1992-93 Wildcats to more pressure than would be the norm in a first-round game against an opponent with modest credentials.

But in the eight years since the NCAA expanded the tournament field to 64 teams in 1985, only one No. 15 seed had upset a No. 2 seed – in 1991 when Richmond beat Syracuse 73-69 – and the Broncos had only two postseason wins (both in the '84 NIT) since 1970. Although Nash had emerged as a freshman to watch on the national horizon, scoring 23 points and making 5 of 6 3-pointers in the WCC championship win over Pepperdine, he wasn't perceived as a take-over-the-game type of player yet. On exhibited talent only, it's unlikely any of Santa Clara's other players even could have made Arizona's roster that year. The Broncos hadn't seriously recruited any players on Arizona's must-have lists since they lost Craig McMillan to the Wildcats in 1984.

Typical of the tangible differences between the team was the link between Santa Clara's John Woolery and Chris Mills. Both attended the same high school – Fairfax in Los Angeles – but Woolery was only a name to Mills, if even that.

"In junior high, Chris lived just around the corner from me," Woolery said. "I never played against him, though. He was a couple of years older, the legend of the neighborhood. I kind of idolized him."

"Not good," Davey told reporters before the game when asked about his team's upset chances. "We've talked to our players about it. We think we have to play pretty close to a perfect game to win. That's really hard to do."

"Making the tournament is always a huge step," Eisenrich said. "Hopefully, we can make it more consistently now."

Privately, though, Davey and his players had what they believed was a coherent road map leading to the destination upset.

Because of the chasm between the teams' athletic resources, Davey intended to use the 45-second shot clock to full advantage, limiting Arizona's possessions and forcing the Wildcats to expend more energy than they had anticipated on defense. He also thought Arizona might become frustrated if it developed that the Wildcats weren't able to put the game away as easily as the 20-point spread indicated they should. If that happened, Davey thought, Arizona's shot selection might deteriorate and the Broncos, though not nearly as big or as fleet or as experienced as the Wildcats, might be able to corral some long rebounds and detonate some fast breaks that way.

"I talked to our guys about putting the fundamental pieces together," he said. "I told them, 'If you're willing to screen out, if you can handle their defensive pressure, if you can be patient and take care of the ball offensively, if you can make free throws … I think you've shown you can do all those things in recent games. I *know* we can win.' And they knew I felt that way. I felt confident and comfortable that we could, and we were really, really ready to play. I've been fooled a couple of times over the years, but I've gone into very few games feeling we didn't have a chance."

Chapter 11
CRAZING ARIZONA

As tipoff approached, the Huntsman Center resounded with the usual Arizona pregame protocol: The Wildcats' band exhorting the crowd with a rhythmic bass prelude, and the red-and-blue clad fans standing and clapping until Arizona scored its first basket.

Some Vanderbilt fans were beginning to settle back into their seats – the Commodores had just beaten Boise State in another first-round game – and supporters of Temple and Illinois (who had the game after Arizona-Santa Clara) were filtering into the building, but it was clearly an Arizona crowd and an Arizona atmosphere. Santa Clara didn't even *have* a band on hand, as it usually didn't in those years even at home games, and the Broncos' rooting section, numbering only in the dozens, was dwarfed by the Arizona contingent. The phenomenon of neutral teams' fans acoustically climbing into the fray on the behalf of underdogs had often played a role in NCAA tournament games, but the Vanderbilt, Temple and Illinois supporters would have to be shown that Santa Clara was a worthy opponent for Arizona before they began to cheer for a team from a school of which most of them probably had never heard.

That didn't take long.

Chapter 11
CRAZING ARIZONA

As tipoff approached, the Huntsman Center resounded with the usual Arizona pregame protocol: The Wildcats' band exhorting the crowd with a rhythmic bass prelude, and the red-and-blue clad fans standing and clapping until Arizona scored its first basket.

Some Vanderbilt fans were beginning to settle back into their seats – the Commodores had just beaten Boise State in another first-round game – and supporters of Temple and Illinois (who had the game after Arizona-Santa Clara) were filtering into the building, but it was clearly an Arizona crowd and an Arizona atmosphere. Santa Clara didn't even *have* a band on hand, as it usually didn't in those years even at home games, and the Broncos' rooting section, numbering only in the dozens, was dwarfed by the Arizona contingent. The phenomenon of neutral teams' fans acoustically climbing into the fray on the behalf of underdogs had often played a role in NCAA tournament games, but the Vanderbilt, Temple and Illinois supporters would have to be shown that Santa Clara was a worthy opponent for Arizona before they began to cheer for a team from a school of which most of them probably had never heard.

That didn't take long.

The retro version of Steve Nash's resume, the one that will be circulated and celebrated when he enters the Basketball Hall of Fame, may well begin with the game that rippled through the basketball world to a greater extent than any other in his alma mater's basketball history. Nash did indeed have an important role in this Arizona game, and he was the primary reason Santa Clara reached the tournament in the first place. In Santa Clara's previous four games, including the three victories in the WCC tournament, he had attempted 27 3-point shots and had made 22 of them – an astounding 81 percent success rate. Because of that, he was featured in most of the pre-tournament synopsis stories, and Arizona coach Lute Olson knew that defending Nash on the perimeter would have to be one of his team's top priorities.

What's generally forgotten, though, was that four Santa Clara players had games for their personal Louvres … and Steve Nash wasn't one of them. In fact, he didn't even start the game, he made only one of the seven shots he attempted, and his impact wasn't fully felt until the final minute.

Recognizing that Santa Clara would have to dictate a low-possession, ball-nurturing type of game to have a chance against Arizona, Davey started his two most experienced ballhandlers and best defensive guards – junior John Woolery and senior Mark Schmitz. Kevin Fitzwilson started at center, although he played only the first five minutes, and Pete Eisenrich and DeWayne Lewis were the starting forwards. Nash spelled both Woolery and Schmitz, and wound up playing most of the game, but only because Davey for long periods went small and played all three of his regular guards, with 6-5 Lewis at power forward and 6-9 Eisenrich at center. Kevin Dunne played about 15 minutes, and Carl Anderson and Jason Sedlock were used briefly in the frontline. Otherwise, Davey went with the smaller, quicker lineup, partly to counter the Wildcats' Stoudamire-Reeves backcourt and partly because Davey included corollaries in his rebounding theorem for the game.

"They were outrebounding their opponents by something like 10 a game," Davey said. "We felt like that would be a major issue. We told them the usual things, like getting off the (attempted) shot quickly, put a body on a guy, make sure you get everybody. We had all five guys go to the boards; we had to take the chance that they'd get some runouts because they were so much bigger than us. We also worked a lot on finding the scams (with smaller, quicker players) and getting somebody through to rebound."

That trying to muscle up with the Wildcats would be futile became apparent when the teams took the floor at half-filled Huntsman Center. With Santa Clara bandless, the Vanderbilt musical ensemble donned Santa Clara T-shirts and stuck around to provide a measure of Santa Clara-directed volume. But the visual effect just before the tipoff must have discouraged many neutral fans who were eager to root for the No. 15 seed against the No. 2 seed.

"They sure look a lot older than us," Davey mused 14 years later as he watched a tape of the game – the first time he had seen the tape in its entirety.

In fact, visually it was more like a varsity-JV matchup.

Eisenrich, a transfer from Boise State, was a sturdy but sinewy sort who looked frail in comparison to Chris Mills and Ray Owes, Arizona's starting power forward and center respectively. Woolery, who was listed at 6-1 but looked smaller, almost seemed gnarled because of the fact he did everything from a crouch. Davey described him as "very spidery," and the description was apt when Woolery was hounding opponents on defense, but he didn't look – at least to Arizona – like somebody who could beat defenders off the dribble or dissipate packed-in defenses with outside shooting.

Lewis was probably Santa Clara's best all-around athlete, but he didn't match up with Arizona's forwards (Ed Stokes was the starting "3") in terms of bulk, or with Stoudamire or Reeves in terms of octane. Schmitz understood basketball geometry and was adept at finding space to spot up and at bisecting a double-team with a pass or a dribble-drive, but he wouldn't have won a race of any distance with any of Arizona's guards, although his troublesome knee was springier than it had been all season.

Basketball orthodoxy might have dictated that Santa Clara play a zone to try to keep Arizona on the perimeter, and Olson certainly saw from any or all of Santa Clara's late-season game videos that Nash was the Broncos' main offensive conduit. But Davey opened – and stayed – in a man-to-man, with one of the guards usually doubling down on the Arizona bigs when they entrenched themselves at the low post. And Nash, who picked up three fouls in his limited first-half time, wasn't nearly as much of a problem for Arizona early in the game as were Eisenrich, Woolery, Lewis and Schmitz.

After Stokes made a 15-foot turnaround jumper for the first points of the game, Lewis glided inside and then accelerated past Owes and Mills for a layup that elicited grunts of surprise from the crowd. Woolery careened into the lane and made a 10-foot teardrop shot over Stokes. Eisenrich railed a 15-footer. Woolery frisked Stoudamire and broke away for a layup.

Davey alternated a motion game with a four-corner delay setup; both drained much of the 45-second clock on each possession, and succeeded in extending Arizona's defense and widening and lengthening the floor. Per Davey's instructions, the Broncos' frontliners not only blocked out against the bigger Wildcats, but also angled themselves to create gaps through which the guards could penetrate to gather rebounds. Arizona's early body language betrayed no chagrin, but the neutral fans all were echoing the excitement of the Santa Clara supporters as the Broncos were one step quicker and Arizona seemed mired.

Lewis' driving layup, Eisenrich's 3-pointer (made possible when he popped out of the low post and nobody followed him) and Schmitz's trey made the score 33-21 in Santa Clara's favor with five minutes left in the first half. The Huntsman Center by now sounded like Toso Pavilion for a St. Mary's game. Stoudamire was on the bench with three fouls, and even Olson's usually impassive visage was etched with concern as he remonstrated with the officials and his players.

But as quickly as the Santa Clara epiphany had appeared, it vanished.

Arizona, navigating the Santa Clara defense like a fleet of Formula One race cars, scored the final 14 points of the first half to take a 35-33 lead at the break, and the Wildcats' basket remained a mirage for the Broncos in the opening minutes of the second half. Davey couldn't wait for the under-16 TV timeout, as he usually did in such situations, but he decided not to vent his frustration on his players, who were still getting designer shots and were defending and rebounding as well as could be expected. As he faced his players in the huddle, he tried to convey to them that winning this game would be a matter of will as much as it would be a matter of ways.

"At halftime all I talked about was trying to remember that we knew we could play with these guys," he said. "We were flat again after halftime; we just couldn't make a shot, and maybe (fleetingly) we were just thinking we were happy to be there. They (the Wildcats) got it going right away (after halftime) and got a little more aggressive on defense."

Just after the second half began, CBS television commentator Larry Farmer, seeing Davey talking to one of his players during a clock stoppage, said: "Dick Davey is reaching into his bag of tricks again."

Fourteen years later as he listened to Farmer's comment, Davey smiled.

"There was no bag of tricks," he said. "When I called that timeout (with Arizona leading 43-33 and Santa Clara's scoreless Gobi approaching nine minutes) I didn't say a word. I looked at them and they looked at me and I looked at them again and they looked at me again. Finally, I just stared at them and said, 'We have to score.' It was going to have to be up to them.

"I liked the way we were moving, though … they were still trying to find a way to create problems. They didn't bag it. It had just been a matter of Arizona doing things to let us back in the game and us not taking advantage of it."

With 15:26 remaining in the game, Arizona's run reached 25-0 and the Wildcats' lead ballooned to 46-33 as Mills completed a three-point play. It was at that point that Davey's unspoken message – take the initiative – kicked in, as Schmitz drove the baseline and flicked in a layup over Stokes. Woolery took advantage of the Wildcats' carelessness, making off with two steals. He converted the first for a layup; after the second, Nash chased down a long offensive rebound and dished it inside to Lewis for a dunk. Stoudamire countered with two free throws, but Santa Clara, feeding on the renewed shouting from the galleries, again had the Wildcats' defenders in a quagmire. Eisenrich scored six straight points, the last on two free throws with eight minutes left, and Santa Clara was within 50-47.

"I think people forget that we got a little lucky in that game," Davey said as he watched the game tape. "Stokes missed a dunk right at that point, and they had some loose balls bounce off them and go out of bounds, and they dropped some passes. Right about now, those things started happening a lot."

Santa Clara was in some foul trouble by now, but so was Reeves, who incurred his fourth foul with nine minutes to play – joining Mills, who got his fourth foul four minutes into the second half, on the bench. With 6:10 left, Woolery made a 10-foot lean-in shot to pull Santa Clara within 52-51, and with the score at 53-52 Arizona, Davey brandished his clipboard during the under-4 timeout and drew up an out-of-bounds play – one of several that caught the Wildcats unaware.

"They (his players) were pretty fired up (during the timeout)," Davey said. "We still knew our people physically weren't as strong as their people, but that's not what wins games. You try to create an environment of success, break it down, make them realize (opponents') shortcomings and then work on those. I never had a doubt, even when we were 13 down, that we would have a chance to win the game, but we were going to have to make a few shots."

Using the inbound play that Davey had sketched during the timeout, Eisenrich darted behind a backscreen and railed a 15-footer to put Santa Clara ahead 54-53. Reeves missed two free throws. Woolery lobbed to Lewis for a resounding dunk. With 1:30 remaining, Santa Clara was up 56-53 with possession and the Huntsman Center was beginning to sound like an airport runway.

"When it started getting tight, just as a general thing you could see them (the Wildcats) getting a little panicked," Davey said. "It wasn't overwhelming, but they were feeling it a little."

But Nash turned the ball over, Mills made two free throws at 1:19 and Santa Clara missed three eminently convertible inside shots. The Broncos' determination, though, yielded them a fourth shot, which Dunne – "our garbageman," Davey said – banked in to boost Santa Clara's lead to 58-55. Mills tried a 3-pointer that missed, and with 31 seconds left, Nash made the first two of what became six straight free-throw conversions for a 60-55 lead.

At that point, Arizona had missed 14 of 15 shots from the field, but Stoudamire drew a foul and made both free throws. Reeves committed his fifth and disqualifying foul against Nash, who raced to the foul line almost as soon as the whistle had subsided, and cashed in two more free throws with 26.2 seconds to go to restore Santa Clara's lead to 62-57.

Arizona wasn't done yet. Reggie Geary drove the lane and was fouled, purportedly injuring his wrist on the play. "I think it was a fake job," Davey said of the play by Geary, not a good free-throw shooter, "but you can't really complain too much about something like that. So they took him out and put in a freshman (Dylan Rigdon, who hadn't played previously) because he was a better free-throw shooter than Geary."

If Olson did indeed have Geary fake the injury, the ploy boomeranged on the Wildcats, because Rigdon missed the first of two free throws. He made the second, with 16.6 seconds left, but Arizona still had a four-point, two-possession deficit. With 8.4 seconds left, Nash made two more free throws – giving him six straight in less than 23 seconds – to make the score 64-58. Mills countered with a 3 just two seconds later to cut the lead in half.

Then, the basketball gods that had treated Santa Clara so kindly became capricious. Nash was fouled with 5.1 seconds left, and he needed to make just one of two free throws to notarize the win. He missed both. Dunne got the long rebound and was fouled – and then proceeded to miss his two free throws.

Arizona, though out of timeouts, ferried the ball upcourt and Stoudamire flung an off-balance 30-foot buzzer beater that seemed to linger over the court like a full moon at harvest time.

"Looking at the video (14 years later), I tend to think more that way (that Stoudamire's shot would go in and Arizona's superior manpower would prevail in overtime)," Davey said. Grinning, he added: "But I shouldn't, because I know it didn't go in.

"I was thinking (at the time) about whether we'd have time to get the ball inbounded, because we were out of timeouts (and at that time, NCAA rules didn't stipulate that the clock be stopped in the final minute after a made basket)."

Stoudamire's shot had sufficient distance, but it clanked off the right edge of the rim, and caromed harmlessly out to Eisenrich on the opposite side of the floor. He flung the ball joyously into the air as the final buzzer sounded.

Santa Clara 64, Arizona 61.

It was an upset that ranked in magnitude with North Carolina State's victory over Houston in the 1983 NCAA championship game, but Davey didn't pull a Jim Valvano and look for somebody – anybody – with whom to celebrate. He says, in fact, that his lingering memory of the moment when the clock hit 0:00 was his pressing need to talk to Dunne about the missed free throws.

"I was looking for Kevin Dunne," Davey said. "I told him he was going to have to be mentally tougher than that. I was really surprised that he missed those free throws, because even though he was a freshman, and so was Steve, I expected them to succeed in that kind of situation."

Davey's pique didn't last long. Nor, for that matter, did his postgame debriefing; he spoke to the media for only a few minutes, excusing himself quickly so that he could scout the upcoming Temple game. He congratulated his players for what they had achieved, then reminded them that they had to scrape themselves off the emotional ceiling for their second-round game against Temple. And he reminded them of the reasons they had been able to shrug off the 25-point run by Arizona and overcome the Wildcats' superior athleticism.

"We had two major concepts we kept re-emphasizing, during every timeout: Board play, and make them shoot the ball on the perimeter," said Davey, whose team outrebounded Arizona 50-36. "We made mistakes, but we had two excellent ballhandlers (Nash and Woolery) who took care of the ball, and we were able to take time off the clock every time we didn't have a breakaway or a layup. We tried to make the game a little shorter. We'd draw things up, and they (his players) were smart enough that even though we were young, we could run something different and they'd know how to do it. The intelligence factor really helped us."

Santa Clara, which had been so dependent on 3-point shooting in the WCC tournament, made only 4 of 22 shots from beyond the arc against Arizona and finished with a .377 overall shooting percentage, but the Broncos limited Arizona to 30 percent shooting (17 for 56). Mills scored 19 points despite missing 10 minutes with his foul problems, but Stokes had only 12 points and Reeves 10. Stoudamire scored only six points, all from the free-throw line, and missed all seven of his field-goal attempts. Eisenrich led the Broncos with 19 points and eight rebounds, and Woolery contributed 10 points on 5-of-6 shooting, along with three assists and six steals.

"They flat-out outplayed us," Olson said. "It starts on the boards, and we were not good there."

After the game, Woolery came across Mills as they were preparing to enter the media room. "Obviously, Chris had his head down, since this was his last game at Arizona," Davey said. "John said to him, 'Don't worry about it. You'll be making a lot of money (in the NBA) down the road.'"

Davey's other overriding memory of the victory was the early morning that followed.

"The phone started ringing in our room at about 5:30 or 6 in the morning," he said. "ESPN, papers from all over the country. The other thing I remember is we got bumped out of our hotel because nobody thought we'd be staying any longer than that day. Luckily, we got to stay. (Assistant athletic director) Amy Hackett came up to me and told us we were going to have to move. I said, 'We're not moving,' Amy said, 'OK, let me go to work on it.' She fought for us, and we got to keep the hotel, as it turned out. Our fans did have to switch hotels, but they got into Arizona's hotel (using the reservations the Wildcats' fans had made in anticipation of a longer stay)."

Meanwhile, the Santa Clara campus was in the midst of a celebratory frenzy not seen there since January 2, 1950, when the football team upset Bear Bryant's Kentucky squad in the Orange Bowl and was met by 10,000 supporters (including California Gov. Earl Warren) at the Santa Clara train station upon its return.

"It had pretty much calmed down by the time we got back (after losing to Temple in the second round)," Davey

281

said, "but we heard it got pretty wild … a lot of partying and mattress burning, things you don't see very often at Santa Clara."

Immediately after the final buzzer, hundreds of students transformed Market Street (which bisects the campus, but has been closed to traffic since the 1980s) into Santa Clara's answer to Bourbon Street. Police blocked the street off, and the celebration – punctuated by bonfires, firecrackers, skyrockets and blaring music and seemingly lubricated by enough beer to float the Queen Mary – continued well into the evening.

Senior Anne Martino was interviewed as she walked quietly through the tumult, a smile creasing her face.

"I went to the airport to see the team off with my friend … not even the (players') girlfriends were there," she said. "We were the only two people to see them off. We wished them good luck and we told them to win. We knew they could do it."

Nobody else was claiming any such prescience. Even though they had set the pregame point spread prohibitively high at 20 points, the Nevada sports books profited as handsomely as Santa Clara, because most of the bettors who wagered on the game still gave the points and took Arizona, according to reports in the Nevada media.

Of course, the victory was priceless even for the Santa Clara supporters who had money riding on the game.

"If it has ever been more fun than this at Santa Clara University, it must have happened 200 years ago on Two-For-One Pita Bread Night at the old Mission," Mark Purdy of the *San Jose Mercury News* wrote. "And that wasn't nationally televised."

It never got quite that uproarious for Davey again at Santa Clara – the Broncos lost their second-round game, 68-57, to Temple – but the freshman class that had arrived on campus amid virtual anonymity a few months before went on to carve out a 73-32 record and make three NCAA appearances during its four-year stay. The Arizona upset also led directly to an NCAA rule change. Olson then and later was one of the most influential coaches in the country, and he felt that the Santa Clara game demonstrated that delay tactics still were possible with a 45-second shot clock. The NCAA apparently agreed with him, because it went to a 35-second shot clock a year later.

And perhaps to an even greater degree than any single Santa Clara player since Kenny Sears in the early and mid-1950s, Steve Nash – the final recruit of what in 1992 had been considered a good-but-not-great recruiting class – became the national face of Santa Clara basketball.

To many not familiar with Santa Clara's program, Davey may be best known for having coached Nash. He got that chance only because the head coach at Santa Clara's archrival hadn't been interested ... and the individual who first made Davey aware of Nash was in the employ of that rival, St. Mary's College, at the time.

Chapter 12
'THE WORST DEFENSIVE PLAYER I'VE EVER SEEN'

If Dick Davey is known to future generations as the man who discovered and developed Steve Nash, Davey won't go out of his way to argue the point, even though he coached basketball for 40 years and would be revered in retrospect even if he and Nash had never crossed paths.

"That's fine," he said of being joined at the hip with Nash in terms of name recognition. "I'm proud of it, truthfully. I'm just grateful to Chris Brazier for leading us to a guy who might be a pretty good player."

Brazier, who had been a graduate assistant at Santa Clara during the 1990-91 season, had just been hired by new St. Mary's coach Ernie Kent as an assistant. During the summer of 1991, a few weeks after he accepted the St. Mary's position, Brazier traveled to Las Vegas for an AAU tournament at which Davey, still a Santa Clara assistant, also was present.

"Everybody else (himself included) was in the main gym of this school watching two of the best AAU teams in the country," Davey said, "so Chris goes down to the small gym to watch another game and he sees this Canadian guard and thinks he's not bad and writes his name down. He mentions to Ernie that he'd seen this Canadian kid who looked pretty good, and Ernie tells him, 'I don't have to go to Canada to find a point guard.'

"So Chris calls me and says, 'I know you guys are looking for a point guard. I saw this guy from Canada and I think he's decent ... not phenomenal or anything, but decent. You might want to take a look at him.' I wrote his name down in August, and in October I asked (assistant coach) Scott Gradin to call up there to see if he could get a video on this kid. He gets the video, and one day I'm walking past the video room and Scott is in there laughing. I asked him what was so funny, and he said, 'Hey, you gotta see this kid. He's making people fall down.'"

"The video was jerking in one corner; it was probably a parent taking it, and it (the overall quality of play in the game on the video) was pretty bad. I said, 'We'd better get another tape.' So we got another tape and we liked it, and (after the WCC tournament in Portland in the spring of 1992) I went up there (Victoria, British Columbia) to see him. I watched him for about 30 seconds and then I started praying nobody else was there. (Nobody was; Nash was otherwise unrecruited coming out of high school, aside from interest from a couple of Canadian universities.)

"I didn't know how special he was when we first got him, but I knew he was pretty good."

Davey offered Steve Nash the final scholarship Santa Clara had available for the coming season – but not before telling the player that he was the worst defensive player he'd ever seen, just to observe his reaction.

"I'll never forget walking out of the gym (at Nash's high school)," Davey said. "There were seven of us walking down the steps – his mom, his dad, his sister, his brother, Steve, myself and his high school coach. You can't talk directly to a player (under NCAA rules) on a school site, so I'm standing next to his coach as we're walking down and I say, loud enough for him to hear, 'This might be the worst defensive player I've ever seen.' I'd just seen him play, and I'm praying we'd get him, but I wanted to test him a little bit.

"Afterward, he got me alone in a restaurant, and his first comment was 'Why am I such a bad defensive player?' I liked the fact he wanted to challenge me and was up for the challenge of proving he was more capable. A month ago (in 2007) a friend of mine visited him in Phoenix, and he said, 'Tell Coach Davey I lead the league in charges taken.'"

Nash, of course, had more than a few other distinctions by then. He was named the NBA's Most Valuable Player in 2004-05 and 2005-06, and by doing so strode into the all-time point-guard pantheon with the likes of Magic Johnson, John Stockton and Bob Cousy.

Bill Duffy remembers the first time he met his future client.

"It was one of the first days he was on campus," he said. "I happened to be in town at the time, and I always came by to see the coaches when I was in town. I was in their office, and they said, 'We've got this kid from Canada, and we think he's really good. He's a really nice kid and I think you'll really like him.' So he comes in, and I mention Leo Rautins (a Canadian who played briefly in the NBA and in 2007 was the Canadian national team coach). He says, 'Wow, really? He's one of my heroes.' I mention that I played with him at Minnesota (before Rautins transferred to Syracuse), and we kind of hit it off from there.

"When he was a sophomore, and I think I was one of the first to tell him this, I told him, 'You'll play in the NBA, and at worst you'll be a Mark Jackson (distribution-oriented) type.' I wasn't really thinking of recruiting him (for the stable of athletes he represented) at the time, but later we developed a relationship, and working with him has excited me more than anything I've ever done in my life. People meet him and are kind of bowled over (by his fame) at first, but he just breaks them down because he's so humble and he's so interested in everybody else."

By 1995-96, his senior season, Nash without much question was the best guard ever to play at Santa Clara, and arguably had become the program's nonpareil regardless of position. It was a given that he'd be chosen, probably in the first round, in the 1996 NBA draft, but gadget defenses, lingering ankle and hamstring injuries, and a less-productive-than-expected supporting cast had undercut his numbers as a senior.

Before Santa Clara's first-round game against Maryland in the 1996 NCAA tournament, Nash revealed a facet of himself that was to resonate later when he became a two-time NBA MVP.

"I don't know if people have stopped doubting my ability," Nash said, "but probably not. They'll probably be doubting me until the day I retire. No matter what people might think, I know I can go into the NBA and help a team. And if I find out I'm not good enough, I'm gonna work and work and work till I am."

"As much as Steve wants to win for the team, what's happening is also about the lack of recognition he's received," teammate Adam Anderson said the same day. "It's like he's saying this is his time, this is who I am."

The next day, Nash went for 28 points, 12 assists, six rebounds and two steals as the Broncos overpowered Maryland, 91-79.

Soon thereafter, the Phoenix Suns made him the 15th selection in the NBA draft. He was a backup to Jason Kidd during his first two NBA seasons, but eventually evolved into a star after being traded to the Dallas Mavericks. He returned to Phoenix as a free agent in 2004, and his two MVP seasons immediately followed.

In Davey's Saratoga home, the only obvious basketball accoutrement is a living-room wall adorned with plaques and photos commemorating high points in Davey's career. The centerpiece of that montage, assembled by Jeanne Davey, is a Steve Nash mini-collection that includes an autographed jersey and a number of pictures of the two of them.

"I try not to bother him during the season," Davey said. "Maybe I'll call him once or twice and leave a message asking how he's doing or whatever. But I've been involved with his foundation a little bit, and this (memorabilia on the wall) has a lot of memories for me.

"If I were to pick a negative about Steve's game in college, it was that he didn't take as many shots as sometimes I would have liked. But maybe the biggest positive about him was that everything he did made everyone around him better. He did so many things so well."

That was equally true of Nash off the court.

Nash, who graduated from Santa Clara with a sociology degree, in 2000 made a $100,000 donation to endow a basketball scholarship at his alma mater. His Steve Nash Foundation is so far-flung that it consumes almost all of his off-season time, and it has impacted thousands of impoverished and needy people throughout Canada as well as in Arizona. In 2007, he was named winner of the J. Walter Kennedy Citizenship Award, presented annually by the Professional Basketball Writers Association to recognize an NBA player or coach for outstanding community service and commitment to serve and give of his time outside the arena.

He returned to Santa Clara in 2006 to deliver a convocation address and to have his No. 11 jersey retired. In his speech, he synopsized his Santa Clara experience and what it has meant to him – not only as an athlete, but as a man and as an individual who believes he owes those around him much more than they could ever owe him.

"From your perspective, you guys are going through life, and sometimes you don't have an opportunity to see the future and to realize what a time it is for you guys to be university students," he told his audience. "And especially at this amazing university.

"I had no idea. I wanted to be a basketball player. I wanted to go to a big Division I school and become a star – those big dreams. But I was really fortunate and, somehow, everything worked out perfectly. I couldn't have gone to a more perfect university for me. And I think that, in many ways, everyone can find that in Santa Clara.

"I had no idea how impressionable and how important my four years here were. I think that it is very difficult for you guys to foresee how influential and impressionable this time is in your life. I remember Coach Davey came to watch me play (in high school). The first thing he said to me was, 'You're the worst defender I've ever seen.' Which was a real confidence builder (laugh). He also used to say that 'I might have rocks in my head,' speaking about himself. I think that's possible, but I'm not a geology major … He had some good ones.

"But he gave me an opportunity to come here to school, and it was one that I didn't have elsewhere. I had no idea what I was in for, and I think a lot of you guys, especially the freshmen, probably have no idea what you are in for and no idea how great an opportunity this is. Not only considering how few people in the world get a chance to go to a center for higher learning, a university, to further their education, and to be in a progressive center; but how many people in America even get a chance to go to one of the elite institutions. That's what we all are fortunate enough to be a part of.

"I say that this was the perfect school for me, and in so many ways it was. I owe so much to my experience here. Obviously, basketball is my career. But I had no chance, obviously, without coming here. And even if I had gone to another university, I don't know if I would have even been a professional basketball player. I owe so much to the coaches here, who taught us a lot. They primarily were extremely honest, as you can tell by the way Coach Davey recruited me. But I think that's such an important quality: to be honest and to be able to be self-critical. They were hard on us, they pushed us, and they were incredible at helping us develop as players … and, as a byproduct, as people. Not a chance would I have had the career, the success, without my coaches. And I want to thank them."

"Those guys (Santa Clara teammates, several of whom were present at the convocation) became like family for me. We were all away in school and experienced this at the same time. Those people are so important to me. We lived together, we played together, we did everything together. We pushed each other through everything. And I'll always feel like they're, without being too cheesy, my family and my brothers. Every city that they live in now, when I have a game, I get to see them, and it's like we haven't been apart.

"And time flies so fast: It's been 10 years since we graduated, and it'll be 10 years later in a minute. So all of you guys really have to take advantage of this and really make the most of your opportunity here. And I urge you to really get involved: To make the most out of your opportunity, to be balanced, to do as well as you can in school, to make as many friends as possible. Your friendships will last forever at this school. They'll be business connections, networks for your career, but, most importantly, you'll have memories and friendships and reunions and people to meet up with and see. My teammates are that for me. And I want to thank them for helping me become, hopefully, a better person and a better basketball player.

"I think that you guys have the same opportunity, as classmates and through the relationships that you develop, to make each other better, to make the school better, to represent yourself and the school and the community better. All of you have a chance and a decision to make about your attitude and what kind of leader you're going to be, because all of us are leaders. In the way we carry ourselves, to the way we decide to be, is so impressionable on our community.

"You have no idea. You feel like one small piece in this world, but each of us have such a huge power and part to play in the world. And you guys together, collectively … this group of Santa Clara students is going to have such a huge impact on the community and our country in the future. I think Santa Clara is taking over the world, by the way. Everywhere you go, someone from Santa Clara is doing something special. So you will be the next ones to do that. And I really want you guys to take advantage and make the most of your time here because, like I said, this will be something that you never forget. Hopefully life will get better and better for each and every one of you, but you will never be able to recreate this atmosphere, this environment. So make the most of it.

"My biggest hobby, outside of basketball, is really my foundation: being involved, getting people together, building relationships that can help people. I was a sociology major, and I can remember my first class in sociology with Dr. Fernandez. I think the term was "cultural sensitivity." That has been such a huge theme in my life: Having an understanding and an acceptance of our differences, of individual psychology, but also as a community as a whole. So I urge you guys to get involved, to give back, to help.

"Father Locatelli talked about some of the ways that we are failing in this country and in this part of the world, and in our society. You guys can all be a huge part in overcoming that, and whether it's politics, whether it's health care, education, poverty, hunger, epidemics, disease ... you guys can all make such a huge difference by just doing small things. For me, there has been nothing more rewarding than building relationships with people, and together helping make the world, hopefully, better. Helping people who need help. So I urge all of you guys to try to at least be interested in the world. Take a deeper look, think for yourself, and try to understand maybe a little bit more about the world. Travel as much as you can, and really get a better understanding of what is out there, and what you can do to help. Because like I said before, you have no idea how powerful each and every one of you is."

Chapter 13
THE TEAM TO BEAT

The Steve Nash-led Broncos were to revel in success often during the three years after the Arizona upset, even though Santa Clara won only one more NCAA tournament game during the remainder of Davey's 15-year tenure. At the same time, the team's youth betrayed it as often during the 1993-94 season as it had buoyed the Broncos against Arizona.

Davey's team still was riding the crest of the Arizona tsunami as practice began for the following season, and not surprisingly, expectations were high. Three of the four leading scorers from the 1992-93 season – Pete Eisenrich, DeWayne Lewis and Nash – were returning, and a promising freshman guard, Marlon Garnett from Hamilton High in Los Angeles, enabled Davey to continue to employ a three-guard rotation with Nash and Woolery and play at the faster tempo Davey preferred.

Jason Sedlock, Kevin Dunne, Brendan Graves and Drew Zurek had developed to the point that Davey could start or play any of them steady minutes depending on the exigencies of the moment. Phil Von Buchwaldt, a 6-11 sophomore center from France by way of Germany who had been infrequently used the previous season, took over as the starting center. Randy Winn, the future major league baseball player, still was on the team as a sophomore, although he was low on the depth chart and committed fulltime to baseball after that season.

But the Arizona upset had put Santa Clara into a position it hadn't inhabited since the late 1960s: That of the place through which the WCC champion would have to travel. Consequently, the Broncos more often than not got their opponent's best game. Additionally, the WCC at that time had a budget-reducing Friday-Saturday schedule that not only tested teams' endurance, but also took away opposing coaching staffs' preparation time. Often, they game-planned for Santa Clara more than for the Broncos' travel partner.

Moreover, the team's mixture of experience and youth still tilted toward youth, especially during a December schedule that fragmented Santa Clara's confidence and chemistry.

"I think we just didn't play up to our expectations," Davey said. "The schedule was part of it, but we were only 6-8 in league. We just didn't have a very good year."

The Broncos split two early-season games with Cal, which was No. 6 in the AP preseason poll, and won at Oregon, but were blown out 89-63 by a vengeful Arizona team at San Jose Arena and lost to Stanford, which qualified for the NIT that year. Nevada, which was only 11-17 that season, and Charlotte also defeated the Broncos during the preseason.

Santa Clara began the WCC season with a rare road sweep of Loyola Marymount and Pepperdine, and was

5-4 entering the final three weeks of the season. But the Broncos won only one of their final six games, including a 76-74 home loss to USF in the first round of the conference tournament, and finished 13-14.

Although Nash was entrenched as a starter by the start of his sophomore year, he hadn't yet emerged on a eye-catching scale as either a scorer or distributor. That changed dramatically during the 1994-95 season, when Nash led the WCC in both scoring (20.9) and assists (6.4) while he and Garnett (13.6) gave the Broncos the most productive backcourt combination in the league.

That backcourt orientation was a departure for Santa Clara, which had been a power-oriented team for as long as any long-time supporter of the program could remember. The Broncos still were a formidable rebounding and penetration-thwarting team, especially after Davey installed 6-10 junior center Brendan Graves alongside Dunne and Sedlock in the front court. But with Nash and Garnett now comfortable forcing a faster tempo and taking outside shots even in transition, Davey was able to present a different look to coaches who long had expected Santa Clara to play deliberately and take only carefully orchestrated, high-percentage shots.

Santa Clara won six of its first seven games, losing only to Oregon State at Corvallis and winning at home against Oregon. The Broncos took seventh-ranked Kansas to the brink in Lawrence before losing 80-75, and concluded the non-conference schedule 8-3, with the only other loss coming against Brigham Young, which had upset

Final Four-bound Oklahoma State earlier and went on to earn an NCAA berth, in the Cable Car Classic.

It was in the first league game, against St. Mary's before the usual rivalry-frenzied sellout crowd, that the Steve Nash basketball odyssey – the one that made him a certain Hall of Famer and a two-time NBA MVP – really began.

He made 21 of 21 free throws (among his 34 points) in a 75-71 victory. The 21-for-21 performance was a feat achieved only twice in NCAA history up to that point, both times in 1959 – by Oklahoma State's Arlen Clark, who went 24 for 24 from the line against Colorado, and North Carolina's York Larese, who made all 21 attempts against Duke. (Larese later played briefly in the NBA, and scored nine points in 14 minutes for the Philadelphia Warriors against the New York Knicks in Hershey, Pa., on March 2, 1962. That game, of course, is far better known as the contest in which Wilt Chamberlain scored 100 points.) No other NCAA player had matched Nash's 21 for 21 as of 2007.

Twelve days later, in Gonzaga's belligerent and claustrophobic Martin Centre, he scored a career-high 40 points – the most by a Santa Clara player since Nick Vanos' 44-point outburst in 1986 and sixth-best all-time among Santa Clara players – as the Broncos beat the Bulldogs 73-68 for their first 4-0 league start since 1980.

"It was a tremendous game," Davey said. "The 21 for 21 was unique, obviously, but I think the Gonzaga game up there was as good as Steve ever played in college. In fact, I know it was. He was uncanny."

The Broncos lost their next game at Portland, then strung together nine straight wins (including a non-league victory over Sacramento State) to match their longest win streak since 1969. The run, during which Santa Clara scored 80 or more points in six straight games and at least 74 in all nine wins, ended with a regular-season ending loss at Pepperdine (despite Nash's 30 points), but Santa Clara was 21-5 and already had clinched its first outright WCC title since '69.

The Broncos' position in the various power indexes was such that most observers thought they already had an NCAA berth clinched entering the WCC tournament at Toso Pavilion. But no home team had won the conference tournament since its inception in 1987 – a hex that wasn't ended until 2003 when San Diego did it – and the Broncos swooned unthinkably against last-place Loyola Marymount in the first round, losing 87-83. (Gonzaga won the tournament to capture its first-ever NCAA berth.)

Santa Clara still got an at-large bid to the NCAA tournament, but the losses to Pepperdine and Loyola Marymount dropped the Broncos' RPI from 30 to 51. The Broncos were among the last at-large teams picked for the tournament, with a No. 12 seed, and were sent to Boise to play fifth-seeded Mississippi State, which went to the Sweet 16 that year and in 1995-96 reached the Final Four.

Santa Clara, which had a 13-day layoff between the end of the WCC tournament and its first-round NCAA assignment, made 1993-ish upset overtures for a time against the Bulldogs, who were led by future NBA player Erick Dampier. But the Broncos lost 75-67, leaving them with a three-game losing streak that blemished an otherwise exemplary 21-7 season.

Despite Santa Clara's disappointing 1994-95 finish, the prelude to the following season was one of anticipation not seen on the Mission Campus in a quarter-century. Home attendance had spiked from an average of 2,992 in 1993-94 to 3,466 in 1994-95, and it reached a school-record 4,141 in 1995-96.

The regular starting lineup – Nash, Garnett, Sedlock, Dunne and Graves – returned intact as the 1995-96 season started, and top reserves Drew Zurek, Phil Von Buchwaldt, and Lloyd Pierce were back. Nash, who was the WCC Player of the Year for 1994-95 and would repeat as a senior, was being touted as a possible All-America (he was honorable mention on AP's postseason All-America team) and a likely high NBA draft pick. Graves was a third-team Academic All-America that season. Garnett had been a first-team all-conference selection along with Nash in 1994-95, and Dunne was named honorable mention All-WCC.

It was a mature team, and paradoxically, one way it showed its maturity was by scoring less.

Davey usually imposed minimal offensive restraints on his team during the Nash years, and that didn't change appreciably in 1995-96. But the Broncos, primarily by dint of their experience, were not as headlong on offense as they had been the previous two seasons. They attempted fewer 3-pointers, nurtured the shot clock more readily, and adjusted calmly when opponents tried to envelop Nash, as occurred frequently.

Nash's scoring average went down, from 20.9 points per game in 1994-95 to 17.0 his senior year, and he made "only" 74 3-pointers, 10 fewer than the year before even though Santa Clara played one more game. His assist total, 174, was the same; only his free-throw percentage went up, to a school-record .894.

"Not to belittle our players," Davey said at the time, "but we don't have the cast of characters that would make him look as good as he is."

"It's true," Sedlock said. "There are times when he'll make a great drive and dish and we'll fumble it away."

Garnett's scoring average also declined, from 13.6 to 12.8, although he led the league in 3-point percentage with .418. Dunne and Sedlock also scored and rebounded less, although Graves' averages went from 7.8 ppg and 5.6 rpg to 9.5 and 7.2 as Santa Clara emphasized its postup game more and thereby enhanced its offensive versatility. Santa Clara also was an improved defensive team in 1995-96, partly because it melted the shot clock enough to reduce the stress on the Broncos on the defensive end.

Santa Clara went from a 76.4-point per game scoring average in 1994-95 to 70.1 the following season, with only five 80-plus outings compared to 13 in 1994-95. At the same time, the Broncos' defensive points-against average dipped from 68.5 to 65.8, and they held eight opponents to 60 points or fewer, compared to four the previous season.

Despite Santa Clara's experience, though, the Broncos' 1995-96 schedule made matching or surpassing the previous season's 21-win total was far from a given. The Broncos began the season with a trip to Hawaii for the Maui Classic, usually one of the top preseason tournaments, and their first-round assignment was against defending national champion UCLA.

The Bruins, directed by former Pepperdine coach (and Santa Clara nemesis) Jim Harrick, had lost Ed O'Bannon and Tyus Edney, the two centerpieces of their 1995 NCAA title team. But they still had three All Pac-10 and future NBA players – guard Toby Bailey and forwards J.R. Henderson and Charles O'Bannon. Center Jelani McCoy, who spent six years in the NBA, was a freshman on that team, and Cameron Dollar was one of the West Coast's better defensive guards and figured to represent a substantial challenge for Nash.

But Santa Clara historically has played relatively well against UCLA, considering the programs' comparative resources, going 13-26 (as of 2007) against the Bruins and dominating the early years of a rivalry that dates to 1921. Santa Clara had beaten one of John Wooden's early teams in a West Regional game in 1952 on the Broncos' way to the Final Four, and although the Broncos had no more success than anyone else against Wooden during his run of 10 NCAA titles in 12 years, they fared better after Wooden departed in 1975. Santa Clara had won 68-60 at Pauley Pavilion to begin the 1984-85 season and the teams also had played three times in the early 1990s, all at Pauley. UCLA won all three games, but by only four, 14 and nine points.

Davey and his assistants prepared for the game as if it were their last of the season instead of their first.

"My kids had geared for that game six months prior to the game," Davey said. "They were really devoted and dedicated and knew they were going to be playing UCLA. It created a real focus in how you practice and how you're preparing."

UCLA was ranked fourth in the AP poll entering the 1995-96 season, but Santa Clara, for the first time since before Pauley Pavilion opened in 1965, had what amounted to a home-court advantage against the Bruins. Santa Clara, unlike UCLA, was used to playing in tiny WCC-type gyms, with the front row of the stands literally within arms length of the sidelines and the walls within a couple of body lengths of the baselines, and the Maui Classic is at the 2,400-seat Lahaina Civic Center.

As had been the case when they beat Arizona in Salt Lake City in 1993, the Broncos quickly won over the neutrals in the crowd, and posted a nationally-televised 78-69 upset that vaulted them into the also-receiving-votes category in the AP poll.

The Broncos, who hadn't beaten a team ranked as high as UCLA since they defeated No. 2 Providence in 1972, scored 11 straight points to break a 47-47 tie in the second half. Garnett scored 21 points, Nash 19.

"While half of the nation's college basketball fans were sleeping (because the game started after midnight on the East Coast)," wrote John Akers of the *San Jose Mercury News*, "Santa Clara pulled off a shocker that eventually will have the country rubbing its eyes."

Santa Clara lost 77-65 to third-ranked Villanova the next night in a game the Broncos trailed by only five points with 3:40 remaining, but defeated Michigan State 77-71 in the third-place game. Wins over Oregon State at Portland's Rose Garden and a 79-51 blowout of San Jose State at San Jose Arena followed, and when the AP poll for Dec. 4 came out, Santa Clara was No. 25 – the first time since 1972 that Santa Clara had been ranked.

Wins over Southern and Fresno State moved the Broncos up to 22nd the following week, but a 78-49 pasting against Marquette in Milwaukee dropped Santa Clara out of the rankings. The Broncos never resurfaced in the Top 25 (and as of the end of the 2006-07 season, hadn't done so since), but they salvaged a split of the Midwest road trip with an 80-78 win at Illinois State, which finished 22-12 and reached the quarterfinals of the NIT.

In their final non-conference game, against Georgia Tech in the consolation game of the Cable Car Classic at the San Jose Arena, Nash played on even terms with Yellow Jackets point-guard star Stephon Marbury – thereby considerably enhancing his NBA draft status – as the Broncos prevailed 71-66 to finish 9-3 against perhaps the toughest non-conference schedule Santa Clara had ever played.

"Jesus, we had a hell of a schedule that year," Davey said.

Indeed. Santa Clara's 12 non-conference opponents that season finished with a combined record of 224-147 (for a winning percentage of .604) and if one subtracts Oregon State's 4-23 record, the numbers become 220-124 and .640. Six of the 12 teams – UCLA, Villanova, San Jose State, Marquette, Penn State, and Georgia Tech – qualified for the NCAA tournament. Three others – Michigan State, Illinois State and Fresno State – were invited to the NIT.

Santa Clara finished in a 10-4 tie with Gonzaga for the WCC regular-season championship, and got the No. 1 seed in the WCC tournament by virtue of a tiebreaker. As in 1995, the Broncos' strength of schedule already had all but assured them an NCAA tournament berth, and for the second straight year, the Broncos would be playing the eighth and lowest seed on their home court in the first round of the tournament. This time, they would face Pepperdine, which was so decimated by injuries, ineligibility and defections that the Waves suited up only eight players for the Santa Clara game. They were only 9-17 overall and 2-12 in the WCC, and had lost eight straight, the final seven by double-digit margins.

It didn't matter, because Santa Clara was beaten in the first round for the third straight year, losing 63-60.

(Portland went on to beat Gonzaga for the title, giving the Pilots their first and only NCAA tournament trip since 1959.)

"Not really," Davey said when asked if a common denominator existed in Santa Clara's first-round WCC tournament exits during that period. "I wish I could put something on it and tell you why, but I think sometimes teams bring out bad things in other teams, especially after you've been successful in league play.

"I never thought we were a super-dominating team, just a nice solid team that was capable of getting beat by anybody but also was capable of beating anybody. We were that kind of team. We were not so strong that we weren't capable of being defeated. But it was discouraging because you think you have a great chance (to make a deep postseason run) and then you have to sit there and fret for a week about whether you get in (the NCAA tournament). And I was pretty much negative about that. It's as if you don't deserve it because you didn't get it done (in the WCC tournament).

"Fortunately, I was wrong."

As in 1995, the 1996 NCAA tournament committee wrote off the WCC tournament loss and granted Santa Clara its third invitation to "The Dance" in four years.

This time, owing to the minefield that was its non-league schedule, Santa Clara not only got into the NCAA tournament relatively easily, but got a better seed than in 1993 or 1995 – 10th – and was matched with seventh-seeded Maryland.

It was as favorable a matchup as Santa Clara could have sought.

As in 1993, the Broncos were ticketed for a relatively adjacent site – Tempe, Ariz. – and actually were favored by many oddsmakers despite the Terrapins' higher seeding. Maryland's RPI was 30 going into the game, while Santa Clara's was 31. Maryland had lost 73-63 to the same UCLA team Santa Clara had beaten, had lost two of its three Atlantic Coast Conference games against Georgia Tech (another Santa Clara victim), and had a less-than-intimidating 17-11 overall record.

The Terrapins also had created distractions for themselves earlier in the season, when it was revealed that guard Duane Simpkins had needed a loan from a former coach to pay off $8,242 worth of campus parking tickets. The NCAA suspended Simpkins for three games for accepting a loan from Donnie Gross, a former AAU coach, although Simpkins was back for the postseason.

Steve Nash, playing in his second-to-last game at Santa Clara, scored a season high 28 points and dished out 12 assists as the Broncos beat Maryland 91-79. The Broncos broke open a 43-43 game with a 22-6 run in the second half. Nash alone drew 10 fouls against Maryland with his penetration, and his dribbling and passing skills helped Santa Clara break Maryland's full-court press. Santa Clara made 34 of 41 free throws; Maryland only 10 of 22.

"He broke through Maryland's trapping defense," wrote Joan Ryan of the *San Francisco Chronicle*. "Maryland knew if the Terps shut down Nash, they would shut down Santa Clara. But they couldn't do it. Nash lobbed balls downcourt, over the heads of the Maryland players. He spun away from defenders, controlling the ball as only a gym rat can."

"They were a vicious pressing team," Davey said. "I don't know how many turnovers we had, but we handled their press reasonably well."

Brendan Graves, responding to a pregame discussion with the coaches about his need to assert himself, scored 12 points – including three crowd-inciting dunks – and contributed eight rebounds and four blocked shots. Dunne had 14 points, a season high, and his nine-rebound total was one short of his season best. Garnett had 18 points, and Zurek had 11.

"They shot it better from the perimeter than we thought they would," Maryland coach Gary Williams said, "and they were strong inside. We saw guys make shots who we didn't think could make them."

Next was No. 2-seeded Kansas, which Santa Clara had challenged the previous year in Lawrence before losing 80-75. That factor, along with the fact Santa Clara had just played its best game since the Maui Classic, prompted many to suppose that the Broncos had another Arizona-circa-1993 upset in them.

The reality was that the Broncos didn't have much of anything left. Kansas scored the first 12 points of the game, led 48-22 at halftime, and won 76-51. Santa Clara's five starters made only 9 of their 42 shots, and Nash, who had aggravated a lingering hamstring injury in the Maryland game, was only 1 for 11 and finished with just seven points.

With the score 69-43 and 4:36 remaining in the game, Davey removed Nash, who received a standing ovation from the 500 or so Santa Clara fans who had made the trek to Tempe. The team received a similar ovation at game's end.

"I knew he didn't want to come out," Davey said after the game. "He's so competitive, but he was hurting, and I know he has a future career in this sport."

"Everyone started to cry in the locker room," Nash said. "So I started telling jokes to change the mood. I talked about what it was like to meet everybody for the first time and what we thought of each other. I think it's more important to laugh than to cry."

"It was a very hard thing for me to talk to the team after the game," Davey said. "Those seniors have been the cornerstone of my four years as head coach. I've been on the coattails of these guys."

Chapter 14
INTERREGNUM

After four years as a head coach, Dick Davey had a 73-32 career record and had brought Santa Clara three NCAA tournament appearances – two more than the program had earned in the 23 years before he became head coach – and NCAA tournament victories over two programs (Arizona and Maryland) that would go on to win national championships in the next decade.

The Broncos during those four years had beaten the fourth- , sixth- and 13th-ranked teams in the country. The Phoenix Suns had made Steve Nash the No. 15 pick in the 1993 NBA draft, and Marlon Garnett, a senior in 1996-97, also was on his way to the NBA, albeit briefly. (He played 24 games for the Boston Celtics in 1998-99, and as of 2007 was still playing professionally in Europe.) Davey was mentioned prominently as a candidate for several higher-profile jobs, although he never interviewed for another position.

Perhaps those on the periphery of the program thought that Santa Clara was about to become what Gonzaga eventually *did* become – the pre-eminent "mid-major" on the West Coast and a fixture on national and regional television. Davey, however, knew better, even though he never stopped believing the achievements of the Nash years could be duplicated, and even though Santa Clara never lost more than 16 games in any of his 15 seasons as head coach.

"I didn't have an abundance of confidence we'd do it on an every-year basis (after 1996)," Davey said. "We'd lost a guy (Nash) who was tremendously critical to any success we'd had, and what happened was we didn't quite get the caliber of guy we'd gotten before. We were never flat-out horrible, but maybe we digressed a bit in our recruiting, and we always had a pretty tough schedule. We settled on guys instead of waiting and making decisions on possible other guys. We ran into a little bit of a buzzsaw that way. It wasn't that we weren't getting athletes, but we weren't getting quite the level of player we had been getting."

Despite the loss of Nash and the other core seniors from the 1995-96 team, the Broncos didn't retrograde precipitously the following year. Marlon Garnett, asked to fully shoulder the scoring load that he and Nash had shared, responded by earning WCC Player of the Year honors, averaging 17.4 points per game, and freshman point guard Brian Jones proved a more-than-adequate replacement for Nash, scoring at a 13.9 clip.

Garnett, in fact, was even more skilled than Nash as a pure shooter, in Davey's estimation, and in many ways was like an earlier favorite of Davey's, Harold Keeling.

"One of the nicest, politest kids I've ever been around," Davey said. "Just a very solid human being. I can say that about most of our kids, but Marlon was very special in that regard. From my perspective, and I'm not trying to short-change anyone, he was the best shooter I've ever seen in our program. He had the best technique, the best stroke, the best concentration, and he had those at an early stage. A lot of times, guys acquire that as they get older, but at 19, Marlon was a shooter, and he's still a shooter. When he got set up and he had time, there was a pretty good chance it was gonna get in.

"When he was playing for the Celtics, the word was that (then-Boston coach Rick) Pitino would take him to shooting clinics just so guys could watch him stroke the ball."

During the one season that Garnett and Jones played together, they provided the same type of torrent-and-stream synergism that had characterized Keeling and Steve Kenilvort during the years they constituted Santa Clara's starting backcourt tandem.

"Brian was a tough, tough, tough kid … one of the most determined kids I've ever been around," Davey said. "He would *fight* you to win; it was important for him to be successful. He was an average to below-average shooter, but as a competitor, most coaches I've been associated with at Santa Clara (after Kenilvort graduated) would tell you he's the most competitive player we've had."

That determination enabled Jones to resurrect his career after an injury suffered during the summer of 1998 almost ended it.

During a summer-league game, Jones was knocked to the floor by Adonal Foyle, then a rookie with the Golden

State Warriors, and injured his right knee so badly that doctors at first feared he might never play again. His anterior cruciate ligament was snapped, and his kneecap was shattered.

"He worked so hard with Mike Cembellin (Santa Clara trainer) ... his rehab was quite an ordeal," Davey said. "He had a cast on his leg for something like four months, and having a cast on your leg, it (atrophies) a little. We never knew if we would have him back. That summer he got hurt, we went 0-6 on a European tour, and that showed we were a little different team without him."

Jones redshirted during the 1998-99 season, and the Broncos slipped from 18-10 to 14-15. The following year, though, Jones was close to full strength and averaged 13.3 points – down from his 15.6 average as a sophomore, but central to Santa Clara's 19-12 season in 1999-2000. As a senior, he was back up to 16 points a game, and Santa Clara went 20-11 before losing to Gonzaga in the WCC tournament championship game.

Like Garnett, Jones was still playing in Europe during the 2006-07 season, helping a German team that had been a lower-division squad several years before to the top of the upper-division tables.

Back in 1996-97, in his third college game, Jones had set a school freshman scoring record with 34 points, including 21 in the last 12:58 of the game, as the Broncos affirmed their growing national reputation as ambush specialists. They rallied from a 19-point deficit for a 79-72 home win over a Marquette team that had been in the national Top 25 the previous week. In the Cable Car Classic at San Jose Arena, Davey's team brought him his fourth victory in four-plus seasons over a ranked opponent, toppling No. 19 Alabama 77-62 as junior guard Craig Johnson came off the bench to score a career-high 16 points and Drew Zurek, usually a complementary player during the Nash years, added 14. Santa Clara also lost with distinction to 12th-ranked Indiana, 86-74, at the Hoosiers' tournament.

Santa Clara finished the regular season 16-10, tied for the regular-season WCC title with St. Mary's at 10-4 and got the No. 1 seed in the WCC tournament at Loyola Marymount. But for the fourth straight year – and for the third time in a row against a No. 8 seed – the Broncos made a first-round exit, losing 70-61 to Loyola Marymount.

The Broncos improved to 18-10 the following season as Jones and Johnson averaged 15.6 and 12.6 points respectively, and Lloyd Pierce weighed in at 11.2 as a senior. Pierce, a graduate of San Jose's Yerba Buena High who later became an assistant coach under Davey, underwent a personal transformation that in Davey's mind rivaled that of Nick Vanos more than a decade earlier.

"The early Lloyd did not talk, basically," Davey said. "I'll never forget going to his home and spending the first half talking to him and the second half talking to his mom, because he did not respond. He would never say anything back then; he just played. He was a great defender, and probably the best athlete I've ever coached. He was three steps above. He wasn't a great shooter, but he could score, and he just developed a personality over the four years ... or if he had it before, he hid it real well.

"At our (postseason) banquet his senior year, he spoke for an hour and five minutes. There were 150 people there and he had a lot of them crying ... he went on and on about his feelings about Santa Clara and his teammates and the whole thing. It was a tremendous tribute to him ... the change that had taken place."

The Lloyd Pierce of 2007 somewhat resembled NBA great Gary Payton in appearance, and he exuded a Paytonesque ebullience both on and off the court. By that time, he had graduated from Santa Clara with a degree in business administration, played professionally for four years in Mexico, Australia and Germany, and had worked under Davey as an assistant coach for the latter's final four years at Santa Clara. He also worked for a San Jose-area financial-services firm, and as a special education teacher at Pinnacle Academy in Santa Clara.

"Lloyd Pierce will be a tremendous (head) coach for somebody," Davey said.

Santa Clara, hosting the 1998 WCC tournament and going in with the No. 3 seed, finally ended its four-year litany of first-round failure by beating Portland 74-53. But the tournament's home-court jinx prevailed the following night, as the Broncos lost 85-83 to eventual champion San Francisco. Gonzaga won the regular-season title that year, and although the Bulldogs lost to USF in the tournament finals and had to settle for an NIT bid, the WCC was about to experience a level of domination approximated only by USF in the years before the Dons' program was shut down after the 1981-82 season.

Even USF's longest period of invincibility – in 1977-81, when it won or shared five straight conference titles – paled in comparison to Gonzaga's run of nine straight NCAA appearances and eight regular-season and eight WCC tournament titles starting in 1999. After winning the 1998-99 WCC regular-season and tournament titles under Dan Monson (son of Don), who left after that season to go to the University of Minnesota, the Zags stunned Minnesota, Stanford and Florida in the NCAA tournament before losing 67-62 to Connecticut in a game for the right to go to the Final Four.

Santa Clara, meanwhile, never saw the postseason again under Davey, and the Zags thwarted the Broncos under the most agonizing of circumstances three times in WCC tournament games – 80-77 in 2001, 63-62 in 2004, and 77-68 in Spokane in Davey's final game as Santa Clara coach a month after the Broncos had ended Gonzaga's 50-game home winning streak (and their own 13-game losing streak against the Zags).

After the Broncos' 20-12 showing in 2000-01, they languished in the middle of the WCC pack for the next five years. Although they never lost more than 16 games in a season during that span, they never won more than

16, and they chinned the .500 bar only once (16-16 in 2003-04). They went 0-11 against Gonzaga, and never finished higher than third in the WCC. Perhaps most galling, they were eliminated by archrival St. Mary's in four of the five WCC tournaments during that period, and alumni frustration and community ennui began to seep into the equation. From a high of 4,141 paying spectators per year during Steve Nash's senior year in 1995-96, attendance plummeted steadily, reaching a nadir of 1,376 in 2002-03. (The crowd-count average rebounded to 2,659 two years later, but even that total was below the norm that had existed through the 1980s and well into the 1990s, and Santa Clara's athletic cash-flow problem by the turn of the century had been exacerbated by the costs of the still-unfinished Toso Pavilion/Leavey Center renovation.)

The one constant for Santa Clara during the 2001-06 period was a succession of injuries that for five seasons made it next to impossible for Davey to cobble together three successive months of excellence. While he never offered the Broncos' chronic manpower shortage as an excuse, some believe Santa Clara would have challenged Gonzaga to a greater extent than it did had the injury factor not intervened almost continuously.

Kyle Bailey, the Broncos' leading scorer in 2001-02, missed virtually the entire 2002-03 season with a knee injury. Highly-regarded recruits like Jordan Legge, J.R. Patrick, Brandon Rohe, Bakari Altheimer, Scott Borchart and Tristan Parham seldom were able to take the floor completely healthy, and Sean Denison and

Scott Dougherty were sidetracked by injuries before finally emerging as standouts late in their careers.

The Santa Clara pendulum swung most crazily in 2004-05, when Santa Clara defeated North Carolina, the eventual national champion and the fourth-ranked team in the country at the time, 77-66 during the Pete Newell Classic at The Arena in Oakland as Travis Niesen – another player who had to fight through a series of physical maladies throughout his stay at Santa Clara – scored 26 points.

The Tar Heels, who lost only three other games that season (in the ACC to Wake Forest, Duke and Georgia Tech), were on their way to Hawaii for the Maui Classic, and were playing their first game while Santa Clara was playing its fourth, including a 34-point blowout loss at New Mexico. Carolina was without starting point guard Raymond Felton, who was sitting out a one-game suspension for playing in a summer league that wasn't certified by the NCAA.

"They whacked us," North Carolina coach Roy Williams said in 2007. "We didn't have Felton, but for our season opener, I thought our team would be so fired up it would be unbelievable. But I told him after the game that he did a better coaching job than I did, and I meant it.

"You can see how well prepared the other team is when you change defensive looks. We use a lot of different defenses, and everything – *everything* – we tried, they were prepared for. To me the basic premise of coaching is to play within your limitations and have an understanding of what you can and can't do, and I've never seen Dick's teams beat themselves by going crazy on offense and taking bad shots. Santa Clara played within its limitations that night, and that was a huge, huge factor."

Williams, in fact, said the jolt that Santa Clara inflicted upon his team that night was central to the Tar Heels' subsequent drive to the national championship.

"We were extremely talented that year," he said, "but all year (after the Santa Clara loss) we heard that even though we had all that talent, we weren't much of a team, which was nonsense. You don't win 13 of your last 14 games (including six NCAA tournament wins) unless you're a big-time team, and I believe the Santa Clara game was a big eye-opener for us."

For Santa Clara, the victory seemed to be a portent of a breakthrough season – until four days later, when the Broncos lost 71-65 to Pacific. And the North Carolina win, unlike the Broncos' previous *tour de force* victories under Davey, was almost completely forgotten within a month, after they were embarrassed at home by Central Connecticut State and Yale.

After that, Santa Clara recovered its equilibrium for a time. St. Mary's brought a nine-game winning streak – including a victory over Gonzaga – and a 15-4 record into a game against Santa Clara in Moraga. Stan Morrison, who was the color commentator on the Fox Sports Bay Area telecast, remembers that game well.

"Dick had the team dress at Santa Clara and get on the bus for the drive to St. Mary's, a drive of around an hour," Morrison said. "They only did the formal pre-game warmup. No casual shooting earlier. I had seen the St. Mary's shootaround that morning and they thoroughly reviewed the offense of Santa Clara. They had a great game plan and appeared to be loose and ready. When the Broncos hit the court, they were anything but loose. Not a single kid smiled. They were eyes straight ahead and completely into whatever was said in the locker room.

"The Broncos jumped on the Gaels right from the opening tip. It was a brutally physical and emotional game in front of a frenzied full house in Moraga. Standing room only. Players diving unhesitatingly for anything resembling a loose ball. Santa Clara deservedly won rather handily (65-42). I was stunned and so was St. Mary's.

"When the final buzzer sounded, not a single player or coach from Santa Clara smiled or celebrated. I watched them go through the obligatory handshakes directly in front of my courtside seat as we did the wrapup for the game. I know what I saw. Absolutely no smiles. As is my custom, after we got everything finished, I went to the locker rooms to say hello to the coaches. Santa Clara was gone! They had moved directly to their locker room, gathered everything, got on the bus and went directly back to campus without showering.

"They had come to Moraga for business, conducted business, and returned directly home! They played Santa Clara basketball the way their coach expected them to every night out. They were not very talented or big. But, they knew how to play and they did it to the absolute best of their ability that afternoon. I won't forget it."

But as was the case often during the latter part of Davey's tenure, the Broncos were unable to build on that victory. After a four-game winning streak, the Broncos lost seven of their last 11, finished 15-16, and were knocked out of the WCC tournament by St. Mary's, which qualified along with Gonzaga for the NCAA Field of 65.

In addition to the on-court uncertainties, Davey's personal life, which had been so well ordered for six decades became a virtual continuum of anxiety.

Carroll Williams had retired as athletic director in 2000. Former Stanford assistant AD Cheryl Levick was named to succeed him, and the athletic department was the scene of constant turmoil during her four-year reign. Many of the coaches hired by Williams or O'Connor were fired; those who survived, including Davey, no longer worked with the assurance that they had the backing of their boss. The Broncos also lost Todd Wuschnig, a three-year starter at power forward, just before the 2000 WCC tournament when it was discovered that he had a heart condition.

Then, in early 2003, Jeanne Davey was diagnosed with breast cancer, and Kathleen Davey's catastrophe followed a year later. Dick Davey acknowledged at the time that he was coaching with his mind largely on the crises within his family, and some were surprised when new athletic director Dan Coonan tendered Davey a two-year contract extension in March 2005 – and, for that matter, that Davey accepted it.

After his retirement, Davey acknowledged that he gave serious consideration to stepping down before he signed the contract extension. He stayed, he says, because his players were no less important in his life, and he in theirs, than they had been during the years when 20 victories and post-season berths were the expectation rather than the aberration.

"I think what I tried to do, and I'm not saying it was right or wrong ... when they're there, I try to appreciate all of them," Davey said. "I wanted to make sure they understood they have responsibilities. I'm one of the coaches and they're players, but once they graduate, you take on an entirely different role.

"You have to be a little concerned about not showing favoritism. Brody Angley (a junior in 2006-07) is one of the finest human beings I've ever coached, but he's one of 15 players and he has to be handled kind of equally. But now that I'm gone, we'll have special feelings for each other, hopefully. (On Father's Day 2007) he called me, and this is the kind of kid he is, to wish me a happy Father's Day after just losing his dad. He's that considerate of people. And maybe it's because we didn't do a great job of recruiting (raw-talent players), but the blueprint of the kind of kids we've had is that they're tough-minded and play hard."

Some of the players from the final years of his career whose names evoke fond memories for Davey include center Alex

Lopez, whose younger twin brothers Robin and Brook later became stars at Stanford; Nathan Fast, a Marlon Garnettesque guard who in 1995 became the first player Davey had signed without having seen play in person; Jamie Holmes, who later played several years in Australia, was a non-paid assistant in Davey's final season, and subsequently went to UOP as a full-time assistant; and Brian Vaka, who had been virtually unknown as a high school player in Reno, but had a good career at Santa Clara after Davey signed him out of a summer league in Phoenix.

Vaka, who was short on elegance but was the equivalent of a hockey wing whose job it is to excavate the puck from the corners and relay it to the sleeker centers, later became one of many Santa Clara players to invite Dick and Jeanne Davey to his wedding. Vaka is of Tongan descent, and in keeping with that culture's traditions, he presented the Daveys with a huge quilt prepared by his relatives – an honor bestowed upon only the loftiest of mentors in a groom's life.

"Jim Howell came out of Oregon … he was about 6-8, an undersized post guy. Travis Niesen (from 2002-06) was a three-year starter whom everybody in the league thought the world of. He could score with his left hand over his right shoulder, and he never gave an inch. We had two guys, Brad and Cord Anderson (from 1999-2003), whose grandfather ran twice for governor of Hawaii. Classy kids … one of them (Brad) won the state 100-yard dash as a senior, *and* the shotput in the same meet. That's a pretty unique combination. Kyle Bailey was a guy out of Alaska who was an all-league player and is playing in

Germany. Doron Perkins, who next to Lloyd Pierce was probably the best (pure athlete) I ever coached, is over there also. (Former Santa Clara great) Ralph Ogden lives in Germany, and before our alumni game (in January 2007) he called me to tell me he was coming but that he could have an alumni game over there in Germany with Doron, Kyle, Marlon and Brian Jones."

Before the 2006-07 season, Davey thought that if this was to be his last season – he was in the last year of his contract, and he and Coonan had agreed to put off any decision about his future until March – it had the potential to be one of his better ones. The Broncos had lost their 2005-06 scoring leader, Travis Niesen, but the other four starters – sophomore forward Mitch Henke, senior center Sean Denison, freshman guard Calvin Anderson, and junior guard Brody Angley – all were back, and Scott Dougherty was ready to step into the other slot. Six seniors figured prominently in his projected rotation, and Davey felt the younger players who had joined the program during the previous two seasons would be able to contribute significantly right away. The Broncos lacked overall quickness, but their two massive centers, 6-10, 305-pound junior John Bryant and 7-foot, 275-pound Josh Higgins, had the potential to transform the area under both baskets into a no-fly zone. Danny Pariseau, who had started for three years at Eastern Washington, transferred in for his last college season with the avowed purpose of playing on a team that would knock off Gonzaga.

That, indeed, transpired. Among many other things.

Chapter 15
THE FINAL SEASON

If there's a lesson embattled college coaches can learn from what happened to Dick Davey during his final season at Santa Clara, it's this: Don't schedule a 2 p.m. game when a big-money alumni function is set for that night and people who have the power and desire to get you fired will be there and have a chance to collaborate.

The Broncos were 14-6 overall and 4-1 in league and were coming off back-to-back road wins at St. Mary's and USF when they took on Loyola Marymount – which was winless in WCC play – on the afternoon of January 27 at Leavey Center. Santa Clara lost 74-71. That night, the so-called "Golden Circle Theatre Party," organized annually by the university's Board of Fellows, was held. The Beach Boys provided the entertainment, and more than 2,300 attended, compared to the announced basketball attendance of 2,278. University president Paul Locatelli, Gary Filizetti and John Sobrato all were in attendance, according to several others who were present.

San Jose Mercury News columnist Mark Purdy is convinced that these boosters confronted Locatelli at that party, with the specific objective of convincing him to get rid of Dick Davey.

"Santa Clara has always had this unbroken line of coaches," Purdy said, "so when we'd picked up about three years before that there were rumblings about people not being really happy with the way things were going, we asked around, and (the answer we got was that) 'Nah, Santa Clara doesn't fire coaches.' I think (*Mercury News* college basketball writer) Jon Wilner had picked up early in the (2006-07) season that this may be Dick's last season. When Coonan came in (as athletic director in 2004) I think Dan felt some pressure from some of those (forceful alumni), but Dan isn't an idiot, and he picked up that Dick was also a very beloved guy and ended up extending his contract (through the (2006-07 season). He didn't have to do that, but he picked up the vibes and (decided to take) more time to assess this.

"As this season started, Dan and Dick had kind of left it at 'we'll assess this at the end of the year.' The season was going pretty well, but then it hit that (Loyola Marymount) bump. It just so happened that that was an afternoon game instead of a night game, and I suppose a lot of those guys (boosters) were at the game in the afternoon and then went to the fundraiser that night. Locatelli was there, and the stew just bubbled … it's all speculation, but enough people have told me, and not just Dick's friends either, that's what they believe happened.

"I was at the Super Bowl (that week), and I got a call from somebody very close to Dick who said, 'You won't believe this, but they fired Dick today.' I called Coonan from Miami, and to his credit he called me back … he said, 'No, no, here's what happened,' and he told me as much as he could. My understanding of what happened was that the school president calls the athletic director and says, 'You've got to tell Dick he's got to quit at the end of the season, and you've got to do it (announce the retirement) *now.*'"

In Purdy's mind, Coonan was not the villain of the piece, but merely a vehicle thereof.

"Look at Coonan's position," he said. "He's only been there two or three years, he's got a family ... his alternative if he really disagrees is to quit, which would have been a ballsy move, but he doesn't want to do that. The goofy thing is if they'd gotten to the end of the year, Dan and Dick might have sat down and reached a well-maybe-it's time (agreement). Dick is Dick ... he's the most honest coach I know. I remember one time I ran into him at the airport and I told him, 'Dick, I'm really sorry I haven't been able to come see your team this year.' He said, 'Christ, you don't want to see us right now. We're (awful).' What other coach would be that honest?

"If they'd just let it play out, I think everything would have turned out just fine. The really disappointing thing when all this broke was the way (Locatelli) reacted. I don't know if he thought nobody was going to find out about this, or what. Dick has friends everywhere, and of course they'll call us and tell us what happened. Dick doesn't have to say anything.

"Now the story breaks. I got the call (regarding Davey's removal) from a source, and I told (his editors), 'I can write this from here (Miami) if you want, but it's probably better to hand this off to Wilner.' So Wilner ended up doing most of those stories. But the fact the president just runs away from any kind of explanation … they put out this release saying Dick has decided to retire, but we know for a fact Dick had told his players that there was no way he'd quit on them, that it's going to come out this way but this is not what happened. For the school president to keep saying this is Dick's decision …

"I called and e-mailed Locatelli's office multiple times. I'd had (previous) interaction with the guy … the day they honored Steve Nash (when he spoke at Santa Clara's 2006 convocation ceremony), Father Locatelli and I had a very nice conversation. His PR woman contacted me (after the Davey story broke) and said he (Locatelli) doesn't want to say anything about this, and I said, 'Just so you know, this is what I'm going to write' and (he would also write that) Locatelli had no comment. So she said, 'Please write his 'no comment' in this fashion,' and I said, 'With all due respect, here's how I'm gonna write it, and if he has any objection, he should feel free to call.'

"As fate would have it, Father Locatelli sits down annually with the staff at the Santa Clara student newspaper, and a couple of the kids on the staff were in my (journalism) class (that he taught at Santa Clara) last spring. So I get communication from them saying (Locatelli said) 'Mark Purdy never talked to me' when I had spent all this time trying to get comments from him. That was really disappointing, and it's not true … I tried like crazy to talk to him, and he chose not to, which is his prerogative.

That's when he told them that the reason he wanted Dick to do this (at midseason) was so they could honor him at one of the last few games.

"I was at the last home game, against San Diego (before a sellout crowd that honored Davey with a series of standing ovations), when coaches (on both staffs) came out in argyle sweaters (one of Davey's trademarks). *Locatelli isn't at the game.* Vic Couch flies in from Minnesota; all these other people were there. They had a thing on campus later and Father Locatelli made a speech, but I think Dick just gritted his teeth and smiled through the whole business. Supposedly Dick says, when he and Father Locatelli finally sit down, 'There's one thing I don't understand. Why do you fire somebody and then honor them?'"

Stan Morrison watched with interest, and disgust, as the Davey imbroglio unfolded ... and as usually is the case with Morrison, one of college athletics' most outspoken individuals, he had a strong opinion on what happened and why it happened.

"Dick did not want the spotlight," Morrison said. "He wanted to coach. He did not do anything to bring attention to himself. He simply did his job. He was great with the alumni. Apparently, he wasn't involved with the right alumni. It is a problem when a coach won't kiss the butt of the more affluent alumni. The administration hears about it and they translate that through a prism that has watched (ESPN) SportsCenter and seen the more flamboyant coaches doing any and everything to get in front of a camera.

"Dick Davey was cut from a different cloth. He wanted to be in front of his team. He wanted to be in front of the marking board in the locker room doing Xs and Os. He wasn't a white-wine guy at the local bistro. He is a beer and pizza guy with his assistant coaches and friends drawing plays on napkins after studying film. He was not at Santa Clara because he could play the tuba in the marching band. He was there because he was a great teacher and he had the capacity to get his students to listen to his words in their classroom – the gymnasium. He never polished his academic halo.

"He was the finest professor at Santa Clara University. He didn't use 20-year-old notes for lectures. He had practice plans that were carefully crafted and reflected cutting-edge thinking in a game that has captured the country and continues to grow internationally. Unlike other professors who deal with their students on an intellectual level, he was the one professor on campus who dealt with his students on intellectual, physical and emotional levels.

"Only dance and music, to some degree, reach young people as thoroughly as Professor Dick Davey. And, while other institutional mentors may continue their relationships with their students, the depth of their relationships will never come close to the depth of love generated decades later by the young men who came to play, compete and truly know their mentor, Dick Davey."

A Santa Clara insider said Coonan told him he discharged Davey with considerable reluctance and with an apparent understanding that a firestorm would follow.

"I try to do three things – one, please my bosses; two, provide the best possible experience for Santa Clara student-athletes so that they leave here thinking it was a really good decision to come here; and three, try to provide my coaches with all the tools necessary to fulfill the second (objective) and, within our parameters, support them as much as I can," the insider said Coonan told him immediately after Davey was informed that the 2006-07 season would be his last. "Today, I can only do one of those three things."

Amid all the turmoil, Davey insisted that the remainder of his last season remain a commitment to his current team, just as his previous 39 seasons in the business had been.

He wouldn't let his players immerse themselves in the tumult that accompanied his removal. He sought no personal martyrdom, and except when asked directly by reporters, he kept his differences with his bosses within his inner circle. For the greater good, he accepted what so many people found unacceptable because he knew it was unchangeable. In his mind, 30 satisfying years at Santa Clara couldn't and shouldn't be obscured by the events of the final month. Even before he accepted a fund-raising position offered by the university after the end of his final season, the school he had served so loyally and so well for 30 years remained "us" in his mind and speech – never "them."

While the maelstrom was raging around Davey, Locatelli and Coonan, the Santa Clara players used a succession of wooden canvases to paint, for all to see, their portrait of their head coach.

After the news of Davey's "retirement" became public, the Broncos went on a six-game winning streak (counting the Pepperdine victory the day before Davey's departure was announced) that made them a national-interest story for the first time since the Nash years. The denouement was a nationally-televised 84-73 victory over Gonzaga in Spokane that ended the Bulldogs' 50-game home-court winning streak, the longest in the nation at the time.

In Davey's final home game, the Broncos defeated San Diego 80-72 before an overflow crowd of 5,000 at Leavey Center. The fans gave Davey a minute-long standing ovation when he was introduced before the game, and highlights of his career flashed on the scoreboard throughout the evening. San Diego coach Brad Holland, who himself would be fired at the end of the season, and his assistants wore argyle sweaters to honor Davey, and spectators repeatedly chanted "Thank you, Davey."

The victory kept Santa Clara in first place in the WCC, one game ahead of Gonzaga with two games left to play – against Loyola Marymount in Los Angeles and Pepperdine in Malibu. The Broncos needed only one win to clinch the regular-season championship, and with it an automatic bid to the National Invitation Tournament, at minimum, regardless of how Santa Clara fared in the WCC tournament in Portland the following week. The NIT the previous year had adopted a rule obliging it to accept all regular-season Division

I conference champions that didn't qualify for the NCAA tournament.

"The (WCC) has belonged to Gonzaga for almost a decade now, so much so that envy has been replaced by questions of 'Why can't this happen to us?' at the other seven schools," wrote *San Francisco Chronicle* columnist Ray Ratto, a former high school basketball referee whose ties to the basketball community were deeper and more extensive than those of most Bay Area sportswriters. "It seems to have happened at Santa Clara, to be sure, although nobody in a position to say ever does. It was apparently 'just time,' even though the announcement was embarrassingly premature. Especially given that the Broncos have lost only once since New Year's Day, not at all since Davey's retirement was announced for him on Feb. 1, and now have beaten an admittedly shorthanded but still potent Gonzaga team in Spokane.

"This would be Davey's time to get in his licks for a sympathetic audience, or his time to propose that the school reassess his redundancy. But though he might have had retirement thrust upon him, he is disinclined to return it. 'I mean, you have to retire sometime, right?' he said. 'And how can you go back on something you've done? The die's been set, and besides, I don't want to return the fishing rod Mark Few gave me (as a retirement gift, in Spokane before Santa Clara upset Gonzaga).'"

But on that Southern California trip, the Broncos ran into Pepperdine and Loyola Marymount teams that played with the zeal that usually had been reserved for

Gonzaga during the previous decade. Raked by injuries, fatigue and probably the ebbing of emotion that had gushed forth during the previous three weeks, the Broncos lost both games, 67-66 at Loyola Marymount and 89-82 in overtime at Pepperdine. Gonzaga caught and passed Santa Clara during that final weekend to take the regular-season title and the No. 1 seed in the WCC tournament. The Zags then beat Santa Clara 77-68 in the tournament finals to secure the conference's automatic NCAA bid, and end Santa Clara's season at 21-10.

A week later, Santa Clara's hopes for its first postseason trip since 1996 were dashed by the NCAA and NIT selection committees, even though the Broncos, who were 79th in the final Sagarin national power ratings, had a better body of work than many of the teams that made it to the NCAA and NIT fields.

"I thought the players themselves were pretty good about it (during Davey's lame-duck period)," Purdy said, "but what if they (Santa Clara administrators) had just left the entire (coaching) situation alone until after the season? They (the players) hit the wall there at the end. Had their emotional reservoir just tapped out? Forget the media … just on campus, other students had to be asking them about it constantly. I actually believe that if this had never happened, they would have been in the NCAA tournament. Then Dick announces his retirement and (even if it had come out that he had been) forced to do so, at least these kids would have had that (NCAA) experience.

"I guess the big honchos said, 'I think it would look real bad if we force Dick to retire and then end up in the NCAA tournament.' Like this didn't look bad enough? I guess they figured nobody would notice or something. Just the most mishandled thing."

The Gonzaga loss officially ended Davey's coaching career, but he said he walked away without the sense of emptiness so many coaches and players feel when their season is ended by a vote and not by their team's body of work on the court.

"I've had so many teams and players I've been proud of, almost all of them," he said, "but this group might have been one of my favorites, one of the best groups of people I've ever had. So many things were rewarding this season ... I know there were negatives from all of our standpoints, and I don't want to dwell on negatives, but there are negatives in every season. A mantra about this team was to get better. I think we did that ... the only thing was we plateaued a little and hit a few games where we didn't play as well as we would have liked to.

"I may be wrong on this, but I can't think of anyone in the modern day holding a good team to 12 points in a half (as Santa Clara did in a win over Stanford in December). Utah State here I thought was a great win for our team, and I thought we did good things during the course of the league, capped off by the win over Gonzaga at Spokane. I thought (posting a win total not exceeded at Santa Clara since 1984) was quite an accomplishment."

For public consumption, at least, Davey approached the subject of his departure with verbal moderation and even a hint of bemusement, both during and after the season. He thought the situation was mishandled, and said so, but without rancor and with an eye toward helping the school, Locatelli, Coonan and Keating move ahead in the euphemistic "different direction."

"I thought we had a pretty good year," he said after the season. "The media were OK ... we're not Stanford or Cal, and they get most of the (Bay Area media) attention. Truthfully, everyone in a roundabout way did (defend him). It's nice to know you're appreciated, but Locatelli has just been bombarded and persecuted.

"Wilner tried to catch Locatelli on his way out of the press conference (announcing Keating's hiring) on why all these things were going to be given to the new guy. Locatelli put him off ... he said he was late to another meeting and took off on him. It kinda plays into what Wilner really wants ... (Locatelli) won't stand up and make a comment and tell you why things went on, and (Wilner's) going to continue to be after him.

"After the press conference I got a call from (a high-level university administrator who also was a friend of Davey's). We were talking about my new position, and he said, 'Hey, I have a question. This Wilner guy has the Board of Fellows (a fund-raising arm of the university) upset and Paul upset because the guy keeps going after Paul.'

"I stopped him and said, 'Hold it, let me explain your problem. If you don't face adversity, don't expect any positive results. He will not stand up and explain. (He could have said), 'Hey, Dick was in the last year of his contract, and we haven't been to the postseason in 10 years. We felt it was time for a change. Here's the reasons we decided to do it, and we like the guy and want to keep him here (in the fund-raising capacity).' You do that, everything's solved. Instead, you won't stand up and be counted and explain yourself, so don't expect anything in return. Paul's problem is that he thinks he's bulletproof. Well, he's not now. He's been taken over the coals."

Not content to let a bad situation dissipate with time, Coonan – presumably on orders from Locatelli – in May 2007 fired Dave Lewis, who had been the Broncos' play-by-play radio announcer for 12 years. Lewis sang a sarcastic ditty at a golf tournament poking fun at the university's handling of the Davey affair. The lyrics of the "song" didn't even mention Davey or Santa Clara.

Firing somebody who probably was closer to the program than any other media member at that time over such a trifling indiscretion made the Santa Clara administration look petty and vindictive as well as callous and inept. Beyond that, Lewis did Santa Clara basketball as a professional sidelight; his "day job" was with KCBS, a San Francisco radio station with a 50,000-watt reach and one of the largest listening audiences in the Bay Area. Lewis never did take advantage of that pulpit, but he certainly could have done so, to Santa Clara's detriment.

A couple of weeks after he was fired, Lewis seemed more bewildered than angry as he discussed the circumstances.

"I'd actually thought about the song for a week or so," he said. "It was a song Beyonce sings, 'Irreplaceable.' I got to thinking about (how the song title applied to) Santa Clara and college basketball, how everybody's replaceable, and I thought it would be a pretty funny parody. I ran the idea past some people, including some unnamed Santa Clara administrators, who thought it was pretty funny. I even ran it past (former Santa Clara assistant coach) Jamie Holmes, and he said, 'Dude, that's so funny.'

"I had no doubt in doing this; the mistake I made was that I embraced the AD into our little 'frat party' at the golf course. (St. Mary's coach) Randy Bennett, (recently-retired Hawaii coach) Riley Wallace, (recently-fired San Diego coach) Brad Holland ... all these basketball guys were there, the door's closed, and on a psychological level I invited our AD into that party. I had no reservations doing that song in front of him. I was only concerned about Locatelli. If he had been there I wouldn't have done it.

"I tell the crowd, 'You know what? I'm in the car with my daughter and I hear this song on the radio, and we're always concerned with what kids listen to. The song I heard was 'Irreplaceable,' (and he asked his 16-year-old daughter), 'What are you listening to?' She said it was about a girl dumping a boyfriend, and I said (in jest), 'No, it's about basketball coaches getting fired.' So I tell (his audience), 'I'm going to play some of this song, and you tell me if it's about a girl dumping a guy or about coaches getting fired. Whatever you say, I'll tell my daughter and I'll be a better parent for it (laugh).'

"I purposely wrote it so I wasn't singling out Santa Clara. There was no Santa Clara specificity at all. It could have been about Brad Soderberg at St. Louis or Ray Giacoletti at Utah (two other coaches who were fired after the 2006-07 season). That was my point … one of the lines was 'You're fired, tell the media you retired,' and apparently it touched the people in the room.

"Unbeknownst to me, the AD doesn't have this sense of humor. Apparently there was a little buzz about it that night. The next day I walk by Coach Seandel, and he said, 'Hey, big boy, you might be looking for a job just like the rest of us.' When he said that, I knew there was a problem. What (play-by-play) am I going to do if not Bronco games? I love my job at KCBS, I like doing sports, but I love doing college basketball (play-by-play), and to think I wasn't going to do that … the possibility was devastating.

"Coonan called me the next day and said, 'We have a problem. Two people have asked if you've fired him yet.' He said Keating (who was at the golf tournament and heard the song parody) wasn't one of them. I told him that I have nothing to hide, that I didn't single out anybody, and if you think it's about you, you have your own guilt to deal with. I e-mailed him the song. Next day he calls me at noon at the gym … I missed it. Day after that, I get an e-mail from Coonan. First sentence is 'Let me tell you I'm a big fan of yours personally and professionally ...' and I didn't have to read the rest. I'm looking for the anvil from the Roadrunner cartoon to hit me in the head.

"I called him, and I said, 'Hey, man, after 12 years, don't I deserve more than an e-mail?' He said, 'I don't know how we can proceed. I think this is outrageous. You crossed the line.' I said, 'I disagree. I think in context it was funny, but maybe not to certain people in the room.' I told him 'You're more than obviously welcome to do what you need to do, but don't put anything in the paper while Brody's dad (Jamie Angley) is still alive. It won't make any difference in him living, but it's a negative vibe, I'm close to that family and I don't want that out there.' He said 'I don't want it out there either because it will be negative publicity and we don't need that.' But the next day it was on the Internet (on a Santa Clara bulletin board). The USF and St. Mary's boards picked it up and it kind of exploded from there.

"I had to go to page 34 of the Dick Davey Be Classy Handbook ... be classy when you feel like you've been screwed. These (Santa Clara basketball) people embraced me into their family. People ask me what I remember, and I tell them beating North Carolina was great, going to the NCAA tournament (in 1995-96, his first season calling Santa Clara games) was great, but I remember most Lloyd Pierce crying for an hour at a banquet because he didn't want to leave this place, it meant so much to him. I'll work again doing games (elsewhere) but it'll never be the same as it was here.

"It certainly was another black eye (for the Santa Clara administration), but I get the feeling they're not that concerned. They're trying to figure the PR standpoint, but I don't know how many PR firms want to touch this place right now. It has a self-destructive tendency, and it's ignorant of the consequences of doing certain things. It's not the same place I heard about before I got here, and it's not the same place (at which) I felt lucky to work for 12 years."

The Lewis incident only served to give the administration's critics more ammunition with which to pepper the school about the Davey firing.

"With all the money Santa Clara University boosters have supposedly kicked in to upgrade the basketball program, the school should use some of it to hire a good public relations firm. Or buy itself a clue," wrote *Stockton Record* columnist Lori Gilbert. "It wasn't enough that it forced Dick Davey out as the head coach after 15 seasons and called it a 'retirement.' Last week it stepped even deeper into the muck of its own making when it fired radio play-by-play announcer Dave Lewis for singing an admittedly ill-advised parody about college basketball that included the line, 'You've been fired, tell the press you retired.'

"At the peril of my sister losing the St. Claire medal the university awarded her as the outstanding senior woman in her graduating class, or my brother's accounting degree being rescinded by Santa Clara, I'm outraged on behalf of Davey. And Lewis.

"Apparently to some who support Santa Clara, there's a coach who can make the Broncos competitive year in and year out with West Coast Conference leader Gonzaga. There's someone who can get more players like two-time NBA MVP Steve Nash, the point guard Davey found in Victoria, B.C. There's someone who can produce more wins like the 1993 NCAA Tournament upset of sixth-ranked Arizona, only the second win by a No. 15 seed against a No. 2 seed in the tournament at that time. There's someone who can make a win at Gonzaga, which this year snapped the Zags' 50-game home winning streak, a regular occurrence.

"Good luck with that plan."

Chapter 16
THE FALLOUT

Those who orchestrated and financed the jettisoning of Dick Davey after 30 years of service to Santa Clara undoubtedly figured the undertow wasn't anything more wins and more postseason appearances in the future couldn't dissipate.

Perhaps that will turn out to be the case, but the mood at a barbecue on campus in May 2007 to honor Davey indicated strongly that the entire episode wouldn't soon be forgotten. Carroll Williams, who organized the party, deliberately left all of the top Santa Clara officials, and others involved in Davey's removal, off the invite list. That was fine with the 400 or so people who showed – from UCLA coach Ben Howland to most of Davey's Leland players to Dennis Awtrey to Peter and Josie Vanos to former Santa Clara and pro football star Doug Cosbie.

Williams during his brief opening remarks asked that the affair be upbeat, and it was, simply because almost everyone present had a story to tell about how Dick Davey had enriched their lives. These people had all taken divergent paths in their lives, and many had not seen each other in years or even decades, but all wanted to be there for the final celebration of Dick Davey's college basketball life.

At the same time, it was as if they also wanted the world to know that their vision of Santa Clara had been clouded, perhaps permanently, by the events of the previous four months. Many of them glared over the buildings surrounding the barbecue area, as if they were staring through those buildings and into the eyes of Father Paul Locatelli.

"I would do anything in the world for all the guys I played with and for the coaches I played for," Matt Wilgenbush said. "What you heard was that Santa Clara wanted to be like Gonzaga, but with (any substantive change in a university's philosophy *vis a vis* sports) comes some things you don't think about. And if that's what they want, lowered standards just to win, I don't want anything to do with this place. The kids who come here, the (Santa Clara) community … we've embraced them and they've embraced us back. To kick one of the family members out for no apparent reason … it's just not worth it. It's so not worth it."

Steve Kenilvort: "Taking the high road like Dick has is more than I could do. I might be able to walk away, but I can't compliment people who are screwing me. What was done was *wrong*, the timing of it was *wrong*, and how it was done is *wrong*. If you're going to make a change, there's a way to treat a man who has treated this place as well as anyone who has ever set foot here with a little class and dignity, and they chose not to do any of that. He was very close with the kids in that (2006-07) group, and it (the midseason announcement of Davey's "retirement") was unjust to Dick and unjust to those players. There's a whole pattern of that here. Athletics aren't really important on that side of the campus, and you've got one guy with a lot of power. And this is what happens when you get knee-jerk reactions from people not attuned to what we have here and not appreciative of what we have here. It's hard to believe in a place that treats good people this way."

Jeanne Davey: "You would have hoped that the subculture of money and power would not have permeated Santa Clara. It was one of the last bastions of family and loyalty vs. corruption. But it's not the same now. That library (for which Santa Clara was trying to raise funds) is an empty shell; an earthquake could knock it right down. It's *people* that are of value, not buildings, but they just don't get it. There are people like Carroll, Pat Malley, people like that who are so devoted to the kids and to the university and to the alumni who support it ... when you disenchant those people and take them out of the loop, you've lost something you can't replace. There are people who won't ever come back."

Scott Dougherty: "When people ask me about what went on this year and ultimately where the program is headed now, I tell them a lot of that has to do with people making decisions who haven't spent enough time in the huddles and in the locker room and at the games. They don't understand the work these five (coaches) put in not only this season but their entire careers."

If one agrees with the sentiment expressed by these and other Santa Clara arch-loyalists, the "retirement" of

Dick Davey is yet another example of the university – *their* university – embarrassing both itself and the people who have cared about it the most and longest.

In 1993, when the school announced it was dropping intercollegiate football, it did so in the most ham-handed way possible: on letter-of-intent signing day, *after* Santa Clara had secured verbal commitments from players who were forced to scramble to find niches elsewhere at schools they previously had turned down. When Carroll Williams retired as athletic director in 2000, the school appointed as his replacement former Stanford assistant AD Cheryl Levick, who had no familiarity with Santa Clara before she was hired, and whose name is uttered through clenched teeth by most Santa Clara boosters. Davey was one of the few survivors of a purge by Levick that vacated almost every other office in the Santa Clara athletic department.

Of course, there also were Santa Clara alumni and boosters who believed that the "Santa Clara way," while admirable for its altruism, was obsolete in the corporate reality of 21st-century college athletics. *San Jose Mercury News* columnist Mark Purdy heard from many people on both sides of the issue in the aftermath of the Davey *coup d'etat*, and in an interview for this book in May 2007, he said the Santa Clara situation is reflective of the what-price-victory dilemma with which many modestly-financed NCAA Division I programs must grapple.

Purdy, who grew up in Ohio and worked for the *Cincinnati Enquirer* before coming to San Jose in 1984, maintained a relatively dispassionate editorial stance during the Davey contretemps. But he is one of the few contemporary metro sports columnists whose reportorial vantage point is from within the programs and teams he covers, and not from a distant computer keyboard. He has immersed himself in the Santa Clara Valley sports community well enough to know Santa Clara as most non-graduates don't – his home is within walking distance of the campus, and he taught a journalism class there – and what makes it unique. So the Davey story therefore took on personal overtones for him.

"In the big-picture view, taking the personalities totally out of it, it's a really interesting laboratory case of what's happening with college basketball today," he said. "It's about where schools are deciding they fit in, and how the people who run those schools feel about how they want to fit in. When I came here, I picked up pretty rapidly that Santa Clara was a different kind of place ... everybody uses the word 'family' and I'm not quite sure that's exactly right, but (it's) more of a neighborhood where everything and everybody's familiar. To be able to study and see how that program had moved along ... you go back to Bob Feerick (Santa Clara's coach from 1950-62, and a graduate of the school), who hands it off to Dick Garibaldi, who hands it off to Carroll, who hands it off to Dick. I can't think of any other Division I program that has that kind of unbroken chain of coaches handing the job off to their assistants.

"I thought that said something about what the school wanted to be ... this neighborhood. I was thinking that's kind of cool, and it also told me (Santa Clara has) one of the things I love about college sports in general: This kind of multigenerational thing at games. I ran into Bob Peters (a starting guard on Santa Clara's Final Four team in 1951-52) and he was talking about it ... guys from the Final Four team can walk in that gym and find somebody who knew somebody who knew somebody."

As noted previously, Purdy thinks Davey's termination was handled poorly – at best – and says it may well be that Locatelli, Coonan, Filizetti and Sobrato misread the lay of the Santa Clara Valley basketball landscape when it concluded that a new coach and an enhanced budget would enable Santa Clara to do what Gonzaga has done.

"This group of e-mails and phone calls I got ... people basically said 'Dick's a great guy, but he's not going to take Santa Clara where it needs to go and it's time for him to move on. The school should be winning more.' I would point out to them that during Dick's time there, that program has the second-most wins (in the WCC) behind only Gonzaga. It's statistically and demonstratively the second-best program in the league behind Gonzaga, and this year they beat Gonzaga at Gonzaga. So even if Gonzaga is their measuring stick, they still come out OK.

"People turn on the TV in March and Gonzaga is on, but there's a difference (between the schools), not only academically but because it's the whole town (Spokane). In that town, that's the thing to do on a winter night. In the South Bay alone – forget about the (entire) Bay

Area – there are two other D-I programs within a 10-minute drive, and there are two Pac-10 schools (Stanford and Cal) close by (along with two major league baseball teams, two NFL teams, an NBA team, an NHL team and an Arena Football League team). I ask people, 'Do you go to games?' 'I'd go if they won more.' 'What about this year? They're winning.' 'Well, I went to the Gonzaga game.' Everybody had an excuse (for not attending more games).

"But then what developed was this personal outpouring ... 'How could they do this to Dick? Don't they realize what Dick has meant not just to that school but to basketball in the valley?' He's a guy who will go to the Garret (a restaurant-bar in Campbell) on a Friday night because he knows the local high school coaches will be there after their games. And how many (upper-tier) Division I prospects have come out of the South Bay in the last 10 years? Maybe three. He knows he won't pick up a recruit there, but he just likes being around those guys, and because coaches will ask him (how to refine their strategy or how best to motivate a certain player). I think Dick does it because he likes it; there's no ulterior motive.

"Out of this reservoir of good will, he loves people and he loves basketball and he loves the basketball crowd. Think how many people that touches. We probably heard from every kid who ever went to his basketball camps, and every coach who ever worked his camp, and every coach he ran into at the Garret. That's what Father Locatelli didn't quite understand ... to me (what Davey did) was part of building the basketball neighborhood, and for a lot of people that's the only contact they've had with Santa Clara. So all that just welled up and kind of washed over this business."

Although Purdy didn't want to speculate on what or how well Kerry Keating will do as the first head coach in more than half a century to take the job without a Santa Clara background, he has his reservations, based on what he knows of the interview process.

"I heard this from more than one very good source … I don't know Kerry Keating, and I hope he does well, but with him and a couple of others who were interviewed, very little basketball was discussed," Purdy said. "It was about recruiting, what their vision was for the program, what did they think about Santa Clara? Xs and Os, they were not discussed, or discussed very little, and Carroll wasn't on the committee to (prompt the candidates to) talk about this. That tells me that this is what this is about … I guess they're convinced that Dick didn't work hard enough at finding guys. Well, Dick's strength was development, and that meshed pretty well with what Santa Clara was (as a basketball program and as an institution).

"Carroll told me this … the difference between now and 30 years ago, when Rambis came out of Cupertino, was that they had a real shot of getting him and in fact *did* get him. The best Division I prospect this year (in Santa Clara County) was Drew Gordon at Archbishop Mitty. Thirty years ago maybe they have a real shot at a kid like him, but now schools like Connecticut and Duke are involved, and he ends up signing with UCLA. Dick is realistic enough to know, 'I have no shot at this kid, and I have to find somebody like the Bryant kid (John Bryant, a 6-10, 305-pound center from Pinole Valley who, like Nick Vanos more than 20 years before, showed signs of considerable promise as a sophomore in 2006-07) I can develop. Maybe by his junior year, I've got something, and maybe by his senior year I've got a really good player.'

(Santa Clara has never had a player leave school early to declare for the NBA draft.)

"Dick and his staff were good at teaching basketball. If you look at Keating's credentials, that's not part of his package right now. I want to be fair to the guy, and retaining Sam (Scuilli) was a good move, but the other assistants he's bringing in were not of that ilk. You need somebody on that staff to *teach the kids basketball.*"

During his Cincinnati years, Purdy witnessed first-hand the basketball renaissance at Xavier, another Jesuit university that is like Santa Clara in many ways – metropolitan location, a major conference basketball gorilla (the University of Cincinnati) against which it must compete for players and supporters, tough academic standards, and a reluctance on the part of the powers that be to spend big money on sports. "I remember talking to (St. Joseph's coach) Phil Martelli when he was out here one time," Purdy said, "and he told me that after he graduated from St. Joseph's, he became a volunteer assistant there. 'And you don't know what being a volunteer assistant really is,' he said, "until you've been a volunteer assistant for the Jesuits.'"

Purdy said Santa Clara would have been well-advised to do what Xavier did – identify which program it wants to emulate, find and hire an athletic director and a coach with a working knowledge of the target program, and rally the most loyal boosters instead of alienating them as Santa Clara has done in recent years.

"You want to beat Gonzaga, or you want to beat Xavier, or you want to beat Georgetown?" Purdy asked rhetorically. "If that's what you want to do, you examine those places. How did they do it? Where did they get the money? How did they format the whole thing? Either you hire a consultant or you send your AD to figure that out, and then you come back and tell (the university hierarchy), 'Here's how other schools did it. Do we want to try to do that?' Carroll told me that when he was AD, he'd have talks with Father Locatelli and Locatelli would tell him, 'Geez, why can't we be more like Stanford?' So Carroll went out and got the numbers and told Locatelli, 'OK, here's their budget, here's what they pay. We can try to do that, but we need more revenue and we need better facilities.' Carroll got the distinct impression that Locatelli wants to be the Stanford of their conference (without making a commensurate financial and philosophical commitment). Locatelli isn't naïve, but they want to be *Stanford?*

"At Xavier when I worked in Cincinnati, they had a school president who said (the status quo) was not acceptable. Georgetown at the time was the role model (among Catholic universities that had lofty athletic ambitions) so (in 1983) he went and hired (as athletic director) an assistant AD from Georgetown, Jeff Fogelson.

He came in, and within six months he had it figured out. 'Here's what we've got in terms of donors and support, and here's what we can do.' He developed a plan based on what he had learned at Georgetown, but adapted into Xavier's demographics.

"Santa Clara is probably a little better school than Xavier, but Xavier is a very good school, and it has always had an incredibly loyal group of alums who wanted something better. So (Fogelson) said, 'OK guys, we have to move all our games to the Cincinnati Gardens (where the NBA's Cincinnati Royals had played before moving to Kansas City and later to Sacramento), we have to raise our recruiting budget by this much, and we have to go hire the right coach.' (That turned out to be Bob Staak, who later moved on to Wake Forest.) He was an assistant at Penn when they made the Final Four in 1979, and he was the unsung hero in the (Xavier) turnaround. He came in and worked his ass off recruiting. He got one of the best guys from the Cincinnati talent pool, Dexter Bailey, and people started saying, 'Whoa, what's happening over there?' Then he recruited around Bailey … he picked up maybe the fourth-best player out of Indianapolis, the fifth-best player out of Cleveland, and he figured out what he could get and couldn't get.

"They had a pretty good team that year, good enough for the NIT … he (Fogelson) worked it, and he got Ohio State to come in for an NIT game. It would be like Santa Clara buying an NIT game and then getting UCLA to play at the arena (HP Pavilion, formerly the San Jose Arena). Well, they packed the place, and they won the game.

The NIT let them play another home game ... they lost that game, but the buzz had started."

It hasn't stopped. Xavier as of 2007 had been to the postseason 20 times in 24 seasons, including an Elite Eight appearance in 2004 and a Sweet Sixteen showing in 1990. The Musketeers have won 11 NCAA tournament games (to Santa Clara's two) since 1983, and have experienced only one losing season during that span. Xavier has become "the" Cincinnati college basketball program; the University of Cincinnati program that once dwarfed Xavier has been waylaid by a string of disappointing finishes, academic scandals, and its players' seemingly-constant scrapes with the law.

In 2000, Xavier moved into 10,250-seat Cintas Center, a $44 million on-campus facility that the Musketeers sell out for virtually every home game. Santa Clara, conversely, in 2007 was still trying to complete funding for the Toso Pavilion/Leavey Center conversion, which remained unfinished seven years after it was initiated.

"Coonan is a good guy, a Catholic guy, but his background is Cal, which is entirely different than this (Santa Clara)," Purdy said. "Xavier is a good parallel, but nobody from Santa Clara has ever talked to anyone from Xavier as far as I know."

Dennis Awtrey, who was central to Santa Clara's most glorious years in college basketball, says the current program shouldn't be saddled with the mandate of attaining the levels of excellence Santa Clara reached in the late 1960s.

"It (winning on the scale that his 1967-70 teams did) would be very difficult nowadays," he said. "With TV the way it is, the way it affects recruiting and with all the money out there … really, it was even pretty fluky that we did what we did. I almost went to UCLA or Duke (out of Blackford High), and the Ogden brothers were right next door at Lincoln. It's tough for a small school to get guys like that now.

"I've told Dick that I think he had one of the best jobs in the country if you don't think the only thing that matters is winning a national championship. You have smart guys, guys who are there for the education and will be there for four years, and you're at a place where you've established a tradition of working hard. I'm really proud of what Dick's done at Santa Clara, and he should be too. It just depends on what you want as a coach. Do you ever see an NBA coach looking like he's enjoying himself or having any fun?

"They're free to hire and fire anybody they want, and Dick's been there 30 years and it's their right to make a change. But I think they did it awfully poorly."

As for Davey himself, he remains loyal, at least outwardly, to the program for which he worked for 30 years. At the same time, he said attaining the stature of Gonzaga or Xavier isn't a matter of a university's hierarchy simply wanting to do so.

"Obviously recruiting is important," he said, "but the caliber of player that you get at a Santa Clara or a

St. Mary's is going to be a little different than you'll get at a UCLA. You're going to get (high school) All-Americans there. At Santa Clara you'll get a player on the come who has a chance to develop. That doesn't mean you can't beat a UCLA down the road (as Santa Clara did twice during Davey's time there), but there are talent programs and there are teaching programs. UCLA (under Howland) is a teaching program now too, but Santa Clara always has been a teaching program and needs to continue to be.

"You're not going to overwhelm people with talent here, and I think another thing that's important for Santa Clara is to keep the former student-athletes involved, connecting with the old guard. That's going to be a change now for somebody who wasn't familiar with Santa Clara before becoming coach. Sam (Scuilli) will be able to help keep that going, and I think Kerry was smart to keep a member of the (Davey) staff ... he would not have known a lot of the people and Sam can connect him. That'll bode well for how he's received by the Santa Clara community. The Steve Kenilvorts and the Harold Keelings and the Vic Couches and the Scott Lamsons and the Kevin Eaglesons and the Dennis Awtreys and the Bud Ogdens ... those people *want* to be a part of the Santa Clara program. You've got to make people continue to feel good about the program.

"There are plenty of people in the Santa Clara community who will tell you we could have done a lot better and won more games. That's probably true, but it was not because we weren't committed and it wasn't because we didn't believe in Santa Clara University. We were pretty competitive every year, and truthfully they've always been pretty good for the past 50-60 years at competing against teams that are supposed to be a lot better – USF (before 1982), North Carolina, UCLA, Georgia Tech, BYU over the years. Those are all premier programs, and we've competed with them without (sacrificing integrity). We haven't had anything (investigative) with the NCAA in all those years ... we may have turned ourselves in once or twice for going 10 minutes too long with an individual workout or something like that, but other than that, we haven't had anything.

"I hope they don't deviate too much from the plan they've had. I sat down with Locatelli and went through a litany of things I thought would help the program have a better chance to be successful, with the final comment being, 'Now you're (financially) capable of doing everything I've talked about. Now, will we change the academic approach and standards?' He said no. I said, 'Well ... throwing money at the program won't do you a bit of good. It's not about me making more money or us having a bigger budget; we can live with our budget, (but) we will never have a consistent winning program here unless we get real lucky or we have a different set of admission standards and ways to keep kids in school once they get here (as in the case of Craig McMillan, who said one of the reasons he didn't sign with Santa Clara was because it didn't have a physical education major). They don't have to do a complete makeover (and admit clearly-deficient students). Even a couple of (transitional) classes to help the kids along would help."

Davey doesn't agree with the WCC presidents and athletic directors who think beating Gonzaga means making wholesale changes in the way they do business – including firing coaches and lowering their academic standards. He points out that Gonzaga itself is operating largely the same way it did when his friend Dan Fitzgerald was head coach and the school was still awaiting its first-ever postseason tournament berth. The difference since 1999, he says, has been simply that Gonzaga has done a better job identifying the types of players it wants and then using them to create a continuum – a Gonzaga way of doing things on the floor that both incoming and incumbent players understand and to which they wish to contribute.

"To their credit, the kids they've recruited have been darn good players," Davey said, "and once they get them, they (the players) have improved yearly within the program. They're about 80 percent kids from the Northwest (which always has been lightly recruited compared to major population centers like California) ... schools like Washington and Washington State weren't getting those guys for a while. That's changing, but Gonzaga will still be real dominating in the league, I think. They get the big kid (2006-07 sophomore Josh Heytvelt, who was suspended for the second half of that season after being arrested on a drug charge) back, (Jeremy) Pargo is as good as anyone in our league, and I thought the Daye kid (Austin Daye, son of former UCLA star Darren Daye) was the best high school player in California this year.

"You can't worry about anyone else's ship, though. You've got to handle your own ship, and in college athletics, the playing fields are not always going to be equal. If you're concerned about playing the best without any firepower, you might as well get out because you're always going to run into that. If you're a Syracuse and you're drawing 30-40,000 for a home game, why should you play (non-conference games) on the road? So they don't, and playing at home, they're going to win most of their games. That's how it is, but we tried to convince our players that anything was possible.

"I just hope that basketball doesn't go the route of football. There are 336 schools playing Division I basketball, and all of them have the same incentive and goal (to reach the NCAA tournament and then accumulate wins). It's healthy for the basketball world to have it that way, and once in a while you're going to get a George Mason (which reached the Final Four in 2005-06) or a Gonzaga that will go beyond what people think they can do. To me, that's really a positive, and you'd subtract from it a lot if you took 150 or 200 schools out of that mix (as football does with its Division I-A and Division I-AA breakdown)."

For Santa Clara to consistently be in that realm, Davey believes, the school must make a firm and realistic determination about where it is, where it wants to go and what means it should take to arrive at that destination. Part of that is hiring the right coaches, giving them the resources they need to compete at the chosen level, and not deviating from the school's long-range mission or sacrificing its academic ideals even if a coach's early won-lost record isn't as lofty as the more strident boosters and alumni might want.

Despite the circumstances of his ouster as Santa Clara coach, Davey hopes Kerry Keating will turn out to be a good fit for the Broncos and that the program can reprise the success it enjoyed in the 1950s, late 1960s, 1980s, and mid-1990s.

"If you believe you had a good guy coaching, as Pat Malley and Carroll did when they were AD, the loyalty factor kicked in (at Santa Clara)," Davey said. "Santa Clara (until recently) was never really in the mode of a big business. It was 'Let's be loyal and give (coaches) a chance, and if they're not doing the job let's bring them in and talk to them about it, but let's not just get rid of them right away.'

"If (Keating) wanted to talk about personnel, I'd be happy to sit down and give him my feelings, but I think he'll learn those things. I want to see him keep strong ties with former Santa Clara athletes. Again you go back to the same thing ... you always want to do better and improve, and each year we need to enhance recruiting. We had a four- or five-year period where it wasn't as good as we wanted it to be, but I think this (2007-08) year, we started coming out of it. We think we had, on paper, the best class we've ever had coming in, and they won't (alter their Santa Clara commitments because of the coaching change) because we worked that pretty good before we left. The kid from Wisconsin (6-9, 225-pound forward Andrew Zimmerman) was the Wisconsin Player of the Year. The kid from Idaho (7-foot center Scott Thompson) played in the state title game there, and the Australian kid (Ben Dowdell) I think will be a step-in starter. He's a little more mature than the average freshman."

"I think his (Keating's) philosophy will be like ours – defensive-oriented and aggressive on that end – but they'll never (consistently) get super athletes. Becoming familiar with the Santa Clara family will be important for him, I would think. His dad was an assistant AD at Kansas, so he knows a little about how you're supposed to handle things. I think Kerry will recognize the importance of connecting with the Santa Clara family. I want to stay in the background and let him get established."

From others' standpoints, Davey's legacy will be difficult to emulate – regardless of how many games Santa Clara wins during the Keating era and beyond.

"He's always been open and very accessible," said longtime Los Gatos High coach Jim Marino. "His practices are open to high school coaches and his office is open to you. He is very helpful to the high school coaching community. He is the only coach I know that does it. Carroll Williams did it at Santa Clara and Dick continued it. Santa Clara has been unique in this.

"He is a people person. There is nothing (haughty) about him. He started in high school coaching here and went through the ranks. He has always been very accessible to high school coaches. Because of it, he has made the basketball community here a close-knit friendship. He's one of a kind."

"Dick has his integrity, and he always got guys who could play in his system, like a Dick Motta (for whom Awtrey played in Chicago) or a Jerry Sloan (a Bulls teammate, and the Utah Jazz coach since 1988)," said Dennis Awtrey, who also played for Lenny Wilkens, whose victory total of 1,332 was the NBA record at the end of the 2006-07 season, and Jack Ramsay, who won an NBA title ring with the Portland Trail Blazers in 1977. "He won't have guys around who won't work hard ... in the pros you just trade a guy you don't like, but you can't do that in college. You've got a guy (in Davey) who won't prostitute himself to win games, and you'll win the right way.

"Is there anything to be prouder of than the fact you've lived your life with honor?"

Chapter 17
GOIN' FISHIN' – BUT NOT GONE

Several months after he coached Santa Clara University's basketball team for the last time, Dick Davey was asked what he thought might be said of him by the generation of his grandchildren.

"Who knows?" he replied, smiling. "Maybe they'll say, 'Thank God we got rid of that guy.'"

As it happened, "they" didn't. Not entirely and not immediately, anyway.

Davey thought at the time his Santa Clara coaching career ended that his forced retirement would mean more time for him to indulge a passion – fishing – that he always has considered one of the grandest of many grand inheritances from his father. But if university officials thought the fund-raising job they offered him (and that he accepted) was nothing more than a sop, Davey took it as a new challenge and a new opportunity.

"The competitive juices are starting to come now in the new job," he said. "It's a little embarrassing initially … I'm a little sensitive about asking people for money, but I made 15 calls in my first four days of actually doing this job and I have had 15 guys say yes, they'll give something. So maybe there's something to this stuff. I'm talking not only about basketball, which is in pretty good position now financially, but about the sports that really need some extra help.

"At Santa Clara they've done a great job trying to enhance (the number and availability of) scholarships, but they haven't done a very good job of enhancing the programs for specific needs, whether it's the women's golf team needing video equipment or tennis needing a racquet stringer or cross country needing a bus to get to its meets or women's softball needing an assistant coach. Their budgets don't allow for some of those things, and that's what we're trying to do.

"I got a ledger (containing the contact information) for every student-athlete (in recent history) at Santa Clara, maybe 7,000 or 8,000 names, along with our season ticket holders. I got all those lists together, went to the coaches and asked them for wish lists with the idea that I'll put that together, get an estimate of costs for those kinds of things, and see if we can raise the funds to do those things and get all the sports to a high level."

Beyond the new job, Davey also found his schedule pleasantly crowded by those who wanted to thank and pay tribute to him.

A barbecue at the university and a surprise 65th-birthday party at Mike Davey's house both attracted hundreds of people from three different generations; Davey hadn't seen some of them in many years. The Oakland Athletics and the San Jose Giants (the Class A affiliate of the

San Francisco Giants, his onetime baseball employer) both honored him by asking him to throw out the first pitches of games, and he maintained his previous practice of calling former players at random to catch up on their lives and remind them that he would always be there for them in time of need. He also planned a vacation to Europe with Jeanne, and had been contacted by several coaching peers and former players about running camps and clinics in the fall.

"I'll probably be able to tell you more about that (the direction of his retirement) in six months," he said. "I'm really going to miss it (coaching) ... I'd say that's something I'm already really aware of. I *loved* it. I don't 100 percent feel maybe it's over. I don't see a lot of people calling up a 65-year old guy and asking them to coach a team, but if that were to happen I'd surely have some interest, because I love it and I think I have a decent knowledge of how to do it, although there's no patent on it.

"Six months from now, I might tell you it's relaxing not to be around it or I need to get back in it, but when people talked about what happened (as the furor over his ouster mounted), I'd tell them, 'Hey, you can't do it forever, even if Lute Olson (who began his coaching career in 1956 on the high school level and was still at Arizona in 2007) is trying to prove us all wrong.' But at the same time, you have to back away sometime. A lot of new ideas have come into play, and maybe it's passed some of us by.

"It's so in my nature, because of my family, because of my desire at a extremely young age to go in this direction

… it'll be strange to not be doing it for the first time in 40 years. You've got to get something to get excited about, and I'm not going to have that adrenaline pumping getting ready for a game or trying to get organized with a team. It's not going to be there. I think I can live with that, but I know I'm going to miss it.

"No doubt in my mind I'll miss the relationship with the kids, the X-and-O factor that's involved with coaching, the competitiveness on the court, trying to figure out how we can attack this or how we can stop that. It's the chess within the game. Jim Jennings (a 1930 Santa Clara graduate who was a fixture around Toso Pavilion for decades as an athletic-department volunteer until shortly before his death in 2000 at age 91, and after whom a Steve Nash-financed endowment is named) always told me being around these people kept him young, and it did. I'm sure it's kept me young to a certain extent, too. Maybe I have a few more gray hairs, but I still feel young and I still feel like I have a relationship with kids. Obviously I don't understand their music or get everything they're doing, but in general I feel like I relate reasonably well with kids.

"Maybe Santa Clara builds that into the equation because of the type of kid they ask you to try to recruit. Again, you keep a separation when they're players, but after they're finished, I would do anything within my power for any kid who's ever left Santa Clara, particularly if he's graduated. With the ones who haven't graduated, it's more of a case of getting them to get back there and get their act together and get it done. I'm going to miss all of that probably the most, and yet maybe the biggest positive is that I'll get to spend a little more time with my own family.

"A few (of his former players) have struggled, and I've talked to them on the phone and tried to help any way I could. (A prominent 1980s Santa Clara player) went through some tough times after he left Santa Clara, but now he's speaking to kids about staying away from drugs and handling themselves properly in the community. He's made a turnaround. Another guy became the CFO of a company in Silicon Valley … he got involved with some stock stuff (during the dot-com boom and bust of the late 1990s) and got himself in trouble. He's living in Oregon; in fact I'll probably call him tomorrow. Jens Gordon was another guy we were discouraged with when he didn't stay in (school) and finishup (work on his degree), but I'm encouraged that's he's going to come back (from Germany) and get his degree.

"But really, we've had very few (who didn't get their Santa Clara degrees and use them to full advantage). Carroll or I might have had a disconnection with somebody, but we've always tried to help them. I've only been discouraged by a few."

Could Davey's "retirement" follow a course similar to that of the man most frequently associated with athletics at University of the Pacific, his alma mater – Amos Alonzo Stagg, who coached football until he was 98 years old?

"I don't know about that," he said, laughing. "Nothing's come up that I'm gonna jump at. One (coaching opportunity) involved a little too much travel, and leaving the area, which I'm not going to do because it's important (largely because of his daughter-in-law's situation) that we stay close right now. If Stanford or San Jose State were interested, even (in having him) as an assistant, I'd have some interest along those lines, but probably not further away than that. I'll help my son's team a little, and I got a call from a good friend who wants me to do a clinic in October, so I'll do that.

"And I even helped out with Rachie's (his granddaughter's) softball team this summer (of 2007). We finished 27-2. Maybe I should have coached softball for a living."

Although Davey had no way of knowing during the summer of 2007 what his post-coaching life would include, he was certain that he would approach it with a rod and reel in hand.

"The guy I first started fishing with, when I was 6 or 7 years old, was my grandfather," Davey said. "He lived in Sonora (in the southern Sierra Nevada foothills) and we'd hike in at 9,000 feet and catch what they call golden trout, which are always at high elevations. We'd go in over Sonora Pass, hike in four or five miles, and fish.

"There's a lot of joy in it for me. It's something I grew up with from my dad, who I have always considered the best fisherman I've ever been around, and there's some technique to being a good fisherman. I'm maybe an average fly-fisherman skillwise. I'm a catch-and-release guy; my wife would never let me keep them when she was with me. She wants them back in the water as fast as I can get 'em back there. So we go barbless, no damage caused.

"Carroll is a big fishing guy, and so is Van Sweet (his basketball coach during his first three seasons at UOP), who's a great guy. (Sweet, in his 80s, was the head golf coach at San Joaquin Delta College in Stockton in 2007). More recently I've gone with (former San Jose State basketball coach) Danny Glines; he's as good as anyone I've been around. And Ben Howland now ... Ben and I went fishing down at Lee's Ferry, which is at the top of the Grand Canyon, and Bob Burton would go with us. Ben and I also have been to Wyoming, and we've fished in Redding (Calif.). Don Bell, who was the AD at Leland and a football and track coach there, and I have gone out a reasonable number of times. He lives by Cal Neva (in Crystal Bay, on the northern rim of Lake Tahoe). Shannon Rosenberg (the basketball coach at Foothill College in Los Altos Hills) is another guy ... he's really into it, a frontline (competitive) fisherman.

"Fishing is something I like to do, and I would enjoy doing it on a daily basis, but now I'm finding I'm doing it more on a monthly basis (because of other commitments). I went in May (2007) and that was the first time I'd been since the end of basketball season. It's not a daily thing unless you really live it. I can fish the percolation ponds in Campbell ... there's trout in there and you can fly-fish for them, but it wouldn't be too exciting.

It doesn't have the thrill of going up in the Sierras and the fresh air and walking the streams."

While Davey makes no secret of his love of fishing, he makes it even clearer that his first love remains basketball – and more specifically, the lives he has touched through it. It's a profession he still loves ... and a profession for which he holds out more long-range hope than a lot of his more jaded coaching contemporaries.

"I think the NCAA is trying to play an active role in keeping the sanity of college athletics," he said. "Obviously once in a while they get hit by a problem, but a lot of people there are concerned about college athletics, and hopefully they'll be able to keep it together. In the same breath, I'll tell people I was very fortunate to have coached when I did, where I did. I hope (college athletics) will keep some stability as far as recruiting and academic standards that are kept. I like to think it will.

"(People in decision-making positions need to) put an onus on kids to perform in the classroom, and take away from programs that don't meet standards. You're just now starting to see that happen; if a school falls behind on the NCAA scale (in terms of athletes graduating on time and maintaining academic requirements), you're in trouble and you've got a chance to lose scholarships. In the long run, it's almost like SAT scores years ago when they first came in. You have to meet those standards, and grades started going up right about that time because kids wanted to go to college to play, and in order to do that, they had to enhance what they were doing in the classroom.

"I'd like to see the NCAA continue to maintain solid standards for funding programs based on guys graduating. We all tend to talk the talk but not walk the walk. I really think one goal we should have is graduating our players. I know that sounds good, but let's see you step up and do it. There are circumstances (at other schools), whether it's a family issue or pro basketball or injuries or transferring or whatever that could change the timing of being able to do those things (penalize a school for not graduating its athletes), but for the most part, kids graduated in four years. They (Santa Clara academic officials) keep them on track for graduation, not on track for eligibility, and that's a big difference."

One coaching-related trend that Davey hopes is reversed, or at least mitigated, is major universities' tendency to hire athletic directors and administrators who have little or no background in coaching and thus tend to give their coaches a win-at-any-cost-or-walk mandate.

"Maybe (he believes as he does) for selfish reasons, but more and more athletic directors nowadays are coming into their jobs with no athletic background," he said. "Many times they're more business people, bottom-dollar guys, more than they are former coaches who have an awareness of some of the problems that coaching brings about. I think that is changing the face of college athletics a bit, and I don't see that as a positive."

But negatives such as those, in Davey's mind, are only tiny fragments of the mosaic that was his career. He left coaching without any rancor and, months after he was deposed, he harbored precious few regrets.

"I tell people who want to get into coaching the same thing I told my son: 'Don't do it because you want to go into some profession where you can make some money,'" he said. "Of course, I say that facetiously, with the idea in mind that again, by 'discouraging' them, you find out if they really want to. From my perspective, I can't imagine anybody going into a profession that is better or healthier than coaching. It's a tremendous avenue to create relationships, and maybe enhance the life of an individual in some manner.

"It was such a positive experience for me. I grew up with it with my dad, and I did it myself. I thought in fourth grade that I might someday want to be a coach, and I've kind of lived the dream from that standpoint. I see a lot of guys coaching their sons and daughters in Little League or softball who are experiencing coaching for the first time, and I realize how much *fun* it can be. People talk about how they handle the stress of coaching. What stress?

"I go speak at high school career days, and the first thing I ask the class is to raise their hands if their moms and dads really like their jobs. Honest to God, there will be 20 to 30 students in a class, and I don't think I've had more than three (in any one class) raise their hands. A lot of adults are not enjoying what they do. I've gone to work now for 40 years in coaching and I don't think I've ever gotten into my vehicle and gone to work and dreaded the day – not one day. Maybe I've had some frustrations …

(because) we lost a game the night before or some guy's injured or there are circumstances that may have arisen, I might have gone to work apprehensive a few times, but never have I not looked forward to going to work. Not many guys could say that. I could say it every day.

"Always have."

548050

Made in the USA